Whiskers, Feathers and Fur:

Veterinary Tales

ORLA
KELLY
PUBLISHING

Austin Donnelly
Illustrated By Ruth Cadden

978-1-912328-57-4

Orla Kelly Publishing
Kilbrody,
Mount Oval,
Rochestown,
Cork,
Ireland

Dedicated to my dad.
You inspired my passion for animals, the
natural world and telling a story or two.

Contents

Preface

Come be by my side as I carry out my day-to-day work as a veterinarian – from the farms of Ireland to the Australian Outback and many more places in-between.

As you will see, from early childhood I dreamt of being a vet. I graduated as a vet in 2009, and today I am honoured to call this my job. I work in veterinary mixed practice, which means I handle a whole range of farm animals, pets and occasionally wildlife too. Getting to spend a lot of time surrounded by these animals, their owners, the countryside, and friends and family – I feel very lucky.

As this collection is autobiographical, many names, dates, locations and place names have been changed to protect confidentiality and maintain respect for my patients and their owners. This also means that the stories are not always in chronological sequence, but rather are organised to show some of the poignant moments throughout the years, including childhood.

I have written this collection to give you an insight into some of the amazing animals I have worked with and some of the touching human experiences I have been privileged to witness. My intention is not to provide veterinary advice, opinions or judgements, but rather to bring you along with me on a journey, in the hope that you might feel some of the magic and wonder that I certainly felt.

Thank you to all my patients and their families, along with my colleagues, friends and family, all of whom inspired my work.

I look forward to what will hopefully be many more years of amazement, humour, teamwork, learning and laughter.

Austin Donnelly

Introduction

The animal-mad boy

If asked, my family would say I wanted to be a vet pretty much from the time I first started to speak. I was raised in Northern Ireland in the orchard county of Armagh, right on the shores of Lough Neagh, on a farm with a mix of horticulture and beef cattle. Growing up in the countryside influenced me from a very early age. I was fascinated by animals and nature. I was also lucky: my dad loved being around animals too, and as a result, we had a whole menagerie, everything from donkeys to aviary birds to rabbits and guinea pigs and freshwater fish. In my younger years, my birthday presents or gifts from Santa started to follow a theme. Most notably, on my seventh birthday an egg incubator arrived, allowing me to populate the farmyard with all sorts of poultry. Then a few years later Santa delivered an aquarium. I spent many hours gazing at the colourful tropical fish, dreaming of the exotic places they must have came from.

My mother found out post hoc that she had a tendency towards carrying au natural twins – she had five kids in three instalments over five years, meaning that, apart from a single-birthed sister, the rest of us are boy/girl twins. People wonder if my twin sister and I look alike. We're fraternal twins, so it's fair to say we look like family members, but I don't think you would necessarily pick us as in utero buddies. All of this proved highly confusing for my eldest sister (the single-birth sibling), who spent most of her childhood wondering where her twin was, and why our neighbours and relatives seemed to only have one kid at a time. Having such fertile parents meant I had a nice tight gang of three sisters and a brother to play and explore with around the farm and countryside.

I was the kid who occasionally had a few escapee pet piglets follow him to the school bus stop and try to get on board. I was also the kid who got called to help rescue the primary school teacher from a bat that had got in through an open window and decided to fly in circles around her classroom. I still remember her screams like yesterday; I reckon the bat was just as startled as she was, just at a pitch that was higher than we could hear.

Right through my childhood I was outdoors a lot. If I wasn't climbing trees and exploring with friends, we were off fishing on the lough. There were large areas of wild Irish countryside just beyond our doorstep, and we travelled every inch of it. Alongside our farm animals and pets, the local area was teeming with wildlife.

It turns out I had a reputation with my mother I wasn't even aware of. I only discovered this last year when we went on a sun holiday together. While she caught a few rays on the beach, reading a book, I went off snorkelling. As I explored, I decided to pick up a few supposedly empty conch shells. My plan was to show her some of these and then probably return most of them to the sea afterwards. Unlike me she doesn't have the animal gene, being stand-offish at best when it comes to non-human life forms.

I had been gone for an hour and had filled my swimming short pockets with several big shells. I got out of the water and walked the couple metres up the beach to where she was sitting on the sand, and then sat down myself beside her to show her my haul. As I was taking the shells from my pocket, just then out of nowhere a decent-sized octopus hopped out of one of them and landed directly on her lap, tentacles a-flapping. The screams! Oh my God she screamed! It nearly gave her a heart attack.

After scooping up the unexpected passenger and returning him to the water, I came back to her. She looked at me with panic-stricken eyes and said, 'That was in your pocket all that time? You have not changed one bit. Even as a kid you always had a creature in your pocket!' Turns out she used to live in fear of doing my laundry. It wasn't uncommon for her to find a frog, an earthworm or even an egg in my pockets.

Because we had lots of farm animals and pets, we were never too far away from needing the services of a vet. As a kid, I loved watching the vets in action. These people with the skills and knowledge to treat a range of animals were like Gods to me, people who spent years studying science and creatures, driving around the countryside all day working with farmers and tending to living things. Over the years, with the vets' help, I got quite good at administering medications, and spent many hours nursing our sick creatures. At the farm we had one shed dedicated as the 'hospital shed' and often it sheltered a range of inpatients, like a duck with a splinted-up leg, or a calf on intravenous fluids.

Looking back on it, I think that duck was almost certainly my first patient, and splinting her leg one of my first 'operations.' I must have been all of seven years old. The duck had appeared out of the duck shed one morning with one leg pointing the wrong way. An examination revealed a mid-leg bone fracture. I thought quickly, fashioning a splint out of matches placed in an upright circular fashion around the break, and fastening them with a series of poultry rubber leg rings. It held well, and with strict hospital shed confinement she was going strong again in a matter of a few weeks. The leg was always a bit wonky thereafter, but she got around just fine.

A poignant moment in my school days came when I was eight, and I witnessed the aftermath of an accident between a foaling mare and a car. It was a stormy night, and in the throes of foaling, the mare had spooked and jumped onto the road into an oncoming car. The car's passengers had a miraculous escape, but the mare and foal weren't so lucky.

My dad and I were driving that way shortly after the accident had happened, and arriving at the scene we pulled over immediately. My dad went to see if the people at the car were OK, as I ran straight over to the mare lying on the road mostly in the dark, illuminated only by the headlights of the damaged car. With the icy cold rain and biting wind I was quickly soaked through and shivering violently. Checking the mare, her chest, her eyes, there were no signs of life. She had already passed away. The foal had been halfway delivered behind her. I ran to the foal and began frantically rubbing it's chest, willing it to take a breath, but there was nothing. I realised they were both gone. All I could do was stand there looking on at their lifeless bodies. I went into a deep state of shock. This was such a harsh reality, it left me numb for days. At such a young age, I couldn't really process the tragedy. Those images stayed with me for a long time – I even used to dream about what I might have done had I arrived earlier, saving the foal, etc. I was devastated.

This had happened almost straight outside the gates of the primary school, and (in an act that probably would cause complete outrage nowadays) a few days after their bodies were removed, a teacher and a small group of us kids were sent down with buckets of soapy water and brushes to help clean up the blood! We can start the adult therapy bill calculations from that point onwards. I still can't decide if that was a crazy move by the school, or if it was one of those mega-lessons about the facts of country life.

It was moments like this that really made me want to be able to help animals. I was drawn by the prospect of fixing them up when things went wrong, but I wanted to help other people look after their animals better too. Watching those vets in action on our farm inspired me. I thought to myself, I want that, that's me! And I was determined to do anything that had to be done in order to get there.

I studied hard in school and eventually got the grades I needed, but in those days there were as many as five applications for every place in a UK or Irish vet school. My first application was unsuccessful and, well, I knew I had to do something. So I went off to Liverpool to study dentistry for a year.

When I reveal this fact, people often ask me, Did you like studying dentistry? The truth is, yes, I really did. The first-year course was taught in conjunction with the first-year medical students, and I met a great bunch of people along the way. The course at Liverpool dental school was hands-on. They had us doing fillings on dummies and practical classes at an early stage, which certainly made the course interesting. The big problem with me was, I was in the wrong place – this wasn't what I wanted, and over many sleepless nights my conscience regularly reminded me of that.

The Liverpool vet school was about a five-minute walk from the dental school, and I used to avoid walking past it, as I couldn't stand the knots in my stomach when I did. The Liverpool vet students were a social bunch who gathered all over the place around the campus, and I would regularly spot them with their customary school hoodies – the ones with 'Vet Student Society' written on the back. Seeing these was torture for me. I dearly wanted to join them and be on that course.

And then an incident occurred while I was at the University of Liverpool that would have made completing dentistry a bit, well, interesting for me: the students' union lured me in to give a blood donation in exchange for free ice cream vouchers. Afterwards, I must have got up a bit soon from the bed, as I felt very dizzy and hit the deck. After a few minutes I came round a nauseous quivering mess, trying my best to feign I was OK, with a gang of nurses staring at me. Thereafter I became apprehensive around my own blood or that of any other human. That fact probably would have made a career in dentistry quite a challenge! It's a silly thing: I can spend the whole day injecting creatures, but turn the needle on me or make me bleed and I'm still a fainting mess. It's also been funny over the years to see the reactions of doctors and nurses tasked with needling me for whatever reason. When I let them know I'm not so good with it all, at six foot five and about as wide as a dunny door, you can see them calculating who to hell is going to lift me if I drop.

Becoming a 'vit'

After a year of dentistry in Liverpool I decided it was worth one last shot at applying for vet school in Dublin. I had made a determined effort to do well in my first-year dental exams, as I knew this was going to be assessed as part of my entry to vet school, and, much to my delight, I received an offer of a place in University College Dublin (UCD), in 2004. UCD is the only vet school in Ireland, and getting that offer of a place was a monumental moment in my life.

And something quite remarkable happened in the weeks after I received that placement. When I started classes at dental school the previous year, one or two relatives had sent me good luck cards and a few banknotes to help buy course books. This time, upon getting accepted into vet school, I was inundated with phone calls and cards and cheques from neighbours, family and friends as far away as America! Everyone knew how much it meant to me, and their support and goodwill was extraordinary. One of my teachers from back when I was eight years old, who had long since retired, and whom we shall call Mrs T, sent me the most charming rose-petal-festooned note, in which – in handwriting as exquisite as ever – she recalled tales of me as a child obsessed with animals. She finished the note writing, 'Donnelly's Abú'. Translated from Irish, this means, 'Donnelly's forever'. It was her magnanimous way, despite the intervening years of no contact, of cheering me on. The note even smelled of her perfume, and my inner child beamed, jubilant as a petted puppy, knowing that I had even made Mrs T proud.

Keen as mustard, I couldn't wait to move to Dublin and get started in vet school. The first day of the course we had a meet and greet with all the first-year students and staff. I had spent such a long and tortuous journey to finally be there, that when I arrived I was on cloud nine. I was also expecting everyone else to be just as delighted to be there. Quickly word spread that I had done a year in dentistry. One fellow fresher vet student came over to get my opinion: he had an offer of a place in dentistry school, did I think he should jump ship? I couldn't believe my ears: surely the first day of university is no such place for career advice. But then again, I thought, hadn't I just been in the wrong place myself?

The vet course in UCD was taught mostly at the vet school on the Belfield campus, with some practical sessions taking place at the university farm outside the city, in the Kildare countryside. The early years consisted mostly of lectures, practical sessions and exams. In later years we trained in the vet school hospital alongside lecturers and specialists in all areas of large and small animal surgery and medicine. As in a human hospital, the facilities were laid out in departments, and before finishing the degree course we students would spend weeks on rotation studying with each department.

The word 'veterinarian,' roughly translates as 'cattle doctor' which would be a bit outdated in this age, for some vets at least. My dad, like a lot of Irish farmers, would usually say, 'Vit,' instead of, 'Vet' – mostly meant as a term of endearment.

'Vit' as a word is perhaps unique to Ireland, although I suspect they say it in some parts of the UK also. It always makes me smile how a word that is already abbreviated gets slightly mispronounced on purpose, as if its original pronunciation was just too much.

My dad sadly passed away during my early years in vet school, but I instantly think of him when I hear someone say 'vit'. He was a caring, kind and witty man. When I first started vet school, he was extremely excited for me, and very supportive. He was always so keen to hear about everything I was studying and what I was up to. He had so much faith in vets that he would have much preferred to have gone to them, rather than regular doctors for his own ailments. I remember him asking vets what they thought of each of his long list of medical conditions while they were out on visits. Some of them were less keen than others to say much, but on each occasion there would be good craic and lots of laughter.

I remember one Friday evening during my first year of vet school, my dad collected me from the train station as I was up home for the weekend, and as usual he was excited to see me and hear about my latest. I was carrying a new pearl of vet school wisdom, and I remember smiling to myself during the train journey home in anticipation of telling him. I knew he would find it hilarious, as we had a similar sense of humour. Driving along the fifteen-minute car trip home I revealed to him some of my new-found knowledge. 'Hey Da, you know that area of uneaten grass around a cow pat, in meadows? I have learned it has a technical term. It's called the zone of repugnance!' He had to pull the car over and hold his forehead, he laughed so much – he nearly split his sides. In fact he kept on laughing about it recurrently for the whole weekend. What was making him laugh most, he later confessed, was that after all my torturous years of school and exams, here I was now down in Dublin in a lecture hall learning about cow pats ! Looking back I must have made him so proud with that gem. He was really quite a humble man, but my dad told everyone he met far and wide about his son at vit school.

At vet school we had a great mix of lecturers from all over the world, some young and modern and others much older and a little old-fashioned. I was fortunate enough to be at vet school while some of the older vet lecture legends were still on the go. It's hard to describe adequately what qualified them as legends, but their reputations certainly preceded them. They were firm and direct but also fair and witty, all at once. We had many great lecturers, but we all had an extra-special fondness for the more senior staff. We found them amusing, set in their ways and disdainful of modern technology. They often gave us handwritten notes, and overhead projectors were their preferred means, almost in defiance of the PowerPoint projectors and shiny new laptops in each of the lecture halls.

Some of my classmates would have conversations with the older lecturers about their parents and grand-parents who had blazed the same trail before them. I had my own (if somewhat tenuous) family link to the veterinary profession: a great-uncle who had been a lec-turer at the college several years before my arrival and who had passed away before I ever met him.

Back in the old days, vet school was a more inti-mate experience. Up until the early 2000s, class sizes were smaller and the vet school was situated at it's own off-campus location in Ballsbridge. Staff and students often socialised together, with the vet students earn-ing and maintaining a reputation as party animals. One of the pubs near the now-demolished Ballsbridge vet school site – the Horse Show House – had been a favourite watering hole back then, and it still found favour with the new Belfield-based vet students, despite being a long trek across the city. This was due partially to nostalgia and partially to the fact that it was one of the only pubs that hadn't barred them.

By my day, vet school was located on the main campus and mixed with other faculties, and class sizes had increased quite a bit, with lots of international students now too. During the course, the vet students would get to know each other really well, but the lecturers could naturally be forgiven for not knowing each of us by name.

One such senior vet lecturer legend, known by many Irish vets, was still on the go – an impressive age for sure. In my class there were third-generation vet students whose grandparents had been taught by him. For years he had been Dean of UCD vet school, and a senior lecturer in anatomy. When I was there he was mostly retired, but he still participated on the anatomy teaching schedule for first- and second-year vet students.

The first time I met him I instantly warmed to him. My father had been a big fan of comedy, and was a huge fan of Frank Carson, a Northern Irish comedian, and this man was, in my eyes, his double. He looked like him, talked like him, and even had a Donegal/Northern Ireland twang. As a result, I was primed to find humour in everything he said, even when it wasn't there. And he was a witty character for sure.

One day, in a second-year anatomy lecture, he caught me off guard. I wasn't focusing on the lesson, but instead had struck up a chat with my nearby vet-student neighbour. Our whispers attracted his attention. I still remember it like it was yesterday. He came over to me with two bones in his hand. Both were reasonably small and fitted nicely in his right hand, although one slightly bigger than the other.

'Mr Donnelly, which of these is in fact a canine femur and which is a feline femur?' he asked, and lay them down on the bench in front of me.

He paced a few steps away, turned 180 degrees, and came straight back to me, glancing at me through glasses that made his eyes look bigger than they were. Maintaining eye contact, he came close to my face and nodded his head up and down in such a way that his eyes magnified and demagnified, all while sternly staring straight into mine. As per usual, I had to steady up and remind myself: this is not a joke; he is not Frank Carson.

I know you are all thinking that the answer would be obvious; the biggger bone is the dog's, the small one the cat's. But no! I had been caught out before, and he wasn't beyond using tricks. He could be presenting me with a chihuahua femur and a bigger cat femur (a Maine Coon, say), in which case the size would be no clue.

'What will it be?' he shouted, with a groan/growl at the end.

He then came right up to my face again.

'Well, what is this?' he said, dangling the bigger one in front of my eyes. 'Is it the 46A bus to Stillorgan, Mr Donnelly?!'

I didn't even get a chance to whimper out a guess before he grabbed both bones and stomped off back to his anatomy preaching pulpit.

He hadn't really wanted an answer. I think it was more that he wanted to make me squirm for a bit, caught red-handed not paying attention. By God, I never messed around in his class again! In any case, we never found out which bone was which.

Another time I was shopping at a Tesco supermarket not too far from the college, browsing the fruit and vegetable section, deep in my own thoughts, when out of nowhere this senior vet lecturer stuck his head up from behind the oranges, looked me up and down, and with a long, slow, low-pitched rumble, he said.

'Mmmmmhhhh – the feeding of the giant.'

Said it in a David Attenborough-documentary-narrative sort of way.

'Here we have … The feeeeding of the giant Human.'

He said this with a mischievous sparkle in his eye, and after delivering this sentence he turned round on the spot and walked off with his hands behind his back – much the way an older man walks around with his hands behind his back, deep in thought.

Right then, yes, he was a little old man, and there I was towering over him with my arms full of food stuffs.

The scene was set. I still laugh at how he delivered one of my favourite comedy incidents from vet school.

Vet school was an amazing place, with all sorts of weird and wonderful goings-on. The staff and students had become desensitised to many of the things that visitors from other faculties would instantly react to. For example, one day there was a dummy model of the rear-end section of a cow that someone had left sitting on the bench in the canteen. A group of art students had come into the vet building to canvas for student union votes. I can still hear their hysterical laughter.

Then there was the Bristol stool chart. The small animal medicine department had wanted to promote its use amongst us students as a way to score our patient's poops. The chart displayed a scale of consistency, from very loose to very firm, and it included photo examples. The department had put a few posters around the place. We vet students didn't bat an eyelid, but visitors were horrified!

Incidents like this weren't uncommon. Many corridors were lined with weird and wonderful things preserved in jars, from venomous snakes to a cyclops lamb, to horrendous parasite specimens.

I used to think at times, when the lecturers delivered their terminology, that it was almost like we were learning another language. I was prone to daydreaming, and used to zone out and then back in right in the middle of lectures; for a moment I would think I had been teleported to wizard school. Take a dramatic, enthusiastic lecturer and for example some outrageous Latin parasite name, and a couple of jars of preserved creatures being tapped at with a wooden cane – who wouldn't think they were in wizard school? Parasites such as *Haemonchus contortus*, *Strongylus vulgaris* and *Parascaris equorum* come to mind. Say them fast under the above conditions and I swear you're on your way to being a wizard.

Those lecturers had magic in bounds – they knew when and where to emphasise the right things just to elevate the whole lesson and make it memorable. Perhaps the more junior lecturers just needed another thirty years' practice and sufficient exposure to formalin, and they too would have this same skill and pizzazz!

Vets the world over have been through this kind of training. We speak the universal language delivered to us by educators. They equipped us with knowledge and an understanding of the skills we needed to master. The degree in veterinary medicine I completed in UCD qualified me to work as a vet in Ireland, Europe and many other countries across the world.

Vet school encompassed some of the best years of my life. Those years of learning theory and practical skills would all come together eventually. Setting out as a newly graduated vet, I had a good understanding of the theory, and had mastered some of the practical skills of the job before me. Those first few years in practice, as with most careers, would be very important for refining my skills. In 2009, I was unleashed from vit school.

As the years roll by

I have now worked in quite a number of different vet roles, on a few continents. To this day, and I hope for many years to come, I continue to work in mixed-animal veterinary practice, working with small animals (dogs, cats, other pets), large animals (farm animals and horses) and wildlife, as you will see.

I really enjoy working with animals, and I feel lucky that I get to. I am the grown-up version of the child with a dream, surrounded by animals. The only difference now is that I am able to deliver some of the remedies the vets of my childhood did, and I really love that. It's a nice feeling to make a difference for an animal in my care. It's that thought that gets me through the tough times and really heightens the good times.

From the day the magic happened of the offer of a place in vet school, to the journey going through school surrounded by people with the same passion, to then moving into practice and working each day as a vet, I am still suffused with this passion.

For me, working as a vet is pleasure; I don't think of it as a job. And that's what they say, right? Do what you love and you will never work a day in your life. I believe I can say that. It really does feel like my natural calling – like it was what I was designed to do, and if I had to stop being a vet in the morning, I have no idea what I would do otherwise. I still have the occasional nightmare that I have to do my final vet exams again, or that I haven't finished yet (which would be a bit crazy nearly ten years later). Vets much more senior than me would confirm these nightmares are not uncommon. I guess with all the years of longing to get there and the false start at university, my subconscious mind on some level still doesn't fully accept that I got there.

There are many pros and cons to working as a vet. I try to focus on the positives. Yes, at times things don't go as planned, and yes sometimes it can get very stressful (more about that later). But I am inclined to think this happens in many workplaces. I really enjoy the diverse range of people and animals I get to meet in my daily work. I am a farmer's son, and I still love that I have an excuse to go onto farms and meet the farmers and work with their animals. Of course, an added bonus is that I often get side-tracked by discussions about their farm systems and, of course, machinery.

Farmers often remind me of my dad and my childhood. Being a farmer at heart and, naturally, being nosy like most farmers, I love to see what other farmers have.

Here are some of the stories from my work and travels as a vet. There have been, and will be in the future, many interesting scenarios that crop up in my line of work – as you will see. One huge source of resilience is a healthy sense of humour. The camaraderie and the people and animals I have met have given rise to some of my stories and have proved to me the importance of an ability to laugh at life and at myself.

CHAPTER 1

Christie Fee and the Crossed Zone of Repugnance

Pottering around in the consult room, I heard Mary, the vet clinic receptionist, answer the phone.

'Hello! Hello? What seems to be the matter? It's a bad line, I can't hear you well. Ah, I see, you have a heifer calving. And who is it? Fee? Ah, Christie Fee. I have you now, and is that at the home place? Yes OK, I have a new vet here and I'll have him out with you shortly.'

As Mary made her way towards me, I already had an idea what message she was about to deliver. It was autumn, and I had recently started working at this clinic in rural County Wicklow. I was keen to get out on the road, meeting clients and exploring the wild Wicklow countryside. This was the type of call – a calving – I used to dream about during those years of vet school, and given it was my early days as a vet, this was my time to shine, so to speak.

'One of the Fee brothers has a heifer calving at Upper Cross and he thinks she needs a hand. Can you go and see him? He's out on the hill there trying to get her in now,' Mary said.

'Sure, no problem,' I replied, and hastily scribbled a few directions (this being before the days of Google Maps). Mary usually tried to be helpful by giving me colloquial details of the farm and client, but this time she just shrugged and said, 'I've never met this brother, although I hear he's a bit of a character. And he sounds like he's in a panic. You should try and get there as soon as you can.'

Mary had a kind heart. I could already see she was a hit with the clients. People said she always went above and beyond to help where she could, and she never had a bad word to say about anyone. I soon learnt that her brief client synopses should always be open to interpretation. A fiery character might be described by her as 'interesting'. Calling Christie Fee 'a character' could mean anything, from he was a bit of a jester to he was a raving lunatic. What exactly she could have meant entertained my thoughts all the way, as I drove out to Upper Cross.

The approximate directions suggested Christie's place was a half-hour drive away, heading up into the Wicklow hills. Upon arriving into Upper Cross, I found the village consisted solely of a crossroads and an old phone box. Relieved to see only two possible road options, I took a guess and turned left. Wicklow's upper hills and mountains are a maze of roads, and there's not too many road signs to be had. Getting lost was a regular thing.

As I travelled up the roadway, I saw more houses than I expected, each about 500 metres from its neighbour, all roughly lined up in a row. The first two appeared to have been recently built – modern with garages and decking – and as I drove along the houses got progressively older, with ivy walls and old-style machinery in their yards. Mary had told me that this was where the Fee brothers and their families lived, with Christie at the far end of the lane, where the lane ended. As I got closer to the end, about three kilometres from the start, the hedges became more overgrown, and the grass in the centre of the lane grew high enough to rub off my engine sump. It has clearly been a while since a vehicle had gone all the way up this road, I thought to myself, and I chanced a guess that Christie's main mode of transport was a bicycle. I started to get a bit worried that I was on the wrong road and had slowed down around house number three when a woman appeared at a window, pointing vigorously for me to continue up the lane post-haste, the distance between us necessitating hand signals. I was reassured that this lady seemed to know my mission and be pointing me in the right direction.

As I approached the end, the lane became very narrow, with the overgrown hedging on either side joining up overhead, to form a tunnel. Behind the predominantly damson tree hedging, with their ripe, abundant dark purple fruit lit by the autumn sun, I could make out an old house. To my right through the thick hedge were lots of old, overgrown apple trees thick with lichen and moss, looking a bit worse for wear, with only a few blighted, misshapen apples dangling.

By the orchard stood the remnants of an old shed with a collapsed roof. Scattered around the tree-covered area were the familiar shapes of old wooden apple bins. Growing up in the orchard county, I had spent many a late summer day picking apples and filling bins just like these. Seeing them made me smile. It was like visiting an old neighbour's house – but in truth, I was far from home.

A path led onto a few stonewall-enclosed paddocks. I assumed the heifer must be in the vicinity, so I parked up and got my things ready – calving gown, ropes, calving jack and obstetrical lube. I left all of this on my car bonnet and set off to try find Christie and my patient.

A quick survey of the house and nearby fields proved fruitless. I didn't see anyone, and all I heard was the faint barking of a dog from within the old house. I found a path through some nearby trees and decided to go that way. In the distance was an area with stone walls and rusty old gates. Perhaps that is where they are, I thought. As I approached, I saw a red Limousin heifer with her tail raised in the air, a sure sign she was calving, but she was nowhere near the race, inside which we would need to restrain her. As I looked over the other side of the stone wall, I saw a hand appear just out of nowhere; it ushered me to get down quick and not make any noise. I watched as the heifer came closer, until she was in the stone-walled area sniffing at a bucket, and in no time a bent-up, rusty gate shut behind her, penning up the heifer. The successful capture of the heifer was followed by a rapturous cheer.

'Yyyyyeeeeerrrrrrrrr oooooooooooooowwwwwwwwwwwwww!'

It was so loud it echoed down through the hills, startling a few wood pigeons along the way, their wings clapping loudly as they made their escape.

'We have you now ya ooohhhh-welled bag ya!

Where are ya vit? Come on through!' A voice shouted.

I revealed my presence by standing up and the heifer immediately looked at me and indicated with a few snorts and tail flashes that she was not happy. Christie, still dancing in a circle to celebrate apprehending the heifer, beckoned me to come in through a gap in the wall.

Christie was elated to see me, and with a big smile he came straight over to shake my hand and welcome me to Upper Cross. 'I didn't think I would ever get her in,' he said. 'She's as headstrong as her mother.' He pointed at a tiny red dot, far away on one of the adjacent hills.

'She takes her stubbornness after the mother too. She could never be led nor drawn, either. Very disobedient cattle, the pair of them.'

He looked at the heifer and, shaking his fist in the air, shouted at her, 'Yah oooh-welled bag ya! You'll come next time I call ya, do ya hear me?!'

I was a newcomer to working with flighty Limousin cattle, and with my presence in her field fully declared, I was getting a bit worried about the ability of Christie's rickety old gates to pen this beast. Back home in Northern Ireland we didn't know how good we had it, with our docile, steady Charolais and Aberdeen Angus farm cattle – they were like a different species. It was a bit of a baptism by fire, learning on the job how to deal with their temperamental Limousin counterparts. Although Limousin breeders have taken efforts in recent years to try to breed them a bit more mellow, I came to think that working with Limousins was more like trying to handle wild gazelle – panic artists equipped with good running and jumping gear and an innate desire to be nowhere near a human. A big advantage to the Limousin breed that helped balance these drawbacks was the fact that they mostly were easy calving, meaning they didn't often need help because they usually were able to do it all on their own. However, this also meant that they were much less used to being handled. On the rare occasion when they did need vet help, not only was there a patient suffering from the distress of a calving problem, but this event was complicated by the fact that she had almost certainly not been handled too much before.

A very common cattle breed in the Republic, they were a steep learning curve for me, on how best to handle them. I asked Christie if he could give me a hand fetching my calving equipment, and we headed off to the car parked out on the lane.

You could tell by Christie's appearance that he was a bit eccentric, an impression his mannerisms and loud, excitable voice only served to reinforce. He was a man of seventy years, I would later learn, and was the oldest of the Fee brothers. He looked light as a feather, and his old-style formal clothes were too big for his small frame and in tatters, patched up here and there. At times during his excitement he would lift the tweed cap he wore and hold it in one hand, revealing a head with a good covering of silver hair. He had a weathered complexion, a narrow chin and a long, pointy nose not unlike a mouse. This mousy appearance was further enhanced by long areas of unruly stubble near his lips, which gave the appearance of whiskers. His trousers were tucked into his socks, and there was baler twine tied around both ankles, while another length of twine served as a belt. It wasn't immediately apparent what purpose the ankle ties served.

Back at the car, Christie fell over himself trying to carry everything at once. I admired his enthusiasm, but his little bony frame was not equal to his ambitions. I took a bigger share of the items than Christie would have liked, and together we walked back. On the way through the field, he noticed my brand-new blue rope, and I soon discovered that Christie described pretty much everything he encountered as 'fine'. While we walked, he said, 'Jeez, you're a fine, big man, and where do you come from? Oh, that's a fine car you have, and that is a fine new piece of rope you have too!'

Unbeknownst to Christie, it was more than just the rope's maiden journey.

On the way back to the heifer we discovered there had been a terrible mishap. Christie's baler-twine gate tie had loosened, and the bend in the gate had allowed it to spring open. The heifer, now free again, was on her way to her mother, the red dot on the far hill. Christie dropped everything and ran off after her in a rage of screaming, fist-shaking and expletives. She got a trot going, and before long she was becoming a red dot in the distance herself, due to her access to an expanse of unfenced Wicklow wilderness. As I stood there staring in open-mouthed disbelief, Christie came back from his outburst almost in tears, he was so upset by what had happened. He rambled and screamed so much that a bit of saliva froth began to form on the whiskers around his lips. He said in a very defeated way, 'She's a goner, we'll never get her back. May she die beyond on the hill, the ohhl wwwwild bag!'

I said, 'Sure, I have no rush on me this morning, we'll give it one more shot at getting her back.' We put all the calving stuff in a safe spot and headed down the hill. Christie, having written the heifer off as a goner, was starting to calm down a bit, perhaps feeling a little more hopeful that we were at least going to give her another chance.

On the walk over the hills, I started chatting with Christie to try to divert some of his distress. I asked him about the history of his family in the area, and he told me he was a bachelor, having lived in Upper Cross his entire life. All the other brothers hadn't moved far, and that was indeed their five houses on the way up the lane. Christie's place was the original family home, and he added that he had been born on the kitchen floor. As we walked, I asked about the local wildlife, and whether they had many deer, badgers or foxes, as I am always keen to hear what's around. This beautiful hillside location seemed like such an ideal place to find these species. He told me, with a sparkle in his eye, that he saw them regularly. The meadows were heavily grazed, because Christie's few head of cattle shared their paddocks with some of the brothers' cattle, but the others had recently been moved to another place, thus leaving the fields well shorn. Marvelling at how many fresh green circles of uneaten grass there were around the cow pats, I decided to try Christie for a bit of humour, with a bit of information I had picked up years ago in vet school.

'Christie you have some very choosy cattle – would you look at all them zones of repugnance?'

He looked at me, taking in the words, and then after a few seconds he cracked up into the most hysterical laughter, repeating, 'The zones of repugnance, ha ha! Ah, go away vit, is that what they are called now?' We both had a good laugh.

As we headed down the next hillside, we noticed the heifer had slowed down her escape trot and was circling a spot looking like she was going to lie down.

Quickly she was down and sprawled out on her side doing some earnest pushing as her labour advanced. We used the opportunity to circle below her and approach her from lower down the hill, thinking if she shot off again at least she would head back up towards the makeshift race.

As we approached, we saw that our plan had worked. She got up and ran off in the same direction we had started, as Christie and I took a side of the field each and ran along behind her, to keep her going in the right direction. After about fifteen minutes she was back near the race and, when she saw the bucket inside, a further small miracle occurred, she went straight in.

But we were still a hill away from her, so we breathlessly watched as she stood exactly where we wanted her to, but with one flaw – the gate was wide open, and she could be out of there and high-tailing it down the field again in a heartbeat. We didn't hang about but running up a hill for the second time on uneven ground and in full calving gear is much easier said than done. As we got about halfway there, willing her to stay put, I could make out just to the left of the scene a human shape appearing, and in no time this figure had closed the gate. As I squinted to try and see who this champion was, Christie started with his cheering again.

'Ah jaysus she's a fine woman! Johnny's Nora is a fine woman! She's after catching the heifer in for us!'

Turns out the direction-pointing lady from earlier, along with a few of her sisters-in-law, had made her way up to lend a hand, and upon observing our strife had lay in wait. By the time Christie and I finally arrived at the race, all three ladies were there.

The chief gate-closer, Nora, turned to Christie and said, 'She's a flighty bugger that one, isn't she Christie?'

I said hello to the ladies, thanking Nora for her earlier guidance when she pointed out the way. I imagine that Christie had likely been in her house when he made the phone call to the clinic earlier. The three ladies started directing play, issuing a list of instructions to Christie on what he should do next – stand here, tie this, go there, etc., of which he followed about half – and then each took up a gate-side position on the outside of the race so as to help prevent another escape.

It would seem that all the other Fee brothers were married, and that Christie, being the lone bachelor on the hill, was well looked after by the team of his brothers' wives – cooking for him, doing his laundry and the likes.

Mary had been right: he was a character for sure, and some might say he was a bit tapped (mad). Yes, he was prone to screaming at his heifer, but it was also obvious that Christie was a big softy, and that despite his raging conniptions, underneath it all he just wanted her to be OK.

Those wives were like schoolteachers with him, perhaps feeling that he greatly needed their guidance. Some people might suggest that he was a little hen-pecked by them, but at the same time I think they had his best interest at heart.

We retrieved my pile of calving equipment and I got out my shiny new blue rope and fashioned it into a head collar, keen to get some more robust restraint going. We did a team effort of corralling the nervous heifer with some gates to allow me to get near her head, and I was relieved when I got the collar on. The old-style yard didn't have anything particularly sturdy to tie the rope to, so we made use of the branch of a nearby tree. This wasn't great either, but it was the best of a bad list of options.

As Christie went off to retrieve some buckets of water, we needed in order to keep all the equipment we used in the delivery nice and clean, I took a few moments to give the heifer an epidural anaesthetic to help ease her straining and make her more comfortable. I stood back and took a breather for a few minutes, allowing the epidural to kick in and awaiting the arrival of Christie with the buckets of water. In those few moments, I admired the beauty of the location overlooking the hills and the relative tranquillity. Not so long previously, myself and Christie had been running like maniacs through those fields, but now it was all so peaceful.

Just as Christie returned with the buckets and was bent over organising them at the far side of the heifer, the silence was mercilessly broken by a very loud fart – startling the already nervous heifer, who gave a jump and then turned her head around to stare directly at Christie as if to show her displeasure. I went straight into giggling as the offence was undeniable, and the 'who done it' unquestionable! Christie continued about his business completely without a second thought.

Next thing Nora pipes up.

'Ah quit that Christie, that's shocking behaviour in front of the vit and not a hint of remorse either.'

Christie looked at me with a little mischievous grin, then looked back at Nora and said, 'Ah quit yer giving out Nora dear, the deed was in fact done prior to your disapproval, and there is no retracting it now. The heifer had me out running around, what do you expect?'

To which we all stood and laughed.

We got the heifer lined up against a gate next to the tree and Christie held the heifer's tail to one side. I tied on my calving gown and set about applying some obstetrical lubricant and examining the heifer internally. I was thinking to myself that these Limousins usually calved without much help, and I had a feeling that there would be an explanation why this heifer appeared to be having trouble. As I felt through the vulva and advanced my hand forwards, I expected to feel the calf's forelegs and nose, but what it was that I felt, took me a few moments to fully determine. Her cervix was open, and her waters had broken, but there wasn't a hoof or nose to be found. As I felt around, I knew there was a calf there for sure, but I wasn't immediately recognising any body part. Working my way around with my fingers I tried to make sense of the structure I was feeling, and then I found a little calf tail right in the middle. Quickly I realised the rest was the calf's rear end. This calf was breech – coming backwards.

The birth canal examination stimulated some strong contractions, and the heifer gave some big pushes. Soon the calf's rump was pushed as far as the start of the vulva, just reaching daylight. There was now a little red calf tail and rear presenting at her vulva lips. The heifer and calf were the same colour of red, I could also see the calf was a female and seeing the mini-hind quarters issuing from the heifer's hind quarters, it looked to me like a strange Russian nesting doll – little arse inside bigger arse.

The big problem was that there was no way a calf could be delivered vaginally in that position. It was essentially sitting in the heifer's pelvis, both of its hind legs projected forwards inside her mother's uterus. In reality, the only way this calf could be delivered would be with the legs projecting backwards and coming through the pelvis first. I didn't have to explain this predicament to Christie, as he was now so anxious that he was standing almost on top of me and was therefore able to see this all for himself.

'Thank God we got her back in, Christie,' I said, whispering, 'She would never have survived this.'

He nodded in silent agreement.

The first option here was to attempt to gently push the calf back in a sufficient distance so as to get the hind legs up into the birth canal in order to deliver it. We could still deliver the calf backwards, but we would need the hooves and back legs to lead the way. Failing that we would have to do a caesarean section.

In this breech position there was a very real risk that the umbilical cord could be compromised, so I was keen to deliver the calf right away. I got my calving ropes ready; these are used to secure each calf limb individually and would allow me to move the limbs around from within the birth canal and apply traction at the right time. Once again, I got a big handful of lubricant and applied it all around the birth canal. I put my hand on the centre of the calf's rear, over the coccyx, and started gently pushing her forward back into the uterus. Initially there was some resistance but slowly the calf started moving away from me, just as I hoped she would. Christie was beside himself watching on, doing some deep breathing through his nose, almost as though he was in labour himself.

As the calf made her way back through the heifer's pelvis, there came a gentle pop as she finally tumbled back into the uterus. Christie noted the resulting release in pressure as my arm quickly went inside, and he smiled at me, acknowledging that we had made some good progress. Keeping my right hand on the calf's rear, I started searching with my left hand, feeling downwards for a hind leg, thinking to myself that this heifer was surprisingly roomy inside for a first timer.

I found a little cervid-like (deer-like) hock and fetlock, then, continuing down the limb, I got to a fairly pointy little hoof. I tucked the calf's hoof into my hand

and started to draw the leg upwards towards the heifer's birth canal, using my hand to protect the uterine lining from the hoof. The hoof and leg moved upwards, and I placed a calving rope on the calf's fetlock as it arrived into the birth canal, then got Christie to hold a gentle tension on the rope so the leg didn't disappear back inside. With my right hand I now went searching for the second hind leg, which took a bit more effort, as the heifer was now pressing against me again. I eventually found it and moved it up into the birth canal. It was very nice to feel the leg extend and slot into place. This made more space in the uterus for the rest of the calf to line up better. I applied a calving rope to the second leg and Christie held that one too. The calf was now in the correct position for delivery, albeit back end first.

I had a quick look to make sure that the heifer's head collar was secure as I got ready to deliver the calf. I kept tripping over Christie now as he fussed and panicked, trying to pre-emptively fulfil my every need. After getting my calving jack lined up, I attached the calving ropes with Christie leaning on one side of the heifer, her standing and me gently pulling. Slowly the calf made her way into the world. Christie couldn't see sufficiently from his side, so he abandoned his heifer side-support role and came around the back to get a closer look, then got a bit impatient and started sliding his hand in all directions between the calf's rear and the surrounding vulva in an attempt to stretch and loosen and make way. With gentle traction and a bit of leverage, the calf's tail and rear came through the vulva, and after a short repositioning of the calving jack, her abdomen and thorax came through, quickly followed by the head and forelimbs. Christie caught the new arrival in his arms and lay her gently on the ground to save her fall.

We dropped everything and went straight to resuscitating the calf. She had been stuck in there a while, and there was a real chance that she wouldn't survive the delivery. I knelt beside her and cleared the foetal membranes and fluid from her mouth as best I could, then sat her up on her chest. After about a minute of intense chest rubbing, she let out a big bawling noise, took some nice big breaths and coughed out the remaining fluid. I felt with my fingers along the left side of her chest and found a nice strong heartbeat. I heaved a sigh of relief – she was alive!

Christie did not quite recognise these positive signs of life, however, as he was still frantically rubbing and cleaning the calf, blowing into the calf's nose and poking straw into her ear (a trick that sometimes stimulates breathing). I don't think in Christie's panic he had observed any of her breathing, and I practically had to stop him giving the calf mouth to mouth. Eventually he stood back a couple of inches and smiled, declaring, 'She is a fine calf.' Christie couldn't have looked any more chuffed. I smiled in agreement. It was such a great feeling of relief, that it had all gone well.

Seeing that little red calf sitting on the grass taking nice big breaths and calling to her mother just made the moment, as did Christie smiling so much that he was momentarily speechless.

The heifer, a bit sore and getting agitated, started to test my rope halter and the strength of the tree, which she intermittently shook. It was time to double-check the heifer internally, so I asked Christie to hold her tail to the side and said, 'We'll check her for spares and tears.'

His eyes bulged out of his head and he said, 'Jeez vit! There wouldn't be another one in her sure, look at the size of this fine calf!'

To which I replied, 'Sure I'm a twin myself and look at the size of me!'

Tales from other vets I had met through my undergraduate training years had me on high alert for accidentally forgetting to check for a twin – I didn't want to be that guy.

The heifer was quite impatient by this point, but I had a chance to do a quick internal exam and confirm all was in order just before we heard a loud crack and the old tree branch snapped in two.

Christie, in sheer panic, jumped straight onto the end of the rope that was still tied to her head and held on tight. In no time the disgruntled heifer found herself less restrained and took off with Christie in tow, howling expletives at her. He was down and field-skiing, holding onto the rope for dear life, going head-first, his body weight offering no resistance to the heifer's escape. Over the general racket I could make out his mumbling, about the vit's fine blue rope.

He came to a stop about fifty metres downhill to me, right in front of an impressive-sized cow pat. As he fought with his last bit of strength, we both watched as the remainder of rope was pulled through his hands the whole way along its length through the cow pat.

He shouted, 'I'm awful sorry vit, every inch of your good rope has crossed the zone of repugnance and is well and truly covered in shit!'

At that, the heifer, realising her freedom but also interested in her calf, had a battle between her desire to escape and her oxytocin-driven urge to be a mother. She was having a stand-off a sufficient distance away from us so that there was no way we could easily retrieve the now greenish-brown rope anyway. Christie was very cross about losing my rope and shook his fist in the air shouting after her, 'Ya, ooo welled bag – twill have to rot off ya!'

I started gathering my things and Christie reluctantly accepted there was no catching the heifer for a third time and that the rope was staying put, so he helped me to the car. He was sincerely grateful for the helping hand and the successful delivery. As we walked out, the calf was making a good attempt at standing and was up on her knees just about to find her hooves. The new mother started coming closer – the mothering instinct having overcome her flightiness. The ladies who had been watching on throughout bid their farewells and headed off through the field and down the lane towards their respective houses. Christie and I lagged behind. Once we were over the fence, I glanced back to see the heifer now licking her new daughter, bonding underway.

As we walked back towards the car near Christie's old farm place, he asked me if I could keep a secret. I assured him I could make a determined effort to do so. He said, 'Have you got another minute or two? I know you like your nature, vit. I have something to show you.'

We went through the overgrowth near to his house, taking a path that led into the old orchard. I pointed to the old apple bins and said, 'Christie, it's like I'm up in Armagh.' He looked at me and thought for a second or two and then, making the connection, he said, 'I had forgotten of course you hail from the apple county.'

I asked how long it had been since apples were harvested here, and he said he had given up about twenty years previous, as the prices weren't worth the effort in the end. I agreed, as my father had had a similar experience with his orchards. I momentarily smiled and thought back to a friend of mine in Armagh who compared the price of everything to bins of apples. Walking through town with this friend, for example, he would look at a fish-and-chips shop menu and say, 'How much for fish and chips?! £10! That's half a bin of apples! Don't they know what it takes to pick half a bin of apples?' Not many people would know what he was talking about, but by God I did.

Walking closely behind Christie through the narrow path, I was filled with intrigue, wondering what I was about to see. As we made our way through the overgrown scrub, he looked at me a few times a little uneasy, and finally on the third instance, with slight discomfort, he raised his left arm to halt my progress and said, 'Hold up there, vit!'

As I looked on, he went down on one knee, presumably trying to be inconspicuous to nearby wildlife. I was thinking I needed to do the same perhaps, and just as I was about to join him on the ground, he said, 'Me twine has got loose. Wait here till I tighten it.'

He then started unravelling and retying his ankle-level baler twines. There was no time like the present to enquire as to what their purpose was, so I asked him straight out, to which he replied, 'Since tis near fruit season isn't so bad as they are distracted, but there's times of year here, vit, you wouldn't get far here without a rat running up the inside of yer leg! Tis OK, vit, sure you have the wellies (wellingtons / gumboots) on, they would have it hard getting up yours.'

Being around farms my whole life I had never even heard of this being a thing. Surely not, I thought. Maybe the Fee's rats were organised and were in fact crazed leg climbers – the uncertainty was too much. Was Christie a misunderstood genius or a raving lunatic? I couldn't decide fast enough. Maybe he was pulling my leg? Christie got up and as we walked further along the pathway, behind Christie I was trying not to make it too obvious as I took efforts to ensure every inch of my own trouser bottoms were tucked well inside my wellies. Just to be safe like. Christie went on to explain about Digger, his old terrier, who was a good fifteen years old and in retirement. 'He can't hunt them out like he used to – suffering cataracts. He can't see them, and he doesn't have a tooth left in his head for finishing them off either. He's only good for sleeping beyond in the house by the fire these days, vit.'

We walked another 300 metres or so before Christie slowed up and beckoned to me to crouch closer to the ground. We both ended up on our knees crawling through some thick rushes.

I thought to myself that perhaps this was the highest-risk rat-pant-leg entry point of our adventure and tried to not look too terrified. Then Christie pointed up into a nearby oak tree and said, 'Vit, vit – there they are.'

Looking up into the fork in the branches of the tree only a couple of hundred metres away, I saw a red kite standing on the side of the makings of a nest. As I looked on, a second red kite arrived, carrying a sizeable tree branch. The birds greeted each other and set about arranging it on their pile.

Christie whispered out the side of his mouth while still staring ahead at the birds. 'I think they're going to do it this year. I think there will be young reared. Last year was a disaster for them.' He pointed to another fork higher up in the tree that had a couple of misplaced twigs still remaining, evidence of a failed nesting attempt.

'A bad thunderstorm came about last year and put them off, but I think they'll do it this year,' he added.

I stared on in amazement; this truly was a spine-tingling moment, as I knew the red kites had only recently been reintroduced to Ireland after 200 years of extinction. I had spotted one or two already on my rounds, and now here were everyone's ambitions realised – a nesting pair! The larger female was hard at work taking off again, on her hunt for nesting material. She flew directly over our heads – with her expansive wings and rufous red underbelly, she truly did look like a kid's flying kite.

Christie pointed out a few little piles of animal bones and old sheep's wool on the ground nearby, adding that the reason they went extinct in the first place was that they were blamed for killing farm animals. Back then farmers came to check on their stock only to find red kites having a feast on a dead corpse. Christie went on to say, it was only after the damage was done that people realised that red kites eat mostly carrion and were not in fact responsible for the stricken animals – just having an opportunistic feast on their remains. Christie then said, 'This pair will be hard on the rats too. Soon I won't have a single one about.' He was hopeful that rats would be one of the kites' favourite snacks. We sat for fifteen minutes watching them in action, I got repeated goose bumps marvelling at these majestic birds of prey.

Christie then said the scientists involved in the reintroduction knew they were there, for they dropped by on occasions, but he implored me, 'Please, vit, don't tell another soul about them. I don't want them getting grief!'

I thanked Christie for letting me see them and promised I wouldn't tell anyone what I had seen. We made a silent retreat, back through the path.

When we arrived back at the car Christie gave me a very strong handshake, reinforced with his second hand. Amidst a sea of fine vit, fine car, fine job, fine weather, etc., I did a five-point turn in his narrow laneway and then off I headed, smiling to myself at the eccentric character I had just met, the beautiful autumn weather and, well, I guess the fine job of delivering a live calf – a success story. And never once did I mention to Christie that that was the first calving I had ever done as a qualified veterinary surgeon!

About ten days later I was in the clinic doing a puppy vaccination consult when the front door of the practice burst open and I heard a high-pitch voice say, 'Where is he? Where is he?'

'Who are you after?' Mary asked.

'The fine young vet! By God he did a fine job for me, let me tell you!'

The voice was unmistakable – it was Christie.

He paced and shouted in his normal emphatic manner, so loud that I swear I thought he was going to open the consult room door and burst in. He stated that he would do his messages in town and drop back in fifteen minutes – he had something for the fine young vit.

I had finished with the puppy vaccine and the client was just walking out the front door when Christie reappeared. He came straight over to me with a huge smile on his face, and at a very high decibel level declared his appreciation for all my hard work that day. If it wasn't for me, he said, she'd be in an awful predicament up on the hill and only fit for the kites. He beamed.

He then started fumbling in his coat and produced a carrier bag containing my blue rope, spotlessly clean and wrapped into a neat coil. Christie gave me a good tip that day: you got a shitty rope? Put it in the wash machine. But maybe not at your sister-in-law's!

A couple of days after the calving, he and Nora had managed to pen the heifer one more time and get the rope off her. 'Herself and the fine calf are doing great,' he added. He then went to the receptionist and told her the story all over again about what a predicament he had been in and how the new vit had done miracles. I must admit, for my first ever full-fledged calving case it was some very nice feedback to receive, even if my true efforts had been embellished far beyond reality.

As Christie left the office that day, he did a little bow on his way out the door – a final token of appreciation for our work.

Having met Christie, and given that the local town was small, I began to notice him on his bicycle around the town on my car trips out and about. He must have had great eyesight, as he was always stopped and waving in advance of me driving by. This became quite a common occurrence, I soon learned that if there was someone with a bicycle jumping around and waving - it will be Christie! Seeing him was always a nice little bright addition to my day on many occasions thereafter.

A few months later it was time for the local village agricultural show. I was excited to attend, as I had been to many with my dad when I was a kid, and as I mentioned earlier, having a nose around farm machinery, farm animals and country produce runs in my blood.

I spent most of the afternoon walking around enjoying the music, the food and watching displays such as sheep dog trials and horse-drawn ploughing. The entire show was held on some recently cut silage fields on the outskirts of town on a site that featured gentle slopes. It was possible to see the whole site from the top of the field, which was a good vantage point for looking down over the stunning countryside. I even had a great view of the entertainment, which included falconry, show jumping and a tug-of-war competition. I met a few familiar farmers as I explored, and made a few new acquaintances along the way too, the country people being very friendly folk.

As I stood there, noticing busy crowds of people all around, I got chatting with a small group of American tourists who had been driving by and had stopped off for a look, and subsequently were enjoying the show in complete amazement at everything – definitely a stark contrast to a Sunday afternoon in New York City for them.

In the distance I made out Christie waving and shouting, making his way over to me dressed in his Sunday finest. I didn't really have enough time to explain Christie's eccentric nature to the Americans. I had grown fond of Christie and had simply come to expect the unexpected with him. He was liable to say and do literally anything, and I actually found the uncertainty a little exciting. As he climbed the small hill towards us, waving his arms in the air and shouting, 'Ah there's the mighty fine vit!' I must admit I was a little bit embarrassed though, as he was outing me to all the strangers around, proclaiming about what a fine vit I was and attracting everyone's attention. Not that being a vet did much to hold me back, but you see – five minutes earlier I had been in the petting zoo right beside where we were standing, cuddling every critter there and tending not to volunteer that I was a vet. Some might think that was un-vet-like behaviour, and now my cover was blown.

Christie, now about a hundred metres away, was holding the undivided attention of the American tourists and a few other nearby groups of local people, and I was weighing up just what outrageous things Christie might cast upon these American visitors. The suspension was building – what the hell would they think? How would I explain that he was one of the local 'characters'?

He was perhaps fifty metres away when the anticipated unexpected event occurred. As he approached, completely out of nowhere, two shiny, silver, live fish fell straight out of the sky and landed on the ground at Christie's toes. The fish were full of life, kicking and jumping all over the place, as the Aussies would say, 'like cut snakes. Pointing and falling to his knees, leaning back, arms reaching to the sky inches from the wriggling fish, Christie immediately started shouting and waving his arms! He cried out, 'God feeds his people, God feeds his people! Look, vit, look!' I'm not sure if Christie was previously religious, but it looked like he had just found God just right there!

The Americans were amazed and outraged all at once, as was I. They didn't know what to make of it all. Their eyes nervously looked at mine for reassurance that this wasn't a regular occurrence out in the Irish countryside.

I think I was the only one who noticed a European herring gull high up in the clouds overhead – perhaps a bit peeved – do a few small circles and then head back over the hills for the short flight back to the coast, probably to plunder more mackerel from a fishing trawler.

Christie stood and pointed at the frantic, wriggling fish, all the while jumping up and down shouting, 'God feeds his people!' to the crowd of onlookers gathered. It is an image that will stay with me forever and, undoubtedly, something those Americans took back to the States with them. Christie once again had blown my mind.

Finally, catching his breath, Christie made the rest of the way over to me, saying, 'Hello, vit! Such a fine job you did that day. And such a fine young heifer calf she has, running after her now.'

I smiled and nodded and said, 'Sure, it was a great pleasure, Christie.'

He then got excited again, and this time he went to a whisper and got close to my ear, covering the gap with his hand and saying, 'The kites, beyond up near the home place – they have three fine chicks halfway reared!'

I was delighted to hear this news, and I patted Christie on the back and said, 'Do you know what? You have made my day Christie. That's the best news I've heard in a long time.'

Christie's eyes sparkled, a smile stretched from ear to ear and a little bit of foamy spit formed on his whiskers from all his enthusiasm.

Still to this day as I drive around on my daily farm visits, if I find myself up in higher land, I will take a few moments and pull over and get my binoculars out. Red kites are becoming a familiar appearance again, especially in County Wicklow, and each and every time I see one, I always smile, thinking it could be one of Christie Fee's fine red kite chicks.

CHAPTER 2

Marmalade Karma

On a few occasions over the years I travelled over to southern England, to the beautiful Cornwall countryside to work in a small town not far from Padstow. A vet friend of mine, John, ran a clinic there, and he would call me up to come and cover his holidays. I really looked forward to my trips there, as the area is incredibly beautiful, filled with forests, ancient buildings, spectacular bridges and stunning beaches. Lots of the old trades are still very much alive there, with butcher shops, bakeries, fishmongers, coffee shops and quaint country pubs with impressive lists of local brews. It truly is postcard perfect. I love exploring old towns and cities and going on countryside walks and, well, this area had all of that and more.

Everyone down that part of the country seems to be naturally cheery, giving a feeling almost like everyone is on a nice holiday – only those lucky buggers get to live there all year long. The local accents and phrases gave me no end of entertainment. To me, the local speak was just so endearing, hearty and eccentric. I soon got used to hearing the locals thanking their bus drivers by saying 'cheers drive' on the way off the bus, or when something tasted particularly good it was 'gert lush', and those are just a couple of examples of the charming colloquialisms that made me smile often.

Maureen Green was in her seventies when I first met her at John's clinic. One thing is for sure, Maureen loved her tweed. She was always wearing one of her tweed dresses, coats and floral tweed hats, of which she had many. Maureen had a slight frame; medium-length, greying ginger hair with a slight curl in it, just long enough that some of her curls peeped out from beneath the brim of her hats. She had a thick Cornish accent and rosy red cheeks, to go along with her Cornwall cheeriness. A fan of vibrant red lipsticks, and often wearing a perfume that smelled of roses or lilies, her ensemble gave the impression that she was indeed quite a flowery person. Maureen lived in a terraced two-up two-down at the top of town, just her and her cat Marmalade.

Marmalade was an older cat with medium-length, greying ginger hair, but that's where his similarities to his owner stopped, as he was perfectly round in shape. Maureen had taken on Marmalade's care after her older brother Frank had passed away a few months previously. Frank's dying wish was that Maureen would do all she could to look after his beloved cat. Maureen had not really been an animal person, but she had accepted the responsibility for Marmalade, putting her failing brother's mind at ease, and so Marmalade came to live with her.

I first met Maureen around the time she took on Marmalade, during one of my stints at John's clinic. Keen on fulfilling her responsibility with Marmalade, she had taken him to see me at the clinic for a check-up, a vaccination and a chat about how she could best look after an older cat. Maureen had found a few behavioural issues with him and wanted to see if anything could be done. We discovered at that visit that he became an angry, wild lion when we attempted to do anything with him.

Marmalade was a force to be reckoned with, even at seventeen years old, and he soon developed a reputation at the clinic as one of the more challenging patients. His problem was that he was very overweight, weighing in at a good ten kilos (as opposed to the feline average of four and a half kilos), meaning that, to put it politely, self-grooming was not really possible. And for a human to groom him without welding gloves, a welding mask and chain-mail body armour was just not an option either. And so, I was tasked with subduing the lion, to get Marmalade groomed on a few occasions over the years.

Frank had been the town's local beekeeper and was frequently seen out and about on his bicycle, delivering jars of honey to the shops, I am told. He had kept his beehives at the allotments and community gardens around town, where his bees pollinated the crops for everyone and produced lovely honey. Locals recalled Frank as a very friendly chap, and I suspect he may have been a little eccentric too, as he was often seen wearing his full beekeeping attire, while cycling from hive to hive. Maureen told me that one day, while doing his deliveries, Frank found a little ginger kitten in an alleyway, abandoned, cold and only about five days old, with his little eyes still closed. With no sign of the mother cat coming back, Frank wrapped him up and took him home, raising him with a bottle on formula milk. He named the kitten Marmalade.

Growing up a very spoiled cat, Marmalade was treated like the king of the castle, and he truly was, the apple of Frank's eye. Thereafter Marmalade joined Frank on his deliveries, sitting in the basket beside the jars of honey at the front of Frank's bicycle. Frank even fashioned a little bee-proof basket cover for Marmalade so he could come on collection days too and watch from the safety of his basket. Locals soon learned not to approach Marmalade when he was perched in Frank's basket, as any attempt to give him a pat were met with hissing, growls and bared claws; only Frank could handle Marmalade. All this was back in Marmalade's younger, slimmer years, however, before he got too pudgy for the trip and had to stay at home.

Frank and later Maureen had tried and failed to get Marmalade to lose weight. All the common approaches had been unsuccessful: low-calorie foods, satiety medications, more exercise – the list goes on. The primary problem was Marmalade's bad temper; when he didn't get his way, he wasn't afraid to show his displeasure. Frank could just about manage the mood swings, but now that Marmalade was older and (even) crankier, Maureen just bowed to his demands.

She had told me that at an early stage she hadn't been entirely delighted with looking after Marmalade. It would seem that the raging lion Marmalade we saw at the clinic pretty much paralleled how he behaved at home. Maureen had stopped inviting visitors to her house, as Marmalade had started attacking them. Maureen said however, she was going to look after him to best of her ability. She was a firm believer that we as humans should look after animals well, saying, 'You know, what goes around comes around.'

I suspected this might also be a reason for the dieting failure, as Maureen could not bear to see Marmalade look even a little hungry. It was easier just to lay out a banquet of foods for him every day – and this also helped keep him away from her! He definitely was not an affectionate lap cat.

We soon worked out a system for Marmalade's visits to the clinic. We would give Maureen a few sedative pills to slip into his early, light breakfast. Maureen would then tempt Marmalade into his cat carrier with little pieces of smoked salmon, which he simply couldn't refuse. Getting the carrier door closed before the claws and fangs came out, so that she could transport him. This was all very stressful for Maureen. She was determined to do everything to keep him healthy and happy though, even if it meant she would often need treatment for bites and scratches herself. Some days, if Marmalade had been particularly challenging, Maureen would arrive in a shaken state, sometimes wearing plasters and bandages.

Maureen would park close to the back door of the vet clinic so that she could bring him, in his carrier, straight from the car into the treatment room, where he would stay with us for a few hours. Marmalade's arrival could be heard from the far end of the building, a mix of banshee wails and lion growls. He didn't seem to understand that all we wanted to do was help him, as he fought hard against us each time. He would be given some further injectable sedation so that the vet nurse, although not a groomer, could clip off his fur mats and try do several months' worth of brushing while he was out cold. Our work on Marmalade was certainly out of necessity and by no means vanity, as, left to his own devices, his coat would be a matted, festering mess, and would have got pretty unpleasant for him quite quickly.

I was a little afraid that, at seventeen years old and morbidly obese, Marmalade would develop a disease that would require him to be given medications – a task that would likely be impossible for Maureen. My only opportunity to examine Marmalade was when he came in for these visits, under sedation. Marmalade checked out healthy on his visits, his only issue being that his joints were getting a little stiff, but that had been managed quite well with the addition of joint supplements to his food.

It was a few months after my previous visit to cover John's holidays when I had an unexpected phone call from him. He wanted to ask if it was OK to pass on my postal address, as Maureen had asked for it. He also wanted to let me know what had recently happened.

On the previous Saturday morning Maureen rang John at around 9 am, just as the clinic opened. Marmalade had passed away peacefully in his sleep, she told him.

John, a bit taken aback, asked her if she was OK. Had there been any sign that something was up?

'Not one,' she said. He had eaten his dinner the previous night as usual, and that morning there he was on his favourite pillow, dead as a doornail. Maureen went on to say that she was just so relieved that he had had a good life, and that Frank had been smiling down on both of them, ever since the day he passed away. Frank would be pleased that Marmalade had gone peacefully in his dreams.

But, Maureen added, she had a problem. What should she do with his body? She hadn't been in this scenario before and hastened to add, she was too old for digging holes.

She said she had heard of a neighbour who had found a deceased cat in the garden after a suspected run-in with a car and, at a loss as to what to do with the body, she had wrapped him up and put him in the household waste bin. She wanted to know if she could do the same.

John had said he thought that wasn't a great idea, and that perhaps if she brought Marmalade down to the vet clinic they could come up with a nicer alternative, burial, for example, or cremation at the local pet crematorium. She agreed this was a better plan.

Maureen lived at the top of town, about a fifteen-minute walk to the clinic at the bottom of town. She had given up driving at this stage, so she told John she would wrap Marmalade up well and put him in Frank's old suitcase, which she had stored at her house, and walk him down to drop him off at the clinic. She would leave the suitcase to the charity shop on her walk back, she said, as she had no need for that now either.

It was about 11 am, and John was having a quick cup of tea with the receptionist when he saw Maureen coming along the front windows of the practice. From a distance she looked distressed, as though she was sobbing as she walked along. Then the front door opened and in she walked, empty-handed; Maureen wasn't crying, she was doubled up with laughter! John immediately got up to see if she was OK. Gasping through shortened breaths and with eyes full of tears, Maureen told him what had happened.

She had put poor old Marmalade into the suitcase and started walking down through the town. A bit worried that people might figure out what was in the case, she had been trying not to make it look too obvious that she was struggling with the weight. As she came down into town, she encountered two young men at a pedestrian crossing. They weren't familiar to her. Perhaps they were just passing through town that morning, she thought. They noticed Maureen's struggle and offered to help. Reluctant to say no, Maureen accepted their offer. Embarrassed at what she was transporting, she made a bit of awkward chit chat, as the men negotiated the cobblestone footpath with the suitcase. Noticing the bag was a bit of a dead weight, the guys asked what was inside. Maureen, keen to cover up the truth, said it was just her brother's old antique suitcase with a few of his favourite things. Maureen also reported, a passing dog had briefly stopped and sniffed the case, then looked her square in the eyes and trotted off again. As they walked, Maureen was getting more nervous by the minute.

They arrived at a traffic light and were obliged to wait for a minute. Maureen focused on the light changing, deep in thought about how she was going to explain to the chaps, her trip to the vets. Just as the lights changed, Maureen turned to her two acquaintances, only to find them running off down a side street, stuffing her suitcase into an awaiting van and speeding off!

In shock, Maureen just kept on walking around to the vet clinic to let them know the news. They had stolen Marmalade. The ridiculousness of what had just happened now had her in fits of laughter. She said she would pay good money to see the looks on those guys' faces when they opened the case and saw what was really in there. Not to mention that poor old Marmalade wasn't looking his best again. Maureen found the impending karma hilarious.

Only a couple of days later, a postcard arrived at my place from England:

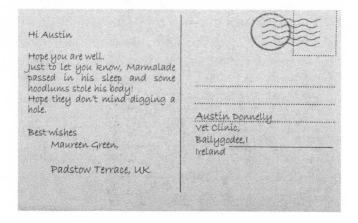

Hi Austin

Hope you are well.
Just to let you know, Marmalade passed in his sleep and some hoodlums stole his body!
Hope they don't mind digging a hole.

Best wishes
    Maureen Green,

    Padstow Terrace, UK

Austin Donnelly
Vet Clinic,
Ballygodee, 1
Ireland

CHAPTER 3

The Craic'd Sheep Farmers

Craic – pronounced 'crack' – has nothing to do with the illicit substance, but it is just as addictive. Craic happens in many different places. Good craic can give you goose bumps, but mighty craic can knock your socks off. It is subconscious and joyful, better than just fun and laughter alone – it enlivens an experience. It's like the MSG seasoning on your chips that elevates them to another level, and just like MSG, too much craic mightn't be good for you either. It has a similarity to the Englishman's banter, but Irish craic is better! You can do certain things for the craic, like an Australian would, just for the shits and giggles. There could be craic even at a funeral, if it's not an overwhelmingly sad one, especially if a previously unannounced offspring of the deceased turns up. There certainly is no craic in misery. A full measure of craic is said to be ninety. Some people have it, some people crave it, and unfortunately some people are completely minus craic, and still other people will never get it at all. It's not just drunken frivolity, and it's more than a gossip's tale or scandal. Any age group can have it. Irish people can detect and find it – they live for it! This farm I'm about to tell you about was full of it.

It all started back when I worked in rural County Wexford. A large proportion of my day-to-day work involved visiting farms to tend to the animals. This area is renowned in Ireland for growing mouth-watering strawberries, being in the sunny south east, by Irish standards. When it came time for local strawberry farms to harvest their fruit in the warmer months, I would often be passing fields with rows of deep-green plants bearing vibrant red fruit, out on my rounds. Being prime agricultural and horticultural land, there were also lots of big farms around, the local landscape being a patchwork of golden-brown hills of grain crops, interspersed with grazing pastures, in a whole range of different shades of green. I was based along the east coast of the county, and on my daily travels I was never too far from the Irish Sea either. In this role I worked predominantly with cattle, sheep and horses. That vet practice also had a small animal hospital, and in the evenings, I would help with pet clinics too.

Spring in Ireland runs mostly from February to May, and that is the time that a lot of young farm animals are born, coinciding with the end of the winter weather and the start of better grass growth. This area had quite a lot of sheep farming underway, and I would often be called to assist with lambing ewes with a variety of different obstetrical issues. Some of the larger sheep farms synchronised their ewes to lamb within a few weeks, housing them in the winter and organising the expectant mothers in pens according to the number of lambs they were carrying (as determined by an ultrasound scan). When I visited sheep farms at this time of year there would be pregnant ewes in pens carrying anywhere from one lamb, right up to triplets and even quadruplets. This allowed the sheep farmers to feed and care for the expectant mothers accordingly – those carrying more lambs would incrementally get more of the higher-energy fodder and perhaps also a bit more special treatment.

The farmers with synchronised lambing flocks had their dates all worked out and knew exactly when their sheep would be delivering. This often tied in nicely with vet students and agriculture students on their Easter college breaks, and as it is a bit of a rite of passage, during college many of us did a stint on such a farm, delivering lambs at a furious rate over many sleepless nights. Many sheep farmers are adept at lamb delivery and can manage a lot of the obstetrics themselves, but occasionally need extra vet help. It's easy for multiple-birth lambs to get all tangled up at delivery, or for a ewe with a single pregnancy to pump all her goodness into the lamb – growing them a bit too much, which results in a difficult delivery (dystocia). Sometimes a ewe with dystocia would be brought to see me in a trailer at the clinic, sometimes even just in the back of a car. Over the years there were many times that I met a farmer and his labouring sheep halfway, usually in the middle of nowhere, and performed roadside lamb deliveries. I used to smile, thinking what the people in the passing cars might make of it all if they knew what was going on, us parked in a rural gateway somewhere.

For farmers with a large number of ewes lambing, it just wasn't practical to leave the farm to meet me at our clinic, so I would call out to see them at their farm instead. Over the years working in that area, I experienced 'outbreaks' of different causes of sheep dystocia. One year there seemed to be a high rate of ring womb, with ewes going into labour but their cervix not opening properly, remaining like a tight ring, and many of those sheep needed assistance lambing (help in this case being gentle massage/manipulation of the cervix to stimulate dilation). This was blamed on weather conditions leading to trace element imbalances in the fodder: low calcium, magnesium and the likes. Deficiencies in these elements then were thought to affect somehow, the ewe's birthing hormone levels, causing sluggish cervix dilations. Another year we had a different problem – the younger, single-lamb-bearing, first-time ewes needed a lot of assistance because their lamb was far too big and, being first-timers, they were comparatively small – good weather and therefore rich fodder, was blamed on that one! My back still remembers all the caesarean sections I performed – all those extra-small-sheep-with-extra-large-vet-bending-over-her scenarios. Caesarean sections on sheep farms, are usually done with the ewe lying on her side on bales of hay or (if luck would have it) on a table as a makeshift surgery.

Over the years I got to know many of the local sheep farmers well, and in spring myself and the other vets at the practice would never be far away, from their lambing sheds. One large sheep farm in particular, called us out a lot for help during those few weeks of lambing. The farm was owned by the Potts family – Cliff and his wife Bridie who were in their late seventies and their son Danny and his fiancée – later to be wife – Trish, were in their early thirties. Cliff and Bridie, being mostly retired, left the farming to Trish and Danny, although they still could be found pottering around the place, and in lambing season they would be in the lambing sheds feeding orphan lambs and doing light jobs. Danny, their only child, was keen on keeping the sheep farming going, and did good work improving the flock's genetics and growing its size. He had quite a scientific approach to sheep farming, and the sheep shed walls bore noticeboards with flow charts and targets. Danny was one of those sheep farmers that gives other farmers tours of his farm and talks on how to do it well.

The Potts also had a forty-foot sheep transport truck, with Trish and Danny being qualified truck drivers. Over the years I often saw them trucking together on the road, shipping sheep for themselves and many other farmers in the county. The Potts ran a flock of around 500 ewes, and in late spring and early summer the fields surrounding their farm were filled with sheep. Trish and Danny had met a few years previous on a Spanish holiday, they would later tell me, love at first sight and all that. Trish was born and bred in Dublin but had moved the 100 miles down the road to join Danny at the farm in Wexford and had embraced country living, grabbing sheep farming by the horns.

Unusually, my first visit to the farm all those years ago didn't come during spring lambing-season but in the autumn, and one of their prized rams had developed an abscess on a very sensitive area between his legs. It was shortly after breeding season, and he had his work done for the year, but having such an issue near his crown jewels meant his future breeding career was in peril. The farm itself was up a laneway off a main road on a gentle sloping hill. Large green fields look onto more hills and forests in the distant north and overlook the Irish Sea way off to the east – spectacular views all around, really. The Potts had big green sheep sheds to accommodate their flock in the winter months, and over my time working there I would experience many hilarious things in those sheds!

The Potts were an interesting bunch, that's for sure, each and every one with their own quirky spirit. When I visited the farm to attend to their flock, I could be greeted by any one of the gang and sometimes all four of them, as they all worked well as a team. Trish really looked the part of a young country farmer, usually wearing overalls and welly boots and a colourful hand-knitted beanie hat or scarf, accessorised with large-frame spectacles in a variety of colours. The only aspect about her that suggested she hadn't been raised in the depths of the countryside was her strong Dublin accent. She was so hands-on and clued-in with the farming; it was impressive to see a city girl with such a flair for all things, country. As time went on it became clear that this was a great source of pride for the Potts family. They treasured Trish's enthusiasm, perhaps in the early days thinking she might not last in the long haul, but she had surpassed all their expectations.

I was reasonably new to the area the first time I visited the Pott's farm, and still getting the measure of the local clients and the vet workload. I soon got to love going out to see the Potts. On trips out to their farm there would be many laughs, occasions of preposterous wonderment and humour along the way, and truly never a dull moment. The Potts were first and foremost a cracked (slightly mad) bunch, but they were also great craic. Affectionately, I came to think of the whole Potts gang – Trish, Danny, Cliff and Bridie – as the Craic Potts.

That first time I went to the Potts farm to see that ram, the message was that Danny and Trish were out in the truck doing a delivery and that, should they not have returned by time I arrived, I was to park near the sheep sheds. 'Go on over to the farmhouse and have a cup of tea with Cliff and Bridie until we get back,' Danny said, adding that he wasn't too far away. Turning off the main road and driving up the laneway, I noticed Danny and Trish's newly built house on the way. Following the lane past the house, I arrived at the farmyard. Just a few hundred meters further along stood a big old Victorian-style farmhouse, right in the middle of the farm buildings. This was where Cliff and Bridie lived. Danny had insisted I wait on him to get there to help handle the ram, as he didn't want his elderly father getting injured, saying, 'Despite his age, the old bugger will still have a go at wrangling a sheep. It's pretty hard to stop him trying.' So, with a little time to kill, I went in to meet Cliff and Bridie.

I parked and walked across the courtyard towards the old farmhouse. To get to the door of the house, I had to pass through a garden gate and go up along a short path between the house on the left and some old stone-walled vegetable beds and rockery on the right.

As I got closer, I noticed a large, colourful cock pheasant sitting on the top of the garden gate, right at my eye level. He was still in full summer plumage, with bright-red wattles, erect purple ear tufts and an iridescent bottle-green-and-blue head and neck. With his plump, round body, bright copper-orange feathers and a red sheen to his undercarriage he was a dazzling sight altogether, catching the morning sun as he turned to look at me. He was like a living piece of art, with his beautiful, vivid colours. Every pheasant I had ever met previously had been naturally wary of humans, and as I approached, I expected him to take fright and fly off, but instead he just sat there observing me from his perch. In fact, as I grew nearer, not only did he not take flight, he taunted me by making that loud screeching call and wing-clap noise pheasants make – at ear-ringing close quarters.

He kept his eyes locked on me as if to say, 'Take that.' We then had a bit of a standoff, as he would have needed to move, if I was going to get through the garden gate. I believe I won the stare down, but he didn't appear at all defeated. He simply jumped down onto the garden side of the gate and strutted across the path to feast on a few scraps of bread sitting in some nearby dog bowls, displaying how very sure of himself he was. He even appeared to pump his breast out a little more than before, so as to remind me I was entering his patch.

I passed by, impressed at the pheasant's audacity, and gave him another sun-squinted glare to try to reclaim some of my manhood. Arriving at the farmhouse I gave a few raps on an enormous wooden door with a cast-iron knocker. These knocks were met with a chorus of barking dogs and the sound of paws scrabbling from a doorway on the other side of the house. In no time I found myself surrounded by a pack of Old English Sheepdogs, barking and keen to say hello. I was mobbed! They weren't threatening or aggressive, just making sure everyone knew I was there. I looked back towards my feathered friend, who was no more than twenty metres away, and thought – there's going to be some kind of clash here. To my surprise, the dogs didn't go anywhere near the pheasant, and he just continued, head down, arse up, in food-bowl-inspecting indifference. Bridie opened the door from inside and called the dogs off, inviting me in. The dogs followed us through, and in a flash, they were all in their beds along the hallway.

Bridie was a small woman, wearing a beige dress and a red polka-dot kitchen apron. As I came through the door, she looked up at me in such a way as to draw attention to what felt like a three-foot height disparity between us. Smiling, she said, 'Well, hello up there!' Bridie had a slightly stooped-forward posture and wore her auburn hair in two loose plaits that just about reached her shoulders. On her feet were a comfortable-looking pair of Crocs, a slightly unexpected modern twist. The dogs kept giving the occasional bark, so Bridie shouted at them again to be quiet, this time walking around to them individually in their beds, waving her finger and saying, 'Call it off, call it off. I see him now!'

There were five freshly shorn Old English Sheepdogs in total, all a lovely light-blue-grey and white. We stopped at each of the dogs in their beds for a few moments, and Bridie introduced me. First up was a nine-month-old pup, the baby of the bunch – Candy. She playfully rolled onto her back in her bed and offered me her paw as I tickled her tummy. Candy's mother Millie was next and resting her chin on a pillow at one end of her bed she gave a few happy tail wags as I patted her head. Further towards the entrance of the kitchen there was Fred; this time Bridie bent down and played with his under chin – saying he was five years old and a stud dog. Fred's ten-year-old uncle, Flash, was in the next bed. He looked at me with a slightly apprehensive eye as I approached, but soon gave in to my back-scratching attempts, making little groans of pleasure and swinging around to look at my hand each time I dared to stop. Further along the corridor, nearest to the heat of the kitchen stove, Bridie introduced the matriarch of the pack, Meg. At twelve years old, Meg was less excited by my approach, choosing to ignore me, as though having a nap now, was more important to her. I gave her a back rub anyway.

Bridie told me that she once had been big into working and breeding the Old English Sheepdogs, but that she was now retired from that. Danny and Trish put the dogs to good use rounding up sheep, amongst other things, she said, and they were also great company for her and Cliff.

I took my boots off, leaving them just inside the doorway, and we made our way through the hallway, towards the living room, to meet Cliff. The door was already open and as I walked in, I saw Cliff sitting with his back to me in a red suede armchair. His seat was in the centre of the living room, right in front of a large window which overlooked the farm, with the distant paddocks and hills on one side and the Irish Sea in the distance at the other. At his elbow stood a coffee table with a knitted-tea-cosy-covered pot of tea and a cup freshly poured, steam still rising from it. Fitted neatly underneath the coffee table was an old chest of drawers. Cliff was busy looking out over his farm and scribbling notes as he went, an old-style tobacco pipe hanging from one side of his mouth. There was no smell of tobacco smoke, however, and in fact the room was filled with the lovely aroma from the turf burning in the large central fireplace. The living room was huge, with a high ceiling and walls painted a deep red with a rich golden wallpaper border. There were quirky tasselled lampshades on the lights and a couple of large vases on the floor filled with peacock feathers and dried flowers. A gramophone with a huge silver horn stood on a stylish mahogany cabinet, with a stack of records beside it. Near the gramophone was another similar cabinet, this one lined with crystal whiskey decanters, all full, and accompanied by fancy glasses, on a shelf above.

As I made my way across the squeaky floorboards towards him, Cliff took the pipe out of his mouth and exclaimed loudly, 'A young vet approaches.' Thinking perhaps he could see my reflection in the window, I smiled at the window. He put his notes down on the table, pushed his glasses up onto his forehead and shuffled forward in his seat so that he could stand and greet me. Cliff was a bit unsteady on his feet and on standing he reached out for my hand to help support him. But when he was up fully standing, he was actually quite a bit more mobile than first appeared, and after taking a few steps, he muttered about getting his hearing aid and made his way over to a bowl on top of an old piano nearby. He put a hearing aid in each ear and then said, less loudly, 'Happy to meet you son,' as he shook my hand. I hadn't seen a tobacco pipe in years, and, noticing my interest, Cliff just chuckled and said, 'Old habits die hard, I haven't smoked this thing in forty years, but I like to hold it in my mouth anyways; it helps me concentrate on my weather forecasting.'

He collected his teacup and saucer and walked to the nearby window, holding the saucer in one hand and looking out. Cliff, who was tall and thin, was wearing quite a twee mix of colours, including khaki-green trousers, with lemon-yellow socks on show, tucked into shiny black leather shoes, a dark-green waistcoat, complete with a blue cravat and a yellow shirt. He also wore a camouflage baseball hat, the kind you would see someone wearing whilst hunting deer. His face was thick with wrinkles, and there were patchy red areas of vessel-lined skin on his cheeks. He was down a tooth or two at the front, giving him a slightly hollow-gapped smile. The laughter lines around his eyes and mouth connected to larger folds of skin that dangled from his face, which came together to form a little pouch under his chin. The wrinkles seemed to disappear when Cliff smiled and returned thereafter. He had small, skinny hands, with long, knobby fingers like whips of willow.

I joined Cliff by the window, and we looked out over the fields; grazing sheep dotted the surrounding landscape, the clear-blue sky giving great visibility into the distance.

I said to Cliff, 'What beautiful scenery you have here.'

He looked at me and said, 'Well, son, as a wise man once said, 'You can't ate scenery…'' ('ate' being his colloquialism for 'eat').

I was momentarily quiet, nodding in agreement with Cliff's statement, while also trying to comprehend what he had said. I was a bit stumped, trying to figure out why you would even think about the nutritional value of such beauty? I wasn't fully sure what this meant or how wise the quote truly was. It momentarily cast me back to my dad, who always used to joke about people making such a fuss over food presentation. He would say, 'No need to be so fancy, sure I'm only going to eat it!' Food was food to him; there was no need for artistic flair.

I looked back over to Cliff and said, 'In fairness, those sheep of yours are having a good munch on it.'

To which Cliff looked at me, then back out the window, and said, 'I suppose you have a point,' although I was still a little confused. I think Cliff was too. He went silent for a few moments, scratching a patch on his head just above his right ear, pondering deeply.

Just then the house phone began to ring, an old-style fire-bell-type noise. Bridie came in from the kitchen and shouted to Cliff, 'That will be Fiona from the radio asking for the weather.'

'Oh, keep her talking for a minute or two,' Cliff said, 'I'm nearly ready.'

Bridie went back to the kitchen from where I could hear her loudly asking about Fiona's family, and how they were all keeping. As I looked on, Cliff popped his glasses back onto his nose, grabbed his pages of notes and made a few last scribbled additions. He then apologised, saying he would have to go and take the call for a few minutes.

Bridie came through again and said, 'Oh please excuse Cliff for a minute or two; he has an important phone call.' She explained that Cliff always had a call with the local radio show at 11 am of a Monday, to give the weather forecast for the week ahead. Bridie invited me to have a seat and I accepted her offer of a cup of tea, which she poured into a bone China teacup with matching saucer. She got out a set of knitted placemats to save her tabletop and, noticing more and more knitted items in the room, I asked if they were her work. 'Yes, they sure are,' she said. She told me how she had loved knitting, since she was a girl. She pointed out a knitted throw on the sofa behind me, then her knitted jumpers on a hanger by the door; she even had knitted the curtains around the window – all her handy work.

We dunked a biscuit or two in the tea and as we chatted, and I couldn't help but overhear Cliff in the background, relaying his forecast. He was saying things along the lines of:

The sheep are close together on the lower hill this morning – there will be rain tonight and tomorrow, but mind you not too much, as the starlings are murmuring overhead too. The pheasant is tending to stay at the south, there will be a northern gale for a day or two. The grey lag geese were on the wing at dusk last night – there could be an early frost before next weekend is over.

It was fascinating what he was saying, but I couldn't quite hear all of it despite my best efforts to train my ear in his direction. Finishing the call, Cliff came back in the room and carefully filed away his notes in the chest of drawers under the coffee table, which I noticed was full of similar notes – I suspect years' worth of Cliff's weather work.

A very old television in the far corner of the room had been on the whole time with the volume turned down, and just as Cliff was getting settled back into his chair caught a glimpse of it. The news channel had gone over to the weather presenter, who was pointing to maps and charts. Cliff reeled in horror, pointed to the television and said to Bridie, who was nearest to it, 'Will you ever turn that bollox off please?' Cliff covered his eyes with his hands for a moment or two before Bridie got it turned off, I think to fend off any meteorological influence. I couldn't help but smile, as my dad used to call the weather forecaster a bollox too. But that was only really after he had given a bad weather forecast!

Changing the subject, I decided now was a good time to ask about the pheasant I had met on my way in. 'What's the story with him?' I asked. Cliff said that the pheasant had been there for a decade. 'It's an old pet of a thing really,' he said, 'And he's very helpful with my forecasting. He's my weather pheasant.' Bridie also pointed with a proud smile to a framed picture hanging on the wall, a nice crocheted piece depicting the weather pheasant.

A few moments later Cliff got up, cup of tea and saucer in his hand once again and walked back to the living room window. I stood with my own tea and resumed my position next to him. To my immediate right was the old piano, and from that vantage point other old furniture pieces in the room began to catch my attention. I was keen to have a look at them, most of them almost certainly being antiques. On a shelf above the piano were two glass cases, one holding a stuffed barn owl and the other a stuffed mink; I went to have a closer look. Cliff noticed, and with another chuckle he came over to me, tapped me on the shoulder and said, 'I reckon you vets should train in taxidermy. You know.......... for when things don't go so well. It could be a great sideline!' He looked at me with a mischievous smirk, and we both had a laugh.

As I followed along the wall looking at the random assortment of photos and artworks, I came to an old black-and-white professional photo of a baby in a flowery dress. I was sure the Potts had said they only had the one child, Danny, so I assumed this must be of someone else. Bridie joined us now by the furniture and we got chatting about the various pieces. Some were heirlooms from her grandmother, and she enthusiastically told me a bit of their history. As I continued around the living room, I came to a second and then a third old black-and-white photograph of what appeared to be a bouncing baby girl. I decided to ask who this was in the photo. Bridie looked at Cliff and then at me and said, 'Well, that's Danny as a baby.' Seeing the confused look on my face, after a moment or two she added, 'Ah yeah, we had to dress him as a girl – well, you know, to keep him safe.'

At that Cliff lifted a walking stick and, moving to the middle of the large window, beckoned me closer and pointed the stick towards an enormous oak tree in the middle of a nearby field. Taking a deep breath, he said, 'There was a faerie barrow (where faeries live) dug up under that tree there, many moons ago back when I was a boy. My father and a couple of the neighbours did it.' His face now assumed a concerned expression, and he added, 'And, well, that was the start of a run of bad luck for us up here at the farm. The faeries left after that alright, but not before cursing us. That year we had dreadful problems with pregnant ewes delivering rotten lambs, weeks too early,' (sounded to me like abortions). He added, 'Later, with a lot of ewes that did make it to lambing time – many lambs were born dead – stillborn, not even fit to take a breath. Surviving lambs didn't thrive very well either and quite a few went missing too.'

As Cliff talked, I drifted into a light daydream for a spell, and in those few moments, I got to thinking of what diseases or conditions could have been responsible for this 'curse'. *Deep in the inner cogs of my brain, Steve (my memory guy) was making his way towards my mind-bank filing cabinets, in particular, the section C7 area, where all my vet knowledge about sheep is kept. I could visualise Steve dusting off the file entitled, 'Austin's vet school essays on the causes of still births and abortions in sheep'. As Steve flicked through the pages, the memories came flooding back. Common infectious agents and diseases causing abortions and stillbirths in sheep: the top of the list? A protozoan infection causing toxoplasmosis (Toxoplasma gondii), then some bacterial ones: Enzootic Abortion of the Ewe (caused by Chlamydophila abortus), Q fever (caused by Coxiella burnetti), campylobacteriosis, salmonellosis, listeriosis and then, getting down to less common things such as nutritional issues, bad moulds on fodder and exotic diseases not often found on these shores. Following that list came my go-to, vet school essay gap-filler: stress. Although, right there, part of me was slightly upset that no one had ever told me about the faeries being implicated. I so would have put them in my essays as a causative abortifacient of sheep back then had I known, if even just to give my lecturer a laugh. Strangely enough, I'm reasonably sure this lecturer would have seen the funny side of that, as he was prone to a bit of folklore chat himself.*

I returned from my brief reverie soon enough to hear Cliff say that, by the time Danny was born, they were on high alert that the faeries might try and take him, or even swap him, changing him with one of their own. 'The best thing we could do was disguise him as a girl,' he said. 'Back then the faeries only wanted baby boys.' Looking off into the distant horizon, Cliff then exhaled the last part of a large breath with a sigh and said, 'I believe nowadays that's different. They'll take either boys or girls.

'I came from a big family myself,' Cliff continued, 'And would you believe it, I'm the seventh son of a seventh son. Back in the early days me and my darling wife Bridie here had ambitions of having a big brood too and filling this big old house up with children. Why do you think we built so big? Having our own, seventh son ourselves was a dream. Danny was the only child we were blessed with – those faeries had us cursed, I'm sure of it!'

Bridie spoke up and said she would have loved a daughter too. She added that all these years later she would get a wonderful daughter-in-law, Trish, and at least that was something.

Cliff now said, 'The only thing they couldn't touch was my special talent. You see, some seventh sons,' seventh sons get healing hands, some take a notion and can predict the future – but me? With the help of nature, I got the gift of being able to forecast the weather.'

To which Bridie added, 'The last thing you would want is the faeries to get their hands on your child. Back then they were known to steal a few children in the night, around these parts, some parents finding nothing but a rotten piece of timber, or a few hen's eggshells, in their baby's cot in the morning.'

Cliff's face now turned into the picture of worry, as he recalled those very real and torturous, fears of yore. 'Those people unfortunate to have their babe swapped with a faerie baby had an awful curse on their hands too,' he said. 'The faerie babes just would never do well being raised as a human, always craving their own kind. Even after a few years of rearing, out of nowhere they could disappear and never be seen again, after having their fill of human milk and nurture. Meanwhile some people's human children were later returned and that never went well either,' he said, shaking his head firmly, saying, 'No, no, it was never good. Old folk around here got good at spotting the swapped babies too. They just never thrived as well as the human babies, always looking a bit thin and slight. The unsuspecting parents may not notice a thing different, but a newborn growing a full mouth of teeth in only a matter of a few weeks would be a sign.' Cliff adjusted his glasses and closed one eye to help focus the other then came close to me, screwing up his face and momentarily gazing into my eyes, one at a time. As he did so he said, 'If you looked deep into the blacks of the swapped infant's eyes, you would know something wasn't quite right either. Deep in the eyes you could see there was a sapience, far beyond the infant's years.'

He pushed his glasses back onto his forehead and raised one long finger out in the air in front of him, saying, 'That was especially true if they had swapped your child for an older faerie made to look like a human infant, those ones could never quite hide that uneasiness; if you peered deep into the blacks of their eyes, you'd see it.'

Bridie stood beside Cliff as he spoke, making head gestures and the occasional gasp as she relived those same fears from Danny's infancy. 'Thank God we got him raised without any of that nonsense,' she exclaimed.

Through the window we saw a large sheep truck approaching down the lane. 'Ah, there's Danny and Trish coming now,' Bridie said.

Then, out of nowhere, Cliff shouted, 'Ah, there's my grandfather! Bridie, look, he's back!' He got excited and fumbled at his forehead to get his glasses on once more, then pointed to a nearby paddock along the laneway with his stick just as the truck passed, and there I saw a beautiful big sandy-brown, hare. Cliff, his right hand held over his left collarbone, stared on gleefully.

'That's my grandfather,' he said, 'He comes to visit occasionally.' He was elated, smiling from ear to ear and looking anxiously towards Bridie to ensure she saw the hare too.

Bridie smiled and said, 'The hare – Cliff's grandfather – keeps an eye on us here. He's been away for a few weeks. It's nice to see him back.' I smiled in acknowledgment, as this phenomenon was not new to me. I came from a farm with a drove of hares, all reported by my father to be my reincarnated ancestry.

We watched as the hare, startled by the truck, initially galloped through the field towards us, then slowed to a more relaxed hop, arriving at the lawn in front of the living room window. He stopped a few meters away and, sitting on his back legs, looked straight at us before setting about licking the dewdrops off the fur on his tummy. He then lay down and sprawled out, basking in the morning sun, completely at ease with his proximity to the house.

Getting ready to go out and meet Danny and Trish, we walked out of the living room and back past the row of sleeping dogs in the hallway. Cliff pointed to a shelf high above the dogs that I hadn't noticed earlier. On it stood an old dusty glass cabinet with a big stuffed fox in it. 'Ten years ago, the next-door neighbours shot that fella. That was the last fox we have seen at the farm since. We haven't lost a lamb to a fox in years,' Cliff said. 'I suppose you would like to know why that is?'

Intrigued, I said, 'Yes, tell me, what's your secret to keeping the foxes away?'

Cliff pointed amongst the sleeping dogs to Flash. 'That's my secret right there. By God is he a formidable fox chaser. And not only that, he's taught all the others to do the same. These dogs patrol the paddocks all around, keeping any foxes away. The younger dogs are faster than Flash now, and by gosh can they get some speed going when they need to. It would be a sorry fox if Flash and the gang got near them!' Cliff's long hand now gesturing across his neck an -off with their head motion. He added ' The local foxes are terrified of our dogs.'

At that Bridie and Cliff smiled to each other, Bridie adding, 'The local wildlife gets protected from the foxes here by the dogs too.' Cheerfully she asked whether I had ever seen a pheasant or a hare as tame, to which I shook my head – I wasn't sure I ever had.

I must admit that I was quite surprised to hear this about the dogs. I had never had the pleasure to meet a pack of working Old English Sheepdogs, and I certainly didn't know that they could have this protective trait. To me the Old English Sheepdogs were considered more the clowns of the pastoral dog world – more playful and chilled out than other more serious, diligent pastoral working breeds. I had come to think of the Old English Sheepdogs mostly as pets, and occasionally for marketing paint on the television, although the Old English Sheepdogs I had met over the years always appeared smart and highly trainable. As they had mostly a boisterous, goofy energy, I had kind of forgotten their origins as sheep herders. The Potts' dogs were very much a working gang, it would appear, being born and raised on the farm. They had sheep herding in their blood, and now, what's more, they were doing a pretty good job of being sheep protectors too. No doubt their woolly coats kept them nice and warm as they patrolled the fields in the harsh winter weather too.

We made our way to the front door, and as I was getting my boots on inside the doorway, Cliff said in a whispered voice out of earshot from Bridie, 'You know what they say around here?'

I said, 'What's that, Cliff?'

'Well people say I'm a bit, you know,' making a circular motion with his extensive index finger over his right temple, 'Well they say I'm a bit tapped, you know a bit cracked, if you will?'

Smiling, I said, 'Thanks for the heads-up Cliff, but sure who isn't these days? To me, mad people are the most fun and interesting.'

He looked at me again with a smirk and his eyes full of devilment – there was no need for any more words. Cliff may have been cracked, but that was quite OK with me. Perhaps surprised by my acceptance of his condition, he went a bit smiley and quiet. We shook hands again as he opened the door and waved me off.

Shouting goodbye to Bridie and Cliff, I went down along the path past the weather pheasant, who was still pecking around the dog bowls, and walked across to meet Danny and Trish, who were just rolling into the yard in their truck. Trish parked the empty sheep truck alongside one of the sheep sheds and they both hopped down from their truck shouting Hello! As they made their way over to me. Danny was a medium, muscular build, bespectacled and balding with the remains of some red hair and a constellation of freckles across his face and head, perhaps as a result of the lack of hair cover. Trish was a similar height, with long, black hair tied in loose plaits, one on either side of her shoulders. (I briefly noted the similar hairstyle to Bridie, and how Bridie had called Trish the daughter she never had). Danny wore blue jeans and a navy body warmer over a checked shirt with rolled-up sleeves. After shaking hands with them both, I went to get gloves and a stethoscope from my car so I could examine the ram.

When I got back Trish asked Danny if he'd like a hand catching the ram. He agreed the ram would probably take some holding, so the three of us set off to have a look. The sheep flock were out in the paddocks, but this ram, being unwell for a day or two, had been getting special attention in a pen in the sheep shed by himself. Apart from a few sparrows on the lookout for grain amongst the straw bedding, inside the shed was quiet, with gently swaying cobwebs and dust particles dancing in the sunbeams, that shot through the cracks overhead. When Danny opened the large sliding shed door further to let more light through the ram let out a few bleats – perhaps a little startled and eyeing up his scenery-eating comrades just a few hundred metres away. I noticed that the sheep in the nearby fields were mostly Texels or Cheviots, with the occasional black head of a Suffolk in the mix as well.

'He has a big swelling on his balls,' said Danny. 'It's been there for a few days. He's just finished breeding season. I think that's how it started.'

Trish giggled at the inferred possibility that this was a sex injury.

'OK,' I said, 'Let's have a closer look.' In a moment, Trish and Danny had hopped over the gates, caught the ram, and turned him up to sit on his hindquarters for examination. He was an impressive Cheviot ram – hornless, well built, with a large frame and nice strong legs. I was a little concerned that this swelling could be part of the contagious lymph node disease CLA – caseous lymphadenitis (caused by *Corynebacterium pseudotuberculosis*), which typically presents itself as abscesses all over the body. I had a good feel around the ram's lymph nodes, which all felt normal. I then felt around his scrotum, and his testicles felt normal, but this abscess was in a very inconvenient place, in the skin dangling right in the middle. It seemed that this abscess was more likely a scrotal skin infection gone bad. I let Danny and Trish know it was best we lance it, flush it all out, and give him some antibiotics and anti-inflammatory injections.

At this point Danny said to Trish, 'You know what you have to do here, Peig. I'll go and get the lunch on.' He then swapped positions with Trish and made an exit from the pen.

Trish shouted after him, 'I'll have a roast beef sandwich so, dearest Fred!'

It turns out these were their pet names for each other. Trish's farming enthusiasm had earned her this new name, with all the Potts fondly calling her Peig (pronounced 'Peg'). Danny later explained that, as Peig was more of an older country lady name, it was mostly in recognition of the country blood now flowing through Trish's veins.

Trish conversely affectionately called Danny 'Fred', and if you met him, you'd see that the name kind of suited him, although I was never to discover if there were any deeper reasons, she gave him the name. Either way I soon got accustomed to the fact that, at the

Potts' farm, Danny and Fred and Trish and Peig were respectively interchangeable.

With Trish holding the ram, I went off to fetch more equipment from my car. I returned and set about clipping and cleaning the skin around the scrotum. Some people get great satisfaction out of lancing abscesses: the bigger the flow and the more congealed and custardy the pus, the better – again, for some. Holding the ram's scrotum in my gloved hand in such a way so as to separate the testicles and abscess from the approaching scalpel, I lanced the skin overlying the abscess, and a small stream of bloody pus started pouring onto the ground. The ram looked directly at me from Trish's arms as I worked, already starting to look relieved. Trish's eyes bulged, and she started making ooh, aaww noises. Even with Trish being fairly new to farmyard abscesses, she said she was already fond of a nice satisfying one. I never did develop the love of zits, boils or abscesses that some people seem to have. Some people get very excited by them, like Trish.

From behind the ram's head Trish said, 'Poor old Fred isn't so good with the bloody jobs around here. You want to see him in lambing season; he's like a nervous wreck pulling lambs.' Saying she always got stuck with the gory jobs, she added, 'I suppose I love him anyway, and in any case, he makes a great sandwich! Half the reason we are to be wed,' she smiled. I certainly agreed it was an important consideration for marriage. We both laughed.

After some injections, we let the ram back up and he went over to his hay rack and started nibbling, seemingly not too fazed by what had just happened. As he stood there munching, keeping one eye on us, the pus flow from his lanced abscess slowed to the occasional bloody drip onto the ground beneath. I said to Trish, 'It will be up to his body to push out the infected material now, and in time the abscess will close up. We'll find out in due course if he returns to breeding, but it all looks promising.'

Trish, looking at him, said, 'Ah, Romeo and his sore bollox,' and that got us laughing again.

I got my equipment packed up, and as I drove past, Trish waved me off from the shed door.

It was about three months later, on a crisp January Saturday morning, that I had my next visit to the Potts. Trish had called through to say that she was at home minding the fort for a few days. Danny was on his way back from his stag do, and I had heard on my local rounds that their wedding was imminent, but I didn't know the full details. The sheep were in the winter sheds now and a few of the neighbours had been helping Trish with feeding. Trish had noticed that one of the ewes was having a bit of an issue, and so she asked if I could drop by and have a look. Being still a month before lambing, Trish was a bit concerned the ewe would go early. She sounded unsure of what was going on with the sheep altogether.

'She's in a bit of trouble I think, Austin,' she said. 'When she walks around, I can see something hanging out from her Mary.'

Not really hearing her well, it being a bad line, I asked her, 'Sorry, Trish where is the thing hanging from?'

To which she replied, 'It's a long, red tubular thing hanging from the ewe's Mary – you know, her lady parts,' adding, 'I bloody well hope she's not lambing – it's too early! And we're off on holiday to New Zealand next week!'

Finally catching her drift, I said, 'It sounds like a prolapsed cervix peeping out of the ewe's vagina. I'll come by shortly and have a look for you.'

On arrival I parked by the sheep shed and Trish met me there. She was wearing jeans and work boots and was wrapped up in what must have been one of Danny's coats. Her make-up was unusually well done, and I remember thinking her hair all done up, wasn't looking half bad either.

Trish caught the stricken ewe and held her for me to have a look. A quick check over revealed the problem: a prolapsed cervix for sure. Giving the sheep an epidural and the cervix a good wash over, I replaced it and did a purse-string suture (an enclosing circumferential suture) on the vulva to keep the cervix in place. As I worked, we chatted about their trip to New Zealand. Trish said that herself and Danny were excited to see the country, and that they had plans to visit a few sheep farms over there too. After finishing the suture, we let the sheep get back up and Trish got a can of sheep-marker spray paint to flag it as needing special attention at lambing time; as we had discussed, she would need to have the suture removed before lambing. As it was a Saturday morning and I was on a half day and hoping to make the most of the fine weather, I inquired what Trish and Danny were up to for rest of the day.

Trish, now washing her hands at the shed sink in a rush, checked her watch and said, 'I better get going. I'm getting married at the church at 12 o'clock. They're waiting for me up in the house with the dress!' She shouted thanks, and off she ran.

I was so gobsmacked watching after her as she raced up to the house that I didn't know what to say. No sign of a Bridezilla in Trish anyways.

Apparently that three-week trip to New Zealand was actually their honeymoon. Lambing was due to start in mid-February, and they would have a welcome reprieve from the Irish winter, as it was summer over there.

It was shortly after their return that lambing season started, when I next got called out to their farm, upon noticing their shiny new wedding rings and beaming smiles I congratulated them both. Trish was telling me about what she had seen in New Zealand, with their different sheep breeds and enormous farms. They had even taken a tour of a sheep dairy. Trish said that those New Zealand folk were very entrepreneurial, having a wide range of sheep products Trish had never even heard of, from woollen toys for kids to soaps, to lanolin (an oil harvested from sheep wool used in a range of products from lubricants to shoe polish). Trish had even tried some age-defying sheep-placenta face cream. She was inspired and was thinking there could be a niche in the Irish market for something like that.

As lambing season was underway, there was a lot of work for Trish and Danny in the sheep sheds, helping the lambing ewes where necessary. They were assisted by a few students from agricultural courses too. Shortly, the sheep sheds resembled a huge ovine maternity ward – all the individual sheep cubicles filled with mothers and their newborn lambs. There was also a nursery pen of orphan lambs, where some ewes hadn't survived lambing, or failed to produce any milk, and some cases where the newborn lambs had been rejected by their mums. The team of Old English Sheepdogs patrolled the yards, keeping a watchful eye out for any escapee lambs, gently nudging them back indoors. The newlyweds were very busy handling their first wave of lambing ewes. As the lambing days became a few weeks, I was a regular in the Potts' sheds. I overheard Trish giving out to Danny on a few occasions for wearing his wedding ring while lambing ewes. He just nodded and said he would take it off later, saying he was too busy to stop.

Cliff and Bridie also could be found pottering around the sheds, mostly for moral support for the students and for Danny and Trish. Bridie regularly delivered pots of tea (showcasing her range of hand-knitted tea cosies) and thick, well-buttered slices of barmbrack loaf to the sheep shed for the workers. Overseeing the orphan lamb nursery, Cliff and Bridie were also tasked with putting jackets on the lambs, ahead of them getting turned out into the fields a few weeks later. The little hand-knitted blue-grey jackets had a loop at one end to fit over the lamb's head and a little Velcro belly strap in the middle. The lambs looked incredibly snug running around frolicking and playing with each other in their snazzy jackets, despite the brisk temperatures. On one of my visits to help deliver some tangled-up twins that had defied Danny's efforts, I arrived as Bridie and Cliff were standing in a pen of newborn lambs, fitting them with jackets. I couldn't help admiring Bridie's handiwork, so I asked her how she managed to make so many.

She explained, herself and Trish organised the local stitch-and-bitch meetup group. Ladies from all over the local area came together to work on stitching projects, learning and teaching each other new skills, and importantly, having a good old gossip about all the local goings-on. 'This time of year, I have a whole gang of ladies stitching lamb jackets for us,' she said. 'They can't bear the thought of our lambs getting a chill. And you know, these jackets are potent fox deterrents also,' she added with a smile, looking at Cliff.

Cliff nodded in agreement and said, 'And they keep the little folk away too.'

Bridie then held up one of the jackets and asked if I noticed anything unusual about the colour. Taking the jacket in my hand and examining the wool further, I agreed it was an unusual colour, but said I couldn't see how this helped keep the foxes or faeries away.

She looked at me and said, 'You'll keep this quiet, won't you?'

'Of course, I will.' I said.

In a fit of cackles, Bridie said, 'Go on ahead there and see the lambing ewe and have a good think about it, and if you don't get it, I'll share my secret with you on your way out.'

Still befuddled, I moved on as instructed.

The twin-untangling defied me too, and that lambing became a caesarean section. I did this on a bench in the shed, with Danny holding the ewe. Thankfully it was a success, and two healthy Suffolk lambs were delivered. As I worked, I tried to solve in my head the puzzle of the wool jackets. Candy the pup kept coming up to me and playfully rubbing off my legs as I stitched up the ewe. She was looking for pats but, focusing on the job at hand, I couldn't get to her for a while. As I finished and packed up Candy came over and lay on her back in the straw once more, and I knelt down to give her a good tummy rub.

Just then Bridie and Cliff arrived beside me and Bridie said, 'Have you solved the mystery yet – where we get our special wool from?'

At that moment I had two handfuls of Candy's fur in my hands.

'Well, you're holding it!' she said.

I was so shocked I couldn't help but burst out laughing!

Turns out Bridie, keeping the pack of Old English Sheepdogs well shorn for most of the year, had saved up their fleeces and found a good use for them. Some years previous, she had discovered that their wool could be spun into yarn and used just like sheep's wool. I was blown away with the ingenuity. The lambs in those jackets were snug and warm, and with a smell of dog, there wasn't a self-respecting fox in the locality that would try to snatch one. Bridie was on to a winner.

This was all in the year of the big lambs. The Potts' single-lambing ewes were delivering proportionally enormous lambs. Some we managed to deliver, while others needed caesarean sections, as the lambs were just too big to come out the way nature intended. That same year the Potts had three ewes have quadruplet lambs, and it made much more sense to foster some of these lambs out to the single-lamb mothers, although fostering was challenging – where it worked, it wasn't unusual to see a ewe in her pen with a big lamb and then a second little one, from all the lamb spreading. The lamb jackets, I suspect, helped here too, as to the foster ewes their lambs all smelled similar. On one occasion I had just done a caesarean section on a ewe and was packing my stuff into my car when Trish came out to chat with me as I got organised. She looked at me with a glint in her eye and asked if I had a minute, as she wanted to run some ideas past me for a new project she was working on.

'OK,' she said, 'I know you're going to think I'm cracked, but I'm going to make my first batch of sheep-placenta anti-ageing cream; I even have my first customers.'

Having discussed the anti-ageing benefits of the cream with them, Trish told me that the ladies at the stitch and bitch classes were all keen. She wanted to run her branding ideas by me, saying, 'OK, first off, I'm thinking up a tagline – "From our farm to your face, ewe-ter-us cream". What you think?'

'That's quite catchy alright, Trish,' I said, and we both smiled.

She then said that a close second, she was considering was, 'Potts' face-crack cream for eternal ewe-th'!

She said she had specially selected some of the ewes as placenta donors when they lamb, for freeze-drying and powdering. I couldn't help but smile, adding, 'I'm voting for the second one, Trish. I love it,' thinking to myself that it was only fitting that the Craic Potts would make face-crack cream.

A day or two later Danny called me directly on my mobile phone, and he was sounding a bit anxious. 'I have a dreadful case of ring womb here, Austin,' he said, 'And I don't know what I am to do. I'm in a spot of bother. Will you come have a look at her for me?' I wasn't too far away so I agreed I would be there fifteen minutes later.

Meeting me at the window of my car as I parked in the yard outside, Danny seemed very stressed, repeatedly shaking his head, looking like a worried man: quite pale and mumbling to himself. His forehead poured with sweat and his glasses were all steamed up. As I opened the window he said, 'You know when I said ring womb? Well, it's not traditional ring womb! I have gone and lost my wedding ring while lambing one of the ewes, and I'm in a lot of trouble!' he said. The ewe had only just lambed about an hour before and hadn't quite passed the afterbirth when he left her. In his panic he had gone to a neighbour's house to borrow a metal detector and had scanned around the pen and the ewe's hindquarters. The ring was nowhere to be found.

In Danny's desperation he had told Cliff what had happened, but he wouldn't dare tell Trish, who was also pottering around the sheds with Bridie, tending to the flock. Not really having faced this problem before, I said to Danny that the best I could do was examine the ewe internally, as a second pair of eyes on the search, so to speak. Cliff was also inside the shed, feeding the orphan lambs, and he made his way towards us.

As I approached the pen where the ewe was, I saw the metal detector and what looked like an old plumbing camera with a fibre-optic cable, the kind used for illuminating and exploring around blockages in difficult-to-reach places in water pipes. Danny, still panicking, said Cliff had borrowed the camera from a neighbour but it hadn't been of any use. They had tried to pass it into the ewe's birth canal to have a look, but they couldn't quite work out the controls, and it just kept twisting backwards, facing out at them, and after a series of flashes and crackles, he had given up. Trying to maintain some semblance of secrecy, and thinking that

Trish was not far away, Cliff took the metal detector and headed off to return it to his neighbour.

I hopped in over the small gate beside the Cheviot ewe with her newborn lamb attentively suckling at her udder, the lamb's tail wagging with satisfaction. The ewe looked at me disapprovingly; maybe it was just my imagination, but she looked like she was thinking, 'here we go again.' Putting on a glove and some lube, I got her in the corner and proceeded to examine her, willing myself to find Danny's ring but trying not to show on my face, my low expectations. As I inspected her, I could feel already her cervix was closing up, but there was no ring, and worse still, there was no afterbirth in there. I subconsciously acknowledged she may even have passed that and ate it in the time since birth – that was a distinct possibility. Danny, looking at me and picking up on my fruitless search said, 'That's it. I am a dead man!'

Trish turned up at the far side of the shed, out of earshot, but seeing me, came over to say hello and see what we were doing. I said, 'We're just checking this ewe is OK. It was a big lamb.'

Danny looked at me in terror – we both silently acknowledged defeat: the ring was a goner. Right about then Trish spotted the fibre-optic camera and cable on the ground and asked, 'What is this?'

To which Danny replied, 'Ah, you know us boys. Just playing around with an old plumber's toy. Dad and I were seeing if we could have a look inside the ewe's uterus earlier, and well sure we got it going, but I think it's not working right. It kept turning and pointing back outwards at us and sure we soon gave up.'

Trish knelt down and started fiddling with the controls and in no time had some sort of action replay going of the footage and started laughing hysterically, calling us over to have a look.

'The bleedin' hack of ya!' she shouted at Danny (her Dublin way of saying, 'What are you like?!'). 'You're after taking a feckin' selfie of yourself from the aspect of the ewe's Mary! Look! A ha ha! Look!'

We all gathered around the small screen, and sure enough, there was a frozen screen selfie of Danny glaring into the dark abyss of the sheep's vulva, steamed-up glasses and sweat beads pouring down his face, all framed by the sheep's labia. The look on his face was completely priceless. We all cracked up with laughter. Even poor old Danny saw the funny side, as he escaped his cloud of impending doom for a moment.

Trish got her smartphone out and took a snap of the image and was off to send it to her friends, leaving the shed in a haze of belly-aching laughter. As I left, Danny said he was going to have a trip to the jewellers to try to get a replacement, accepting he may have to get remarried to make it official at some point. Adding insult to injury, he texted me later saying the replacement ring would take weeks to arrive.

I was back at the Potts' two days later, and on my way through the shed, I noticed a card in the shape of a sheep stuck to the notice board. It was a novelty card, which when opened let out a Baa, Baa, Baaa. I stood there for a second or two playing with the card. Written inside was a note saying, 'To Fred from Peig XXX.'

Danny arrived beside me and, with a big smile on his face, he pulled a new golden neck chain from under his collar to show me his extra-shiny wedding ring dangling on the end of it!

Trish had presented Danny with the card over dinner the previous night. With all the Potts gathered around, she had asked him whether he had perhaps lost something important, and then gave him the card.

As he opened it, amongst the sound effects, his ring and new chain, wrapped up in a note, dropped out, the note saying, 'I'll forgive you this time but next time you are dead, Fred!'

Danny added, 'Trish thinks it was all worth it for the sheep's Mary selfie!' Amazingly, she had found his wedding ring in the ewe's placenta when she had picked it up for making her face cream – but had left him to squirm for a day or two before letting him know!

As lambing season came to a close and my visits to the farm less frequent, my next call from the Potts' was actually from Bridie. She rang to say that her eldest dog, Meg, was looking a bit out of sorts, and although they had thought she was well past breeding age, she had come into heat again (the tell-tale sign – a bloody discharge from her vulva). Bridie asked if she could bring Meg in to the clinic for a check over, adding she would need to wait on a lift and would only make the evening clinic when Danny got home, as Cliff was going birdwatching in the hills for most of the day. She explained Trish couldn't give her a lift either, as she was feeling under the weather too, and was spending the day in bed, in her own house. Bridie added with a frustrated sigh, 'It will be me next, the lurgy that's going will no doubt strike in threes! Peig, Meg and whoever will it be next!'

Later at the evening clinic, I did a physical exam on Meg, who was looking a bit sorry for herself for sure. She hadn't eaten well for a day or two, and she was now vomiting often and becoming dehydrated. She had a fever, and when I felt over her tummy it was all a bit uncomfortable and bloated. It was apparent pretty quickly what was wrong here – Meg wasn't just in heat; she was in fact suffering a very serious uterine infection (a pyometra).

When I told Bridie this, she looked at me in horror, beside herself with worry that Meg could be so sick. She recognised the condition that had claimed one of her former breeding dogs, some years previously. She asked me what could be done about this and I said the best thing would be to get her on a drip to rehydrate her, start some antibiotics, and get her into surgery to do a spey (an ovariohysterectomy) as soon as possible. Given Meg's age Bridie was concerned that she may not be fit for an anaesthetic, and that she wouldn't make it through, asking me would it be better to put her to sleep instead. I suggested we run a blood test first of all, to see that everything else was OK before any surgery, and Bridie agreed.

While I collected the blood sample and got Meg set up on a drip, Bridie made a call to Cliff from the consult room to ask his advice on what she should do.

'Hello Cliff, it's me, Bridie. Go on turn up your hearing aid there, I've got some bad news. I'm down the clinic with Meg. She's got a discharge from her vagina which could be a uterine infection and they say she might be able to have surgery to fix it, or they may have to put her down instead. What do you think?'

A few moments of silence passed, and then Bridie said, 'What do you mean, am I cracked in the head? Will we put her down or try save her? I need to give an answer here!'

At that there was another long pause, and then Bridie said to me, 'Jaysus, I did not expect that response. Cliff is beside himself. I've never heard him react like that. I'm going to have to hurry home. He isn't good with his nerves at the best of times, but it sounds like he's having a conniption! Put her on a drip sure, and I'll ring you shortly,' she said.

Just before Bridie left the blood work came through, and it showed that, apart from a big infection, old Meg was looking reasonably healthy. I let Bridie know.

About forty minutes later the phone went. It was Bridie, now hysterical with laughter. 'Yes, go ahead and do the surgery, Cliff says, whatever it takes to fix up old Meg. But let me tell you something; when I phoned him earlier, he misheard me and thought I was talking about Peig! Hahaha ha ha! He couldn't hear me right! No wonder he reacted so badly! Hahaha! He only knew Peig was sick today, not Meg. He thought we were going to put Peig down. The darling girl just has a cold! Ha ha ha!'

That evening we did surgery on Meg, and I removed her infected uterine tract in the nick of time, before any intra-abdominal rupture had occurred. The next day she was up and about, eating well and looking much brighter, so we sent her home for rest and special attention at the Potts' place. In a week or so she was good as new, Bridie called to let me know. On collecting Meg that day, I got a chance to ask Bridie something I had been wondering about for a while: How was Trish going with her face-crack cream? Bridie just nodded and, throwing her hands up, said, 'Oh that didn't go anywhere; something to do with not getting public health approval off the pen-pushers in the council.'

That year there was a rare weather event (even by Irish standards): it snowed in mid-March, St Patrick's Day, arriving as a full-on blizzard and sticking around for the best part of a week. The whole thing was accurately predicted by Cliff Potts in the weeks before it happened. A local newspaper sent a reporter out to interview him and take photos of all the Potts gang, and one of these photos appeared in the local paper, making the front page, with an interview showcasing Cliff's weather-prediction talent.

Cliff explained in the interview that he knew the big snow was coming from a few weeks ahead, having observed a range of natural clues. For a start, there wasn't a drop of frog spawn in the ditches laid – the frogs being too wise to spawn before snow. Then Cliff had noticed that the March hares hadn't been seen sparring yet – a sure sign they were holding off on breeding for a bit. 'They won't willingly breed in snow as they live above ground entirely, unlike the rabbit,' Cliff added. Plus, the daffodils were slow to open, which had further aroused Cliff's suspicions that a big chill was still to come.

A day or two before the storm hit, Cliff had also observed with his binoculars that the local grey seals were reluctant to leave the sea and rest on shore. The night immediately before the storm, he noted that the red deer had abandoned the nearby hills and distant mountaintops in favour of lower ground and the shelter of the forest. On the morning of the storm, Cliff's weather pheasant refused to leave his roost – a sure sign of the impending snow blanket. Finally, there wasn't a sea gull to be seen for miles – all heading out to sea to escape the storm, Cliff reckoned.

The front-page photo had Trish and Bridie each holding a lamb, with Danny and Cliff standing beside them and the view from their farm as the backdrop. The last bits of snow were melting on the distant hills. The photographer even managed to get the weather pheasant in the frame.

CHAPTER 4

Peadar and the Lads

Working over in rural County Galway, out on the road doing farm calls, I would often be full of wonder at the natural beauty of the area, with the rugged rocks of the Burren in the distance, as well as all of the historic buildings and castles in the surrounds and the abundance of forests and lakes. The local town where I was based was quaint and full of character. I soon got to know a lot of the regular faces around town. One frequent visitor to the clinic was Peadar O'Grady, the local postman (Peadar, is the Irish equivalent to 'Peter.') Peadar was as regular as clockwork – arriving at the vet clinic at 11 o'clock to collect and deliver mail each weekday morning, usually coinciding with our tea break.

As I was raised in Northern Ireland and later moved to the Republic for university and work, the southern dialectal use of the term 'lads' in an unconventional way was a new one on me. I remember being outraged the first time I heard someone from the south of Ireland address a mixed-sex group of people as lads. Surely there was a mistake? Surely, they must know there were ladies present. The term eventually grew on me though, and I caught myself saying it too. Working as a vet out in the country, I was then further intrigued to find that the term 'lads' could be used for animals too. A farmer could say 'the lads up on the hill,' pointing to his flock of sheep. I was entertained to see just what species could in fact be called lads.

Peadar was a man who always said 'Lads'. He would loudly say, 'Well lads,' every time he walked in through the clinic door, even if it was just Lindy the receptionist, behind the desk by herself. I was surprised Lindy didn't pull him up on this grammatical travesty, given that she was a retired schoolteacher and a stickler for punctuation. Being a born-and-bred local, I guess she was just well used to hearing it.

Peadar's interactions with Lindy would become a great source of entertainment for me. She was a fanatic tea-pusher and loved nothing more than to make tea for everyone. Of course, this was of great benefit to her practice colleagues. We all soon got used to multiple cups of tea every day, and to be fair she made a great cuppa. As Peadar walked in each day, he already had his answer ready, as to whether he would have a cup of tea, giving rise to some of the more interesting ways of requesting it. I still smile thinking of the days he would walk in, wink, and say, 'I'll just let you make me a cuppa tay there, Lindy.'

Lindy would get straight to it, delighted with this development. I'm sure in any other country he wouldn't get away with that. It wasn't that he was pushy, or that he expected it; it was more just his charming Irish way that made this seem less chauvinistic and more endearing. Some days he wouldn't be in the mood and would say no to tea, and those days were worse for Lindy than the days he said yes; you could see that she was visibly disappointed.

There were many subjects covered over those tea chats, from politics to sports, to talk of food and recipes, both Peadar and Lindy being passionate foodies at heart. Chatting over those cups of tea, Peadar would fill us in on the local gossip, mostly of the light-hearted kind. He was always keen to hear if there had been any weird or wonderful happenings at the practice, interesting cases and the like. When I first met Peadar at the clinic, he said that he loved animals but didn't have any himself. Back then Peadar was still harbouring a broken heart for his beloved dog that had passed away a few months previous, before my arrival. After his dog passed away, Peadar's wife Kate put her foot down, adamant that there would be no more pets.

Peadar was a social, kind old soul, always keen to stop and chat and have a bit of craic, unlike our couriers, who came and left fast as lightning. No, Peadar was slow and steady on his rounds. At the vet clinic Peadar knew where the outgoing post was kept, and if we were all busy attending to patients/clients, he would often go in and get it himself, and on occasions he could even be found helping Lindy apply stamps to envelopes should she still be snowed under with a stack of outgoing mail when he came by.

Peadar and Kate lived a couple of kilometres out of town. Both being in their late fifties, they had two grown-up daughters nearby, as well as a small gaggle of young grandkids. Their house was near the main road, and it wasn't unusual to be passing by in the afternoons and see the proud grandparents playing with their grandkids in their beautiful garden, as they often helped-out with their school runs and childminding. Peadar was a big, well-built man with quite a large, round tummy, the kind synonymous with a fondness for pints of stout and a love of food. He often wore a baseball hat and had a good sense of humour and a jolly laugh, with a tendency to go a bit reddish-purple should a particularly intense series of laughter arise, which was often. He was a genial chap, and tended to wink a lot when he talked, just to reinforce the subject matter being discussed. At my first few encounters with him I didn't quite know what to make of it. He would say something like, 'Hey Austin, did you have a nice weekend?' – wink, wink, wink.

At which point I would get a bit disconcerted. What could he be implying? What the hell does he think I was up to? But as time passed, I realised it was just a quirk, a Peadar peculiarity.

It became pretty clear to me that he also cared greatly for wildlife after the first occasion Peadar brought in an injured bird to the clinic. It was an adult male blackbird (a native Irish species), wrapped up in a mailbag. Peadar had found the bird by the road on his countryside mail drive. We examined it together, poor old Peadar was in a stew, perturbed and anxious that the bird would be alright. He was so happy when I declared the blackbird to be pretty healthy, with no broken appendages and just looking a bit concussed and in need of recuperation. Peadar was further delighted when he called in the next day to find that the blackbird was back full of life – a rest and some food and water had done the trick. Together we placed the bird in a small cat carrier, ready to be returned and released where he was found.

Peadar had a spring in his step as he set off on his rounds that day, as he had a very special delivery to make. Peadar by that point knew I was keen on hearing all about his wildlife sightings, and nearly every day he would have something to report. There was a lovely seasonality to Peadar's encounters, with migratory cuckoos in the spring, native kingfishers attending to their nest burrows down by the river in summer, and playful fox cubs in the fields in the autumn. Peadar nearly took the front door off its hinges the day he spotted a pine marten out on his rounds – a distinctly rare sight. He was so excited to tell us about all of these experiences, over those cups of tea.

One day Peadar told me that back before he was married and settled, he had spent a few years working as a sous chef at a high-end London restaurant. This particular restaurant had had an issue with mice infestation out the back of the kitchen in the food-storage area, and the head chef used to fly into fits of rage and go after the mice with a big knife, killing many that way. The head chef also called in pest control, and they used many ways to get rid of the mice, from baits to glue traps. One weekend Peadar was in the kitchen early before the other staff, and found a live mouse stricken on a glue trap on the kitchen floor. As he looked on at the little creature struggling and terrified, he was compelled to do something to save it. He took the glue trap and the mouse and quickly popped back to his nearby apartment before anyone noticed, offering the mouse some food and water. Later that day, using a combination of hairdryer and warm baths, he rescued the mouse from the trap and placed her in a large empty biscuit tin with some hay. Over the next few days, using warm baths and gentle brushing with a soft toothbrush, he was able to get all the glue off the mouse. With all the attention the mouse became tame, and Peadar went on to hide her secretly, for a full two years in his shared apartment bedroom before the mouse passed away of old age. Peadar said with a wink and a smile, 'She was the best-fed mouse in London, getting all sorts of tasty treats from the kitchen.'

On another occasion Lindy told me Peadar was well known locally for a special talent; he had an amazing memory. Being the postman for that area of the county for a good thirty years, he knew almost everyone's birthday off by heart. All those years of delivering birthday cards and parcels, it was only a matter of time before newcomers to the area would have their date memorised too. Peadar's hallmark was to wink and wish a happy birthday, with precision date accuracy anywhere from about five days in advance should he bump into a local person before the day itself. Lindy had a plan up her sleeve for that year. The funny thing was, there weren't many people who knew Peadar's own birthday, but she had managed to work it out with a series of covert questions and chats over many cups of tea; you know the sort. What star sign are you Peadar? What phase of the moon were you born on, etc. This year she was going to have a cake ready for him and make a bit of a fuss. 'The old sod always acknowledging everyone else's birthday,' Lindy beamed. It would be his turn this year.

Most of the tea interchanges occurred with the occasional shortbread biscuit from a seemingly endless tin, but on big occasions there would be more of an effort made when it came to sweet treats. Lindy was a discerning lady. Well-travelled in her youth, she had worldly experience, with a very refined taste in just about everything, and that was especially reflected in her cooking efforts. Lindy had already gained a reputation amongst the other practice staff for being a superior cheesecake maker. Colleagues still spoke of the cheesecakes she had made before my arrival at the clinic. I hadn't had a chance to try one yet, but as Peadar's birthday rolled around, my luck was in. Lindy was religious (but not preachy) and happily married, with a grown-up family. She was quite maternal to us all in the practice, with the multiple cups of tea and the occasional disapproving look should a late night out with the lads at the weekend be mentioned. As such, she commanded a lot of respect, in her gracious and motherly way.

Come Peadar's birthday, Lindy produced the most delicious baked vanilla cheesecake, complete with candles and a birthday bunting, ready for the main man's arrival. It was a fantastic surprise for Peadar, who was caught completely off guard. Scoffing the delicious cake, face beaming red with winks and praises, he complimented Lindy louder with every spoonful. He was also keen to find out her recipe. 'Ah go on tell us!' he said repeatedly, once or twice taking his hat off and placing it on the bench before him in an effort to reinforce the point that he was ready to receive the recipe.

It was apparent Lindy was getting more and more flustered; she was not going to give up what turned out to be her most secret recipe. She kept trying to change the subject to the weather or the price of cattle, her quick go-to topics, but these were shot down, as Peadar relentlessly pursued the recipe. Once Peadar and I had finished our slices and were enjoying a nice cup of tea, he gave one more push at getting an answer. 'Lindy, please give me the recipe,' he exclaimed.

Lindy stood up, looked at him, then looked at me, and with a quick double-check to make sure there were no clients in the waiting room, said something that had us spitting out our tea in surprise. As Peadar asked one final time for the recipe, Lindy stood and said, 'Dammit, years ago I had to sleep with someone to get the recipe in the first place!'

And before the words had fully filtered through, she quickly added, 'And a couple of times it took too, I won't be sharing it, and that's that!'

With that she was up and dusting a nearby bookshelf that was already spotlessly clean.

In the few moments of stunned silence that followed, I couldn't decide if I was mostly shocked or impressed. Peadar blushed beetroot red after that, and swiftly gave up asking. I can see why Lindy kept her top-notch recipes closely guarded – by God that was good cheesecake!

With spring, it came time for Peadar and Kate to head off for a sun holiday in Spain and a few more weeks travelling mainland Europe, an annual tradition for them, I was told. The postal service would be covered by a casual postman from the city, and wishing him off on a safe trip, Peadar said we would hear all about the trip when he got back. And for a few weeks we had another lad doing the mail, the much younger, quieter, earphone-wearing, get-in get-out, smile-and-say-hello-but-not-into-chatting kind. Not that this was a problem, but I guess it made us all realise how lucky we were to have our charismatic Peadar. Lindy never even offered the new guy tea, saying he didn't look like the tea kind. I guess a seasoned tea drinker like Lindy just knows her audience.

Eventually Peadar returned, a bit redder than before and with a big smile on his face. He was well-rested, wined and dined. He told us of a glorious week at a beach resort in Majorca, followed by a flight over to Amsterdam and a cruise down the river Rhine, with a few stop-offs on the way in Frankfurt, Slovakia, Vienna and further along the Danube to Budapest. He said they had a whale of a time.

Peadar wasn't back long till he started ranting about his junior colleague's sloppy work. There was a bit of undelivered post turning up here and there in the van, a load of empty cola cans, and a few too many brown, sticky cola stains in the shared mail van.

On his second morning back to work after his holidays, Peadar turned up to the practice a bit earlier than usual, and I could see him sitting in his parked van outside in the car park. I was heading that way, and as I passed, he called me over, he was not as bubbly as usual. As I got closer, he looked up at me and said, 'Austin, the heart is crossways in me today.' (His colloquial way of saying he was upset about something).

He then said, 'That *eejit* they sent down from the city is after missing out on a post box – not a letter collected from it the whole time I was gone!'(eejit is perhaps a milder word for idiot).

He went on to explain that the previous day he was out on his rounds collecting mail from the rural post boxes when he discovered one full to the brim with mail. He opened it at the back and started pulling out armfuls of post only to find that in the middle of it all, was a robin's nest.

He discovered it too late, having taken it all out of the post box before he even knew it was there, and it quickly fell apart on the ground before him. In the mound of letters and in the middle of the remains of the nest on the ground were baby robins, only about a week old and mostly bald, with just a few sparse feathers starting to grow. He said, that as he stood and looked on in disbelief, the mother and father robin were shrieking in protest overhead, a little too late. Peadar was devastated for inadvertently ruining their home. He thought he might put the nest back together and place the chicks back in, but he already knew there was a chance they would be abandoned. Unsure what to do, he reassembled the nest, re-nested the chicks and waited a while, watching from his van as the parents inspected the box – only to fly off. He had no choice but to take the young robins with him.

As I stood there listening to Peadar's story, Peadar got out, went over to open the passenger-side front door and sat in on the seat. He beckoned me closer.

With a wink, he said, 'Wait till you see these little lads.'

Very slowly and carefully he opened the glove compartment drawer with one hand while raising a finger on the other hand to his lips. In the compartment was a folded-over beanie hat, which Peadar delicately opened to reveal a spectacle of chirping orange mouths. I counted at least six. He then produced a small tub from his breast pocket and with a pair of tweezers began distributing mealworm halves, much to the delight of the little birds. Like an attentive parent, he administered one to every open mouth. The offerings were quickly gobbled up, and in a minute a few faecal sacs (young bird faeces enclosed in a sac for easy removal from the nest, by the parent) were presented for collection, which Peadar expertly removed. In no time at all the lads were quiet again, in closed-mouth digestive contentment.

Peadar closed the beanie, put it back in and gently closed the drawer. Looking at me anxiously, he said, 'Please don't tell a soul. I'll be in fierce trouble. I'm already finding it hard to hide the mealworms from Kate, but if head office finds out it would be another story entirely!'

He then smiled with a twinkle in his eye and said, 'Sure, I'll have them raised and away before anyone knows a thing.' It was obvious he was beating himself up for disturbing their little family. All I could do was reassure him that accidents happen, and that we at the vet's would certainly help him in any way we could. His plan for them to hide out in his van would do for a while, he said, but in time, like all young they would need to spread their wings, meaning he would need to find them more space.

Peadar had already figured out that mealworms were a good food choice, but we decided to seek more experienced guidance, so I called a friend involved in wildlife rescue in the UK, who advised we add the occasional small piece of apple and the odd berry. Peadar was feeding the lads around the clock during daylight hours, which his early mail-run starts perfectly suited.

As the days passed, he quietly reported with a wink, the lads were growing rapidly, like little mushrooms. Meanwhile Lindy had raised an eyebrow on those few occasions when Peadar delivered a letter with bird poo on it, though she chalked it up to there being birds in the letter boxes, not realising they were actually in the post van. But given Lindy's track record of being able to hold a good secret, Peadar decided she was a safe bet, and after a couple of weeks he introduced her to the lads out at his van. At that stage they were already much bigger and well feathered; she was smitten! Lindy thought they were the cutest things ever. 'Plump chirpy merry little cherubs,' were her words.

Peadar also let Kate in on the secret. 'She's like a grandmother all over again,' Peadar told me one day with a chuckle, and within five minutes of finding out about his secret, she had them all named. Being still juvenile with their sexes unknown, and given that Kate and Peadar were avid gardeners, she went with this theme: there was Spud, Perri, Rocket, Beanie, Tomato and, number six being the smallest of the gang, Winky – apparently he tended to wink a lot as he was being fed. I couldn't keep a straight face when Peadar told me that, thinking Winky was just like his foster dad!

In time Peadar started the process of fledging by transferring the lads, who at this stage were feeding themselves, to a shed in his garden. After this he progressed to opening the door during the day while leaving a plate of food for them morning and night. Inside the shed was a stepladder, and the six robins took up residence on its upper steps. Peadar got a great photo of the lads on the ladder and brought a copy of it into the office for us. Lindy later had it enlarged and framed, and after a few months placed it on the waiting room wall for all to see, as a testament to Peadar's hard work and good luck.

Incredibly, all six of the lads survived to fledging. As soon as they were flying and feeding themselves, four headed off on their own. Because they are territorial by nature, it was time for them to find their own patch. Luckily for Peadar, two of the lads stayed around his home a bit longer. Winky and Rocket took up residence in his bountiful garden for a couple of months further and went on to develop their full adult plumage. Peadar said he often had red-breasted company while digging new vegetable beds. The two robins took turns sitting on the cross of his shovel handle, on the lookout for worms or grubs being uncovered. Peadar was only delighted to help fill the undersized Winky out a bit more. Soon the two remaining lads also headed off on their own.

That same year a British birdwatching TV show started a campaign and a public vote to choose a noun for a collection of robins. They had discovered that no such collective noun existed. Peadar had a few ideas to offer for sure. He was absolutely thrilled with the final result. Given that on that fateful day he had become a foster parent to those baby robins he had been out doing his postal rounds, the final result of the naming competition could not have been any more appropriate: a *round* of Robbins!

CHAPTER 5

The Irish Vet Down Under

Working in mixed veterinary practice in Ireland, in a few different locations, I learned a great deal from more senior colleagues and put into practice a lot of the theory and skills vet school gave me. After a few years, I decided it was time to do the young vet shuffle. I call it this because it's a common phenomenon that happens a couple of years after qualifying and working in Ireland. The allure of Australia and New Zealand (down under) becomes impossible to resist and, as I would later find with my Australian/New Zealand vet counterparts, they felt the same draw to Ireland and the UK. Setting off to this other hemisphere was sure to be an amazing adventure, presenting new systems and techniques, new animal species, new people and an amazing outdoor lifestyle. There would be plenty of surprises in store too.

Shortly after New Year's 2013, I set off for Australia, taking time to spend a few weeks touring Thailand on the way. I arrived in Perth, Australia, about a month later. I had been quite disorganised about researching the finer details, and decided it was best just to go with the flow. What I knew about Australia was that it was an English-speaking country, that they drive on the left and that they are fond of a cold beer. I hoped that, with a job already organised before arriving, it would all just fall into place.

I also had a few expectations of Australia from a childhood spent living with *Home and Away* and *Neighbours* addicts. I couldn't wait to hear someone say, 'flaming galah' Or 'struth'. Funnily enough, still to this day I have never heard a native Australian say either of these. But I still hold out hope!

Just before arriving in Australia, I had heard a few tales about what to expect. These comments came from some New Zealand folk I had met in Thailand. Among the things they told me were that I might not get a very warm welcome in Australia, and that I should expect to feel like an outsider. The word 'xenophobia' was tossed around.

Because I had watched a lot of border security shows, I was a nervous wreck walking through the immigration channels when I got there. I expected to be subjected to a third-degree interrogation, a full baggage search, and then be taken aside for a body scan, where they would find traces of ketamine and lignocaine on my clothes, the result of years of using these in my work as a vet. The lignocaine would confuse the beeper machine and cross-react, coming up positive as its close relative cocaine, and I would be on *Banged Up Abroad* before I even knew it.

On arrival I was told - go to this channel if you have food, declare it and have your bag X-rayed. Being Irish and therefore naturally fussy when it comes to tea, I had packed plenty of Irish teabags. Also, someone had given the heads-up that Aussie chocolate wasn't the same as home, so I had stashed some of that in my baggage too – good creamy Irish stuff.

As I approached the immigration officer stations, I was aware there were quite a few Irish accents in the passenger arrival queues around me, even though the plane was coming in from Thailand – not necessarily one of the most direct routes for Irish people to arrive in Australia. While I awaited my imminent arrest and deportation, something quite different happened. The immigration officer stood up and looked left and right to his colleagues in their row of stations, all processing eager arrivals, and he shouted quite loudly, 'What to hell is going on with all the Irish? Are there any Irish left in Ireland? And I suppose you're all bloody carrying chocolate and tea!' I straight away thought back to what the guys from New Zealand had said, and – *gulp* – I got a bit nervous.

But after being allowed to enter Australia through a much less invasive process than the border security shows had me believe, I straight away found a much warmer welcome. I quickly saw that Australians love teasing and joking with visitors (taking the piss) from other nationalities. Maybe that immigration officer had just been hangry?

In contrast, a few years later I went on a trip to New Zealand, and on arrival the immigration officer read my arrivals card and said 'Oh you're a vet, are you? OK this way for a ketamine search!' and pointed to some burly-looking officers behind a bench. About thirty seconds later he gave a huge big laugh. 'Ah I'm only shitting you, bro! Off you go. Enjoy New Zealand.'

The limited information I'd gathered before travelling to Australia had included facts on how many different things there are, that want to kill you – crocodiles, snakes and venomous spiders. I would later discover others that weren't so obvious:

disease-carrying mosquitoes; six-foot kangaroos jumping in front of your car as you drive at 110 kmph along the motorway; honeybees (who knew – causing hundreds of deaths by allergic reactions to their stings each year) and evisceration by territorial cassowaries (emu-like rainforest dwellers), just to mention a few. I still remember my sister waving me off as I left Ireland. She shouted after me, 'Remember Austin, not all fish are your friends', knowing that I am a dedicated sea explorer. Full to the top with fear, she was sure I was going off to Australia to get eaten by sharks.

Whilst in Australia, I spent some time in tropical North Queensland working as a locum (a temporary stand-in for another vet) at a clinic. For one of my first lunch breaks I announced I was going to have a swim at the nearby beach. Alerting me to another of the dangerous local animals, on the way out the door the receptionist, told me I must wear stinger-protection clothing in the sea, due to the deadly arancini. As I walked to the beach, I soon discovered she was having a word mix-up, as there were many large signs warning about the 'Irukandji' (the tiny deadly jellyfish found there) – they were no relative of the delicious fried balls of pasta, arancini! We had a good laugh about that afterwards.

I went on to work in Australia for seven years. This was not uncommon. The usual story is for a one-year working holiday visa to become a more, long term one. In those seven years, the term 'vit' would not be uttered even once, but there were quite a lot of other similarities between vet practice in Ireland and Australia (the temperatures not being one of them). I travelled far and wide as a locum vet. This was a great way to enable exploring between work stints. It was amazing to see the love the Australians have for their native animals, and the opportunities that arose for me to work with this wildlife were pretty special.

Australia had many new species I wasn't familiar with, and I quickly became acquainted with their care. There are many amazing native animals, common examples including kangaroos, koalas, emu and the duck-billed platypus. But then there are so many more lesser-known creatures, from sea turtles right down to the unique antechinus and the brush-tailed phascogales. Have I lost you? Think carnivorous marsupial mouse and rat-sized creatures respectively, with sharp fangs. They are no threat to mankind but bloody terrifying if you are a real mouse, a bird, a cricket or a frog.

I was fascinated with the Aussie bush (mostly unpopulated forests) and spent hours and days on hikes into some of the most amazing places. A lot of the Aussie native animals are unbearably cute. When it comes to cute natives, I think my personal winner is the quokka from Western Australia. It's a toss-up between that and a young wombat. Wombats may have a competitive edge, though, as they produce cube-shaped poos and, well, with that, could they get any cuter?

The Australian echidna reminded me of European hedgehogs (although echidnas are anteaters). The echidna is a fascinating creature. Just like the duck-billed platypus, their young are called puggles (cute native animal contenders for sure), and they are the only two remaining animal species on earth that lay eggs yet are mammals and rear their young on milk. Interestingly enough with their milk-producing and egg-laying talents, it also means that they are some of the only animals that would have the requisite materials to make their own custard. I definitely wouldn't like to try it though!

The Australian jokers in my life kept me going about running into a 'drop bear' out in the bush. Although drop bears are fictional, many a visitor to Australia has been had with this prank. They will have you believe the drop bear is a bloodthirsty cousin of the koala, likely to pounce on your neck at high speed; it may as well be on the list of potential human-attackers too. Just as in Ireland we live in fear of meeting a banshee, you'd be much better off never encountering either of those! (The Koala technically isn't a bear at all, but more closely related to the wombat family.)

Slowly getting used to all this Australian joking about, it could be equally hard to convince me I wasn't being had, as with the day an Australian vet colleague informed me that a female mud crab is called a Jenny and the male is called a buck. It still seemed outrageous to me, but it turns out to be true.

One change for me was the introduction of the term 'Doctor'. Before leaving Ireland, this had not been a part of a vet title, although it is now. Arriving in Australia, where the title is widely used, was a new thing to me. I was keen to follow through during the first few months as Dr Austin '*The vet*' for fear that people would think I could work on humans. On all my travels I'm still waiting on that awkward moment on an aeroplane when they call out for a doctor. I would probably be of limited use, and most likely would pass out in any case, adding to the casualty list.

Although I witnessed a close call of sorts, on a plane trip to an Australian vet conference. Turns out about eighty vets had boarded the same flight. So, imagine the air hostess's confusion when a medical emergency arose – that long list of doctors on the passenger list. The hostess then clarified the need for a non-vet, a doctor of the human variety, and a retired GP, a lady who was at least eighty years old, was found sitting close to me down in the back. After a slow, reduced-mobility trip up the aisle to the patient, she returned pretty quickly, having solved the emergency in a matter of minutes. This was astonishing, because for one thing, she had no medical equipment. I couldn't help but ask her – how had she done it? She said, 'Ah, he was just having a panic attack and needed a good slap!' Tough, but effective in this case.

Australians have a witty sense of humour that is largely familiar, as I found it to be pretty similar to us

Irish. Like us, many Aussies seem not to take life too seriously, and are able to laugh at themselves and (even more so) at others. They have a tendency to abbreviate words, which entertained me greatly. Nothing was safe. Mosquitoes were 'mossies', morning tea break at work became 'smoko', fuel service station were 'servos', the off-license bottle shop became the 'bottle o'. I could go on and on, providing an enormous list here. Some of the abbreviations were impressively succinct, such as kangaroo being a 'roo'. Even the term 'selfie' is an Aussie creation.

On the subject of memorable abbreviations, one weekend when I was off-duty during a term working as a vet locum in a mining town in Western Australia I took myself on a trip to another nearby town (by Aussie standards, only about 300 km away) to explore the hiking trails and try a few craft beers. I stayed at a small, intimate hotel run by the owners, Bob and Marnie Downes, real salt-of-the-earth, country-type Australian folk. Bob was a retired dirt farmer, as he put it, an apt term for sure (as he had been a miner). When I visited there was a lot of dirt-farming still ongoing in that area. I saw a hive of activity: trucks, trains and even distant ships full to the brim with freshly harvested iron ore – everything and nearly everyone was covered with a fine smattering of red dirt.

After my second night at the hotel Bob caught me mid-yawn as he handed me the breakfast menu and asked me how I had slept. Quite honestly, I hadn't slept too well. Both nights I kept waking up, watching the shadows play weird tricks on the wall in front of the bed. I told him I had seen the outline of what looked like an old lady moving around on a few of the walls, her eyes half open. It was eerie. I assumed I must have been working too hard, or perhaps had drank too much of the local craft beverages.

Bob looked at me with a raised eyebrow brow, then offered me coffee to start breakfast and headed off into the kitchen to get it. As I sat there with a few other guests having breakfast nearby, he loudly shouted at the back of the kitchen, in earshot of all of us, 'Marnie, Marnie! The guest here says the chick on the wall is back!'

I guess he didn't realise that a swinging kitchen half-door doesn't constitute soundproofing. He then came out and poured my coffee with a straight face – no hint of what he had just shouted.

My shock was twofold: first, how could he have abbreviated an old lady ghost to 'a chick'; and second, why was such a chick in my room? I omitted these details on my TripAdvisor review – Marnie and Bob were so lovely and hard-working; they didn't need that negative press.

With quite a few years spent in Australia I definitely began to feel more at home. I did encounter many Australians along the way who had enjoyed a trip to Ireland. Amongst all of us Irish visitors, I also stumbled upon one very unexpected Irish ex- pat who was now enjoying life down under. An endearing piece of Irish heritage with a great story of her own, right in the middle of metropolitan Sydney. Outside the Queen Victoria Building (QVB) in central Sydney stands a large bronze statue of Queen Victoria that demonstrates both a good relationship between Ireland and Australia and, I think, a mutual sense of humour. The statue bears a plaque that reads, 'Donated in a spirit of goodwill and friendship', and while I was on a history tour it was pointed out that the Irish government sent this statue to Australia in the 1980s – on a permanent loan basis. Her statue had originally been outside Leinster House (the Irish parliament) for many years, but after the end of English rule in Ireland this didn't seem like a good place for her anymore. Australia had been searching high and low for such a statue for the QVB, and Ireland had been thinking of ways to get her offloaded – and so she was rehoused as a gift down under!

As I travelled and explored the continent, I encountered many wild animals, from foxes to camels, on my bush walks, and I was fascinated with how many species had been introduced to Australia from Europe over the years. I was amazed to discover that there were no placental mammals in Australia before the first settlers arrived – just marsupial, pouch-bearing mammals.

In some areas of Australia there are paralysis ticks – a completely new parasite to me. Over the years, I would spend many hours battling to save domestic (pet) animals from tick paralysis, and I was intrigued to find that tick-paralysis doesn't affect the native animals; thanks to evolution, they are immune to its paralysing toxin. Only our immigrant mammals suffer.

I was also surprised that there were similar circumstances in New Zealand before settlers arrived. Sea mammals and, on land, two species of bats accounted for the entire mammalian animal population there. In other words, any other mammals you encounter over there are not indigenous and have been introduced.

I met many young Australian vets who told me about having Irish adventures. I was impressed to hear of one fellow Australian vet's tales of a year spent working in County Donegal and surfing in Bundoran. He used an extra-thick wetsuit of course. Another chap I met at a conference – Barry – turned out to be the epitome of our unofficial vet exchange programme. He looked Middle Eastern, had a strong Australian accent and used random Irish phrases with confidence. He would go on to explain that he was Australian born to Irish/Australian parents, that he had taken Irish traditional (Irish trad) music classes in Australia since he was a kid and that he was back from two years working in West Cork. Well that explained a lot.

Turns out he was an accomplished Irish musician and had used the opportunity to work in Ireland and develop his traditional music skills. As an Irish person in Australia, I was acutely sensitive to Irishness in all its forms, and as I stood there talking to him even the idea of an Australian who knew random Irish phrases and was good at trad music inspired a row of goose bumps down my back. In some ways this guy was the mirror image of me. Here I was in Australia, accidentally saying random Aussie phrases and spending a few hours each week learning the didgeridoo. We had a lot to chat about.

My favourite story he related to me was about old Paddy Murphy. Paddy was a well-regarded fiddle player and a bit of a local celebrity in West Cork – quite a way from anywhere. He had a herd of beef cattle, drove the local school bus, and was in the pub a few evenings each week playing trad music. He would often call the vets to arrange callouts for sick calves, and he wasn't having a good year with calf health. He had got to know about Barry, the Australian trad-playing vet, and they had even played a few times together at Irish trad sessions in Cork City. Barry had been to see his calves a few times and they became pals.

With a sparkle in his eye, Barry told me an amusing story he was sure I would appreciate. One evening Paddy called him, as one of his calves was blowing (this is a colloquial term for a respiratory infection). He wanted Barry to come visit, around 10 am the next morning, and to be sure to bring the fiddle. Paddy's wife would have a cup of tea ready for them, and they could have a few tunes on the fiddles, after which Barry could have a look at the sick calf. Then they would both be on their way again at about noon, just in time for Paddy's junior school bus run. Barry had dutifully gone through with the plan, and months later he was still beaming about his private fiddle lesson with none other than Old Paddy Murphy. For the record, I still have no idea who Paddy Murphy is, but he sounds like a legend, nonetheless.

It takes a lot to shock a vet, but I must admit there is one thing that can shake me up a bit at times. It's when a human, mistakes my explanation of their pet's condition as an opportunity to tell me all about their own. Sometimes this phenomenon can give rise to hilarious scenarios, and I encountered some of my favourites during my travels down under.

In Tasmania, I was in the local village café for a coffee one Saturday morning when I met Mrs English, one of my clients, along with her flock of friends. I say 'flock' because she was definitely the chairperson of the group, and they followed her and hung on her every word. Mrs English, a British ex-pat in her sixties, was as regal and proper as the Queen of England herself. You know the sort: a prominent local participating in many local groups, from the weekly book club and flower-arranging classes to being a formidable head judge of baked items at the local agricultural show.

She was the dedicated owner of Clyde, a beautiful, middle-aged black labradoodle. Mrs English and her husband Tom used to come in regularly with Clyde for check-up appointments for his heart, and they diligently wrote down every word I said and followed my advice wholeheartedly. Because Clyde's heart issues were complicated, we decided he needed more intensive management, and sent him off for review at a specialist. He was on an impressive cocktail of medications, and the specialist tweaked these and added a new one. I hadn't talked to Mrs English since her trip to the specialist, and she was keen to tell me all about what had transpired.

She was already loudly telling her flock when I arrived, informing them all about Clyde's new medication and how it might turn things around for him. She had carefully written down the drug name and was enthusiastically telling the gang. 'Sildenafil citrate it is called ladies, and Tom the husband is on it too,' she exclaimed, looking down and patting Clyde's head as he napped on the café floor.

I tried to appear as though I knew what the medicine was, expecting it to be a drug for humans. I nodded and agreed it was definitely worth a try. Later that day my interest got the better of me. If there was a new heart medication I had to research and update myself on it, thinking surely it must be something that had been developed in the years since I was in vet school.

It took about fifteen minutes for the tears of laughter to stop and allow me to read my computer screen properly. It was Viagra! And poor old Mrs English would die of embarrassment if she knew what she had been revealing about Tom. I never had the heart to tell her. And no, it doesn't have the same effect on our canine friends, in case you are wondering. The most useful effect for dogs, is its ability to reduce the pressure in the blood vessels around the lungs, improving blood flow in this area, rather than mostly just in and around the nether regions of men.

In a similar theme of vet/human crossover, while I was working at a clinic over by Sydney for a stint, one day a regular client of the clinic rang up and the nurse answered the phone. They exchanged pleasantries and then the lady said, 'I need to book in to get my crow's feet done. You know, the injections like the last time?' I could hear the nurse say, 'Well yes, Mrs Lavelle, what can we do for your crow – the poor thing – are his nails overgrown?' After a couple of moments, the phone went dead, Mrs Lavelle had hung up. Mrs Lavelle then rang back a few minutes later and said, 'Oh my God, I rang the wrong clinic! I'm not wearing my glasses and I thought I was talking to my cosmetics clinic.' We all had a good laugh, Mrs Lavelle included!

When I was working in Australia, I had a large gang of my Irish vet associates living and working all over Australia and New Zealand (back then; they are mostly back in Ireland now). This meant that on various occasions we would have reunions.

It was truly a fantastic thing, to have a big gang of good friends and colleagues all in one place at the same time, all of us going through the same journey. We met up often, making the most of the Aussie experience together.

One such get-together was the Port Fairy Folk Music Festival, which took place on the Great Ocean Road, a few hours' drive out of Melbourne. A gang of us, including both Irish vets and some non-vet friends, had gone for the long-weekend festival. We were having a few drinks in the campsite, getting ready to go to the nearby festival and enjoy some of the music. Lots of people were doing the same thing, and the campsite was full of groups barbecuing and drinking and enjoying the balmy evening weather. Immediately beside us was a group of fifteen or so Australian senior citizens. There were about ten in our gang, and all but two of us were all Irish, so I guess our accents were quite noticeable in the crowd.

These older Aussie folks couldn't resist the odd 'fiddle le dee potatoes' comment, said with much the same jest as our 'put another shrimp on the barbie' exchanges. They were surprisingly lively for a group of seniors and were intent on throwing a few jokes our way – about us. Experience told us that when Australians start their piss-taking, inaction is the worst possible response. We had to act!

Colin, one of my UCD vet friends, had been working in Australia for a few years. He was also a pretty good musician and could sing and play the guitar till the cows come home. What he did next was ingenious. He simply stood up, lifted his guitar and, leaning with his foot on a nearby chair so that he was facing the seniors, started to strum. He then proceeded to loudly sing 'Waltzing Matilda', the unofficial Australian national anthem.

As he went through the verses and it became clear that he knew it word-for-word, the seniors grew quiet – silenced, you might say. As the scene unfolded before us, I experienced a proud patriotic moment: here we were in a faraway land, and there was my Irish friend singing 'Waltzing Matilda' to a group of Australians!

The genius stroke happened when he then slowed down and gently encouraged their group to join in. A couple of random words were added here and there, but no one consistently could join him. It was obvious that the words evaded them. He went in for the kill by repeating the whole thing again, receiving rapturous applause from both them and us.

Colin was prone to singing at parties too. He had a gift and he used it, although I was slightly surprised that an *eejit* such as Colin would have the wherewithal to stage such a coup. I don't know if it was premeditated or accidental, but it was highly effective, nonetheless. The Australian jokers relented after that.

Port Fairy Music Festival was a fantastic weekend for us all. The international line-up included lots of

Irish folk artists, and we went to see the famous Irish songstress Mary Black. She had a great crowd gathered, and it was fantastic to hear her sing on foreign shores with so many international fans in attendance. Then she came to 'Bright Blue Rose', a song written by Jimmy McCarthy and made famous by Christy Moore. A lot of us were immigrants in Australia, and many of us didn't know how long we were going to be there. Booze flowed freely, and an Irish legend was standing on stage singing another Irish legend's song. A high percentage of the audience in that giant marquee began to cry. Some people howled. Sure, a stone would cry – a beautiful song in such a setting. It was only about fifteen minutes later that I bumped into Mary offstage, a few tear streamers no doubt still visible on my face.

'Ah jaysus Mary you wiped us out with that Christy number,' I said. 'I'm here booking my flight back to Ireland!'

She smiled at me, came over and gave me a reassuring pat on the back, and said, 'Yeah, that always happens here at Port Fairy.'

Ladies and gentlemen, Irish expats – you have been warned!

During all my years working and exploring in the Asia Pacific area, Australia was my home. Many places in Australia welcomed me warmly and I made many good friends. Moving around a lot meant I took a lot

Leabharlanna Fhine Gall

of lone taxi/aeroplane trips where I had the dull ache of goodbyes in my chest and a tear in my eye. It was always sad to move on, and that feeling that you might not see some of those faces ever again would become a regular sentiment for me.

Travelling gave me so much. I guess people might wonder about a travelling locum lifestyle – would it eventually be tiring? It certainly is a great way to travel and see the world, but by the time I was done I craved stability and the benefits of the mediocrity of routine didn't look so bad by then. When I visited back home over the years, the pain of leaving Ireland each time only got worse, and the call to be home became impossible to ignore.

CHAPTER 6

Eileen and Eddie

Having worked on a full-time basis during my first few years in Australia, I was keen to do more travelling and exploring. One way to do this, was to offer my services as a locum vet. I went on to travel far and wide all over Australia, and found myself in some very interesting places, from the big cities, to outreach animal clinics with Aboriginal communities in the Northern Territory, to pregnancy testing on enormous cattle stations in Western Australia.

Some of these working trips became more regular, meaning I would often revisit the same practice for at least a few weeks each year. This allowed me to get to know some of the animals, clients and practice staff much better. In many of those places I felt like part of the team, even if only for short stints.

One clinic I worked at on several occasions, was a small animal hospital on the west coast of Australia in the outer Perth suburbs. Of all the clients I got to know there, one that sticks out in particular, was Eileen Kinsella, and her dog Eddie.

Eileen was always accompanied on her visits to the clinic by her friend and housemate, Frances. Both ladies were widows, and rather than living alone, they had decided to share a house together. Although I had lived in Australia for nearly five years at that point, I was fairly sure that there had been no perceivable changes to my strong Irish accent, although I did catch myself using Australian phrases quite a lot. Many clients, upon first meeting me, were able to identify my nationality quickly. Others were a bit shy and would go through a whole consult at the clinic with me, and then hazard their guess at the end: 'By the way, are you Irish?'

Some would ask me, 'What part are you from?' And I would say Ireland, much to their disapproval. They wanted to know which town I was from specifically! This worked the other way too; sometimes people hadn't got the Irish bit at all and were even more confused when they asked where I was from, and I said Armagh. I had to choose my audience carefully; what made things easier was if someone let me know in the first instance if they had been to Ireland before, a surprisingly high number of Aussies had.

Eileen Kinsella was the quickest of them all. When I first met Eileen, I walked into the consult room and just said 'Hello'. Immediately Eileen looked over to Frances and said, 'Oh my God, he's Irish!'

I then accidentally made Eileen get a bit tearful by pronouncing her surname as 'Kin-chella' as that's how it's pronounced in Wicklow, and I was used to saying her surname that way. She got emotional because she hadn't heard that in forty years. After the 'Kin-chella' incident, Eileen went on to explain that she was Irish, having moved to Australia those forty years previously with her husband Paddy. Even at mentioning Paddy's name, she welled up further and the tears trickled down her face, as she told me that it was nearing the third anniversary of his death. She hailed from Connemara in the west of Ireland and had met and married Paddy, a Wicklow man, when they were both nineteen. A childless couple, they had moved to Australia together all those years ago, and she missed him so much.

The ladies were attending the clinic that day with Eddie for a check-up after a recent surgery at a specialist vet surgeon. He had had a mass removed from his liver and, at the time of surgery, blood tests had showed evidence of kidney failure as well. The liver surgery was a huge gamble for an old dog with an underlying kidney issue, but in an attempt to prolong Eddie's life, Eileen accepted the risk. 'Deal with the liver problem and then we will deal with the kidneys,' had been the agreement with the vet team.

Eddie was a sixteen-year-old Labrador, mostly black with grey hairs around his muzzle and lower legs. He had a bony frame with lots of pendulous areas of loose skin, perhaps from being a bigger dog in his younger years. The ageing process had not been kind to Eddie, with his stiff joints and areas of muscle wastage over his thighs and shoulders. He walked with a marked head bob due to his stiff, knobbly joints. He was a very friendly boy, keen to make his way straight over to me and say hello, but only able to do short bursts of activity at a time. There were lumps and bumps all over his body and thick skin callouses over his elbows and hocks. He had noticeable old age eye changes, mostly showing up as a milky cloudiness across both his pupils, probably giving him much-reduced vision. Frances explained Eddie was largely deaf also, but these afflictions were well compensated by a first-rate sense of smell. I soon discovered that he could have smelt his favourite snacks -Liver Treats- from the far side of the road outside, he loved eating them. Eileen would joke that Eddie would nearly write a letter, to get one of them.

Eddie's body may have been weakened with ageing, but his spirits were high, and he greeted everyone in the practice with tail wagging. I noticed he couldn't stand for long before having to lie down and I quickly caught on that it was up to me to sit down beside him for examinations and patting time, as it was much easier for him at his level. He was able to go for short walks only, with lots of pit stops.

During my time at this clinic, I came to learn his owners (I'm including Frances as his step-owner also) exercised much in the same way: a couple of kilometres walk each day from their house to the coffee shop and then onto the deli to get something for lunch and then back with regular stops in the shade, from the Western Australia heat. The ladies told me, on good days Eddie would go too, but those days were becoming less frequent.

Since Paddy passed, Eddie had been Eileen's only family left, and she treasured him dearly. I learned that Eddie had been Eileen's rock of support all the way through losing Paddy. Eileen would tell everyone she met that Eddie had saved her life. The companionship, love, kindness and happiness that Eddie had given Eileen had helped heal her broken heart from the ravages of grief.

Eileen certainly looked Irish. She was in her sixties, with short black hair, a medium build, a lovely, toothy smile and eyes that sparkled when she smiled. Although I had only just met her for the first time, there was an undeniable aura of familiarity, mostly in the way she reminded me of an Irish mother. Quite quickly I began to feel as though I had known Eileen for a long time.

At the first appointment with me, Frances explained Eddie was there for a post-surgical check-up and blood test to see how his kidneys were coping since they had discovered the problem. The head vet who I was covering for had got him on a special diet to help his kidney function. The blood test I ran that day, suggested that things had got worse again with Eddie's kidneys. I had to break the news. It was apparent that Eileen was completely devoted to Eddie, wanting only the best for him. She was clearly anxious, her face creased with concern and displaying visible panic as I discussed the test results.

She needed a lot of reassurance along the way that all avenues of therapy were being covered.

As the weeks passed thereafter, I got to know the trio very well. Eileen would come straight to the clinic if Eddie even so much as sneezed for a second time. Soon we saw them almost on a daily basis, as Eddie's kidney failure slowly got worse. Eileen considered Eddie's condition a part of ageing, and one day lamented to me, 'Age is an awful thing, but I suppose it beats the alternative.'

Frances was of a similar age and build to Eileen, with red hair and a more freckled complexion. She was clearly devoted to both Eddie and Eileen, and perhaps had some medical experience, at the visits she was the one who asked me the pertinent questions and helped explain the answers to Eileen. Eileen seemed to be the less able-bodied of the two, as Frances often appeared to assist her when it came to heavy lifting or driving their car on visits when Eddie wasn't able for the walk.

Eileen, Eddie and Frances made regular social visits to the clinic as well, often extending their daily walk just to drop by and say hello. Watching how much they loved and needed each other, at time I felt a bit deflated, as I knew deep down that, at sixteen years old and with signs of failing kidneys, Eddie probably had months rather than years to go.

Within a few days of meeting Eileen, she took on a rather motherly role towards me. She was concerned I wasn't getting enough food. At first she dropped off a sandwich from the deli, as the receptionist had mentioned I was having a busy day at the clinic, and then it progressed to all sorts of delicious things – from a tin-foil-wrapped cheese-and-ham baked potato to lunch box-sized home-made roast dinners. Each time I would thank her sincerely and make sure she knew there was no need to go to all that effort; this would do nothing more than to steel her determination – although Eileen had never been a mother, she sure had the Irish mother's desire to feed people. All those years away from Ireland and she still had it.

As I got to know Eileen throughout all their visits, she began to remind me of my father too; it was uncanny. I think it was mostly that they were both older Irish people, with perhaps a similar upbringing in an older religious Ireland from back in the day. Although not appearing overly religious, Eileen, like my father, used a lot of biblical terms in conversation.

They had several other little quirks in common too.

Eileen would start a conversation halfway through, and it would be up to me to fill in the blanks. My dad was a master of this trait, although I could never decide if it was part of a twisted genius in order to watch the listener's squirming attempt to make sense of it, or a completely unconscious omission.

Being well-travelled, Eileen loved to talk to me about Australian places we both had been. She would start a conversation about these places by simply saying something like, 'Did you go on the camels up there?'

I would think for a minute and then say, 'Ah, no, sure, I was too busy drinking mango beer, Eileen!' Having figured she was talking about the camel rides on Cable Beach in Broome, Western Australia.

I would come to learn that Eileen loved food, much like my father, and I could say with reasonable certainty there was not a day in either of their lives that didn't involve at least one dinner of meat, two veg and potatoes. Also, more importantly, an 11 am and a 3 pm pot of tea and a biscuit. Yes, I said pot meaning pot – a cup wouldn't cut it!

The better I got to know Eileen; the more similarities cropped up. My dad had a long list of medical maladies, and despite all the doctor's best explanations, his understanding was at best questionable. This didn't impact him too much, and perhaps he was better off not knowing. However, it did often lead to some funny, well, word mix-ups on his behalf. Prostate checks, for example, he would call 'Phosphate checks'. My family got used to his version of medical words, so that if he said a word that was even vaguely similar to the intended, we understood. I would soon learn to do the same for Eileen.

Eileen gave us all a huge belly laugh, herself included, the first day she was tasked with collecting a urine sample from Eddie. She later returned to the clinic well, with a sample of number two instead! It brought about some deep questions in terms of her understanding of the anatomical pathology regarding Eddie's kidneys. We went to great efforts to try to explain it all again. This was exactly the kind of stuff my dad did on regular occasions, and like Eileen, he certainly laughed at his little mishaps.

A lot of Irish people say 'krathur' from the Irish *créatúr*, meaning creature or thing. Usually it is used in reference to something or someone less fortunate, or perhaps cute, and could be an animal or human subject. My father said krathur all the time, mostly to describe our family pets, from our dog to the pet goldfish and even some of the farm animals; a newborn calf certainly was a krathur, in his book.

Eileen had no doubt been saying krathur for years in Australia, but I suspect there were not many people who knew what it meant. Now she could let loose and say it to me about Eddie, and I knew well what it meant.

Eileen went ahead and added '-een' to the end of words when in my company too, from the Irish suffix (-*in*) meaning 'small'. Eileen also took this a step further, and said 'krathureen' (a saying almost exclusive to the west of Ireland), which she used a lot in reference to poor old Eddie, literally calling him a small creature, very much an Irish way of showing her compassion, care and love for him. The term 'loveen' was heard on a few occasions too, I might add.

Eileen didn't just jumble up medical jargon; she also had a few non-medical mix-ups, such as the day she was talking about her new *incest* and wanted my opinion if it could be impacting Eddie. I couldn't keep a straight face. Further questioning solved the mystery – it was her new incense she was talking about. As usual Eileen got a good laugh out it when she realised her mistake.

Eileen, Frances and Eddie, knew that around 1 pm we would all be in the clinic kitchen having lunch, and sometimes they would drop in and join us for a quick of cup of tea. This had delicious consequences, as they often brought cake or other such tasty treats from the deli. Eileen loved her food, but she also enjoyed making sure that everyone else had plenty too.

Although the focus of Eileen's visits was Eddie and his failing health, I think it was fair to say that sometimes we sidestepped the elephant in the room and often found ourselves chatting about unrelated matters. I encouraged this because, with the emerging downward trend of Eddie's health, I didn't want every visit to be confirmation of the devastation that lay ahead for Eileen. It was nice when little things happened other than tests with spurious results, even little things like the visits where we groomed Eddie or clipped his fast-growing nails. When he had been an especially good boy (which was often) there was usually a short detour on the way home to a local takeaway for chicken nuggets – Eddie was a big fan of those too. Eileen would say 'nuggets' and look at him, and even with his hard hearing, eventually he would prick up his ears, he would look back at her and then on further clarification of his favourite word – helicopter tail! And off they would go.

One line of management of chronic renal failure we use quite commonly in veterinary medicine is feeding a diet specifically designed to help the kidneys function. Important features of this diet include balanced salt levels and lowered protein. I have used this diet with success on many occasions, but with a small number of patients the lower levels of tasty stuff can mean that they won't eat it. Sometimes owners have a real struggle with giving just this diet and water, especially if the patient had many years of eating all sorts of tasty, heavy, proteinaceous meals before their kidney issues. Kidney disease can also cause nausea and vomiting, which really impacts appetite too. Although Eileen tried her very best to get Eddie on this diet, she had failed. All she could get him to eat was a pellet or two each day, so she made him home-cooked meals instead. Chicken nuggets were not our advice, but a couple of times a month for a sick older dog – it would take a harder man than me to try to stop them.

The well-travelled Eileen had done an Australian grey nomad trip with Paddy and Eddie a few years before Paddy passed. They had packed up their possessions into a camper van and set off for an eighteen-month trip circumnavigating Australia. Being an enthusiastic traveller myself, on many occasions we would discuss places we had been, and each time Eileen's face would light up, her eyes would become especially sparkly, and she would come to life and recall some amazing experiences she had had along the way. She was a fountain of Australian tourist knowledge, and I got lots of great destination travel tips off her this way.

It would be fair to say that we also bonded over our combined Irishness. When you have been away from the motherland for a while, in my experience anyway, Irish people generally long for it. The work I did with Eileen and Eddie had a slightly different feel because we were two Irish people on another continent and, if I may say, I think this added a special dimension.

Eileen loved a bit of craic and had lots of stories to tell from her years in Australia. She loved animals and had in the past done a bit of volunteering at a wildlife rehabilitation park, hand-raising numerous kangaroo joeys. Frances later told me that back in the day it was most unusual to see Eileen without a baby joey kangaroo in a handbag over her shoulder. If the weather was a bit nippy, they may even have been tucked safely inside her jumper, the little rippling movements and kicks of their feet over Eileen's belly being especially entertaining for passing children.

We could have talked and traded craic for days; Eileen was great at telling me stories of her Australian experiences. One notable tale was an incident with a trampoline and a dangling koala. While living over on the east coast a good while ago, she was staying out on a friend's bush block house-sitting with Paddy for a few weeks. As she was standing looking out from the balcony one morning, she saw a big male koala bear hanging by one arm in a very high gum tree. The poor fellow had gone beyond the strong branches and was clasping onto a few leaves, already down to only holding on with one arm, and just about to let go. Eileen said that she could see the panic in his face, and then of course did a little impression for me.

They thought quickly and in no time herself and Paddy were down shifting the big circular kid's trampoline to the estimated impact spot. About ten minutes and ten chewed fingernails later, she watched as his facial expression changed to a grimace. He was ready to fall to his imminent death and unable to hold for another second, and they watched as he let go.

Eileen's face brightened as she said, 'Well he got three good bounces out of it.'

Landing right in the centre of the trampoline, he then stood up on his back legs, looked at her and Paddy and, not believing his luck, practically did a fist pump in the air before shaking himself off, clambering off the trampoline and wandering down into the forest again. The whole story, along with Eileen's acting and demonstration, was fabulous.

As the months rolled on, especially after I had been away for a while, on meeting Eileen she would give me a hug, with a great big smile on her face and then announce each and every time, 'Ah, God Austin, you are after losing a sight of weight!

Will you have a bit of lunch?' Thanks to Eileen, 'A sight,' is still one of my favourite measurements of human body weight.

Eileen continued her routine of visiting me pretty much daily at the clinic with food. Certainly, no complaints from me about that, although on one memorable occasion herself and the gang turned up and caught me red-handed, eating my own sushi at the table in the clinic kitchen. I was in a spot of trouble.

After walking in, Eileen looked at me in complete horror and said in a downbeat way, 'What is that?' with her head down, talking to the ground before me.

'Ah it's just a bit of sushi, Eileen,' I said, quickly trying to cover up my transgression. I had a feeling she would be none too happy.

Eileen looked puzzled and then turned to Frances and said, 'Sooooo-sheeee,'pronouncing it incorrectly on purpose to show her disapproval.

'I think that might be raw fish, Eileen,' said Frances.

The ladies started discussing this in front of me, for my ears but to each other.

Eileen raised a hand to the base of her neck , in shock and looked at Frances, she said, 'Oh Jesus, no. Frances, raw fish!' Then she stared at me with a look to suggest that I was a raving lunatic, having committed the worst act of betrayal on her.

I was quite surprised that she hadn't heard of sushi – or if she had, she was doing a good job of hiding it. Either way it firmed up my suspicion that there wasn't a day in her entire life that she hadn't had meat and two veg, and that forty years in Australia hadn't changed this fact one bit.

Eileen became just like my Australian step-mum, that is for sure. I had a sad feeling that in the not-too-distant future we would be looking at Eddie's declining kidneys failing and the end of his life. As a vet and a friend, I just hoped that when it happened it would be as smooth as possible, and that although it would likely be devastating for Eileen, I hoped she would somehow find the strength to get through it.

CHAPTER 7

Love and Loss

W hen I wasn't at the practice, I often got text messages with photos and a few words of an update on Eddie from the ladies, Eileen and Frances. Eileen, not fully understanding that the phone bill wasn't based on the number of words in each text message, was usually brief and to the point. As time passed, questions of when I was returning increased, until I had a confirmed booking at the clinic meaning I would be back shortly after Easter. Eileen had become aware that Eddie's health was definitely failing. In the week before I was due back, I got a text:

Austin it's going to be time when you get here.

Another text:

Austin, we want you to do it
we're going to give the krathureen a good Irish send-off

I was sad to hear that things were not going so well for them, though I tried to focus on the fact that Eileen had asked me to euthanise Eddie. As heartbreaking as that would be, it was also the delivery of a gift – the gift of ending his suffering and giving him a peaceful death.

Easter came and went, and I arrived back to Perth to help-out at the clinic once more. I hadn't been in the clinic five minutes when Eileen came to visit, beginning the conversation I had been nervously anticipating.

'I need to book you in on Wednesday afternoon to come out to the house. It's time for Eddie's…' She couldn't finish the sentence.

Eileen welled up.

'I'd love some nice Irish music for when it happens. It's been a while and I'm out of the loop. Could you make a suggestion? A good sad tune I want and nothing cheesy,' she said.

Later that afternoon it came to me: I had seen the aftermath of Mary Black's cover of 'Bright Blue Rose' at Port Fairy – maybe I would suggest the Christy Moore version.

I texted Eileen the details, and later that evening I got a text back:

> It's perfect, he loves it! Me and Frances have been crying all afternoon.

Euthanasia, a word of Greek origin that roughly translates as 'good death,' is something we vets deal with regularly. A lot of people, when chatting about my job, say to me that it would be the part they would struggle with most, and I guess that is understandable. It certainly can be very emotionally charged. I have several vet colleagues who suffer great emotional distress from this element of our work, and although I have developed some coping strategies, it invariably gets me at times too.

People often ask me how I do it, how I cope. In the majority of cases of animal euthanasia, there is an ill patient, and I get comfort that I am ending or shortening suffering. I watched my dad go from walking, talking and able-bodied, as he was admitted to a hospice, to failing badly and suffering all the ill effects of his terminal, invasive cancer, until he passed six weeks later. What I found most hard to watch was the nausea, inappetence, anxiety, depression, drug dysphoria, unknown timing and compromised dignity, as he became completely dependent on others. I know that when we have reached a grave prognosis with one of our animal patients and everyone agrees euthanasia is for the best, I can give a gift to that patient and owner, one that we as humans largely cannot have for ourselves.

On the day of Eddie's euthanasia, I set off from the clinic with a heavy heart. As I drove to Eileen's house, I was worried for Eileen and how she was going to handle all of this. She had tirelessly tried everything to keep Eddie going, and it is probably fair to say that her own psychological and mental health was fickle. I am no psychologist, but I suspected that the bereavement she had experienced, and the one she was about to, would certainly shake her to the core once again.

I arrived at Eileen and Frances's house – a short drive from the clinic. I had not been there before, but it was as I had imagined: a bungalow house in a reasonably new estate with a white picket-fenced garden, front and back. I parked outside and made my way through the garden gate. I saw two cosy-looking seats on the veranda ahead, and imagined the ladies enjoying morning teas there. As is common in Australian housing, there were fly screens on all the doors and windows, and I could see through the fly screen that the main door ahead was open, so I gave a gentle knock and made my way through.

It was pre-planned: the ladies would be inside in the kitchen-cum-living room area with Eddie. He was now mostly housebound, staying in his bed. As I passed through, I noticed that the house had lots of Eddie-friendly features. There was a ramp at the stairs, lots of comfy dog beds from the outdoors to the indoors, an Eddie-sized doggy door, and several large water bowls, most likely so that he never had far to reach water to keep him hydrated, given his failing kidneys.

I made my way through the house hoping to announce my arrival but trying to be gentle and quiet also. I had a basic house-call kit with me in a hold-all carrier, and I placed it on a bench that, I noted, had several small boxes of Eddie's medication on one end. Some of these could have been several years old, and there was quite a range of medicaments, all used in an attempt to prolong his life. I momentarily thought back to the time after my dad had passed, and how afterwards we were trying to organise his stuff at home; incredibly we generated three decent bin bags full of old medications.

Entering into the open-plan area, I saw the two ladies sitting on cushions beside Eddie on the floor, both very tearful. Eddie briefly raised his head and gave a couple of weak tail wags against his bedding before resting his head back on his bed. We all gave a gentle head nod to acknowledge each other's presence, but there was no conversation – we kept to gentle hand gestures, maintaining the peace for poor old Eddie.

As Eddie and the ladies sat there on the floor, I noticed on the wall behind him lots of framed photos; it was like a shrine to his life. There were black-and-white photos of him as a pup, and photos from his birthday each year. I recognised a younger Eileen with a man I assumed to be Paddy, and the more recent photos were coloured, with Eileen and Frances with Eddie. Sometimes the photos would include props, from everyone including Eddie wearing festive reindeer antlers, to what must have been a St Patrick's Day with Eddie wearing a leprechaun hat and beard. It would be hard to convince yourself that in most of those photos Eddie himself wasn't smiling for the camera. Now wasn't the time for questions, but I couldn't help but take the time to look at all of those beautiful, happy moments. Back in the room, a very different scene lay before me.

The mid-afternoon sun shone brightly through the windows at the back of the room. The area where the ladies and Eddie sat on the floor was a shaded, cooler part of the room, with a large wooden ceiling fan silently rotating slowly overhead, tossing a slight shadow on the floor beneath. The hazy sun and relative silence (apart from some intermittent *chit chit* of birds in the garden) gave the room a tranquil feeling.

The house was homely and looked well lived in, with nice old-style ornaments and framed pictures of beautiful scenery on the walls. There was also the odd

Eddie hairball along the skirting board – it must have been difficult to keep those under control as what with Eddie's failing health, he would have been shedding a lot. In the distant sunbeams a few flecks of dust danced in the rising heat, and there was a mustily pleasant smell in which I could detect the faintly spicy odour of Middle Eastern incense, which had probably been burning the previous night.

The ladies made space for me in front of Eddie and I joined them on the floor.

In front of Eddie was a large takeaway box of chicken nuggets; they had gone cold and there weren't many missing. I guess Eddie hadn't been up to having his favourite snack. Next to the takeaway box was a glass of orange juice. Eileen, in her desperation, had asked me the previous day if he wasn't drinking water could she syringe him a little juice instead, and, as this was his final hours and I couldn't think of a reason quick enough why not, I had agreed, although again it didn't look like that had been a go either.

In readiness, Frances leaned over and got 'Bright Blue Rose' playing from her laptop to some nearby speakers. Eddie was resting his head now in a sleepy trance across Eileen's legs. His collar was quite loose, reaching the ground from Eileen's lap – a measure of sorts, of how much the poor old fellow had wasted away in recent times. As I clipped hair off the front of his leg just below his elbow, he looked at me, briefly recognising me, and then his eyelids became heavy again and he settled back into sleepy indifference. His battery of medical investigations had involved a lot of blood samples, and I guess he had an idea there would be another sharp scratch for a second or two coming up as I placed an IV cannula in his cephalic vein. As usual it was clear just what a good boy he was, which just seemed to heighten the injustice of it all – he didn't flinch or object as I placed the cannula.

As the music played, the words were just so poignant in that moment. Eileen, who had remained silent throughout apart from a few head gestures, started to sob loudly, and then Frances started to sob. Eddie remained still and peaceful, and I couldn't help but keep looking down more than I needed to, to hide from Eileen my eyes, which were now filled with tears, and my quivering upper lip.

'Bright Blue Rose' played through, and when it got to the uillean pipe instrumental part near the end I started Eddie's final injection. He was already almost fully asleep on Eileen's lap, breathing gently. As I injected slowly, the frequency of his breaths eased to a gentle stop, and he drifted off.

A few moments later, I had a listen to his chest with my stethoscope. I heard a few tummy gurgles, but there was no heartbeat. I gently whispered, 'He's gone.'

We all just sat there and stared at him, taking in the moment in silence, looking on at Eddie's lifeless body – the little signs of life that had been there only moments earlier, all gone. Despite this being the plan, it was still incredibly sad to think there would be no more wags from his tail, or gentle hand nuzzles from his nose. He just looked so peaceful, finally at rest.

The tune was on repeat, and it must have played through again, because it wasn't until the second go at the instrumental part that Eileen looked up, nodded and mouthed, 'Thank you,' as she cried.

Right there I imagined Eileen's broken heart. She had just lost another member of her family. I was very aware of how losing Paddy had devastated her. Here she was again, the scars on her healing heart freshly opened once more. I momentarily wondered what had gone through Eddie's mind also. It was clear he had been weak and becoming very unwell; left to his own devices he would have passed away in a matter of days himself for sure. Did he know that I was there to help him? If he could have spoken, would he have agreed to his suffering being ended? Some owners in the past have told me that when the time is right their failing pets ask to go; had he? I didn't ask, but I had a strong feeling that the timing was just right.

As we sat in silence, each of us looking at Eddie, Eileen held his head on her lap, and gently stroked him. Frances came over a bit closer and put her arm around Eileen, then gently rested her head on Eileen's shoulder, both of them now crying wholeheartedly.

Eileen shook her head gently, saying, 'He's gone, he's gone.'

I wanted to spend a moment there, but also leave the ladies to have theirs in peace. We had arranged in advance that we would take a print from one of Eddie's front paws, and I had the clinic paw-print materials ready in my kit. Eileen, paralysed with grief, stayed in her position on the floor. Frances helped me apply ink to the pads on his front right foot, we placed the foot over a card and took an impression. Eileen had said, his paw-print would be framed in due course and take up a special place on the wall with the rest of Eddie's photos. I did my best to dry my own tears before saying goodbye to the ladies.

The local pet crematorium had kindly agreed to come and collect Eddie directly from Eileen's house, helping to put Eileen's mind at ease, as anxiety had her convinced that there could be a body-swap mistake when his ashes were returned. The guy from the crematorium arrived just as I was leaving, and he was quick to say that he didn't mind waiting until the ladies were ready. I let Frances know they were ready when the time was right. I sat into my car, hidden behind Eileen's garden fence; I had a bit of privacy there and had a good old cry. This was just all so sad, even with me trying to focus on the positives for Eddie and Eileen; I had lost a little friend too. Rightly or wrongly, when I tear up during euthanasia, I always try hide it and to hold the impression that I am strong and in control.

I still remember the wonderful hospice team where my dad spent his final weeks, and the number of times I noticed staff with red, teary eyes along those corridors, as there is sure to be no end of terrible news in a hospice. Then when my dad passed, many of them stood in the room with my family and wholeheartedly cried with us, a poignant reminder of the human condition.

The grief that comes with animal euthanasia is multilayered, and I have thought about it long and hard over the years. Beforehand the owner will have the pain on finding out a diagnosis or making that end-of-life decision. The grieving can start before the event has even occurred, meaning you are grieving for an animal that is still alive. Then the time comes, and you know what is about to happen, and then it happens, and you are thrown into heartbreak in a reasonably short time. The bereaved owner may get some comfort from the fact they have ended potential suffering, but they are still very much cast into the abyss that is the same grieving process we go through when we lose anyone dear to us. The pain and the heartache, just as real and painful.

It was about a week later before I saw Eileen again. The practice team had organised flowers and a card to be delivered, and along with Frances she came into the clinic with box of chocolates and stayed for a coffee. It sure seemed strange to see the ladies without Eddie. Eileen was emotional on being back in the clinic; I guess it was a trigger for her, making Eddie's absence even more undeniable. She didn't look so well: her face was very pale, and the sparkle was missing from her eyes. We all had coffee and chocolate together.

As the ladies were leaving, Frances give me a nod and a wink to say that Eileen would be getting a bit of help. I took from that she meant counselling and/or medical help. I was so pleased to hear this, as I am a big advocate of getting help when it is needed; there is no need to be a heroine and suffer alone.

Some years have passed since Eddie left us. Eileen would later tell me all within one month of Eddie passing that she knew of at least five other older dogs that had passed away in her circle of friends, believing Eddie to have been the first of a run of pet love and loss. He will be forever remembered by those fortunate enough to have met him. Even all these years later Eileen is still heartbroken, and probably always will be on some level, as the wounds slowly heal, giving way to fond memories.

Eileen and Frances went on to become dog foster carers for a local charity, a task that was made for them. They must be on their fifth foster by now. Of course, I get a lovely photo message and little updates on each one. They help these animals, which often come from troubled backgrounds, by offering love, affection and good care. Through regular socialisation, a healthy routine and any vet care needed, they get back on the road to recovery, and then the charity finds suitable adoption homes. Eileen, in her text message updates to me, makes me smile, as she still describes each and every single one, as a krathur.

CHAPTER 8

John, Mamo and the Three Michaels

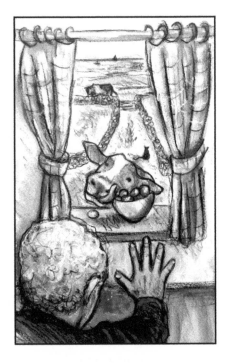

It wasn't a lack of due care and diligence that had got John into the situation he was in. It was more, a series of small accidents that had gone largely undetected.

John had noticed that his old pet cow Mamo had gained weight in the last few months, almost as though she was getting ready to calve, and now, standing there watching her from his garden this morning, there was no doubt left: she was starting to calve. But that couldn't be – she was thirty-five years old at least, John thought to himself, doing the maths from his seventh birthday to now. He led Mamo into the top paddock, beside his house, where he could keep a closer eye on her.

Mamo was a name that suited her perfectly; if you met her you would see why. She was a friendly Charolais with a large, pendulous belly, mostly a result of all the special attention and food she got, being the sole bovine at John's farm.

Over her wide tummy she had a narrow, bony frame with a pointy withers, mostly due to ageing. Her belly hung in such a way that it had done a good job of covering up her enlarging udder up to this point. She was a very sociable animal due to the fact that she was of sufficient age to have been hand-milked in her younger years, but it had been several years since she had had any offspring, she was now an old pet and also lawnmower. John was very fond of her.

Her name was kind of a nod towards the many generations of offspring she was responsible for. In the past she had been very fertile and was indeed a Grandmamo several times over. But that had all ended a few years back, when John took over the farm and, well, didn't do so much farming anymore.

Mamo was mostly grey, with a white blaze down the centre of her face, and white coronets on her back hooves. She was intelligent and inquisitive and was your best friend if there was even the potential rattle of a nearby bucket of feed. She would often come over and nudge her way in for a scratch. John's nephews even used to ride on her back when they were much smaller. She was a gentle animal, and treated those boys almost like a grandmother would, being ever so gentle and careful. She could mostly be found in the fields lining the lane up to John's house, but thanks to a cattle grid where the lane met the road she largely had access to all of the areas around the house, while not being able get out on the roadway past that formidable grid.

Mamo was very good at her job as a lawnmower, and could sometimes even be found at the kitchen window, especially if it was open and John had made the mistake of leaving the fruit bowl too close to it – more than a few apples had met their demise this way. Mamo dutifully munched her way through the old unused vegetable gardens and lawns, and John would often pat her on the back and thank her for her good work. Now, the gardens weren't going to win the Chelsea Flower Show, but Mamo did keep the place looking good in her own cowy way.

Mamo tended to display her affection via her tongue. She licked hands and the occasional exposed leg with her long, coarse, pink tongue. Anyone who knew Mamo would be prepared for a few licks, on approach. Mamo didn't discriminate, and almost anyone who found themselves in close proximity to her (the new postman, the canvassing local politician) got a few licks. This seemed like a funny thing to do. John would often wonder, was she enjoying some human saltiness? Or was she using cow language – if I lick you, will you scratch me? In fairness, it did usually result in a few pats and scratches from the licked human, or at least from those who didn't run away screaming.

John's family were also fond of Mamo. She had been a long-term fixture on the farm. John's nephews, especially when they were kids, loved to watch her eat. She could demolish kid-sized armfuls of hay in record times. Her large jaws, rhythmically chewing and grinding – with accompanying nose twitch as she hoovered her food – was great entertainment for them, and then later seeing her chewing the cud was just as captivating. The cycles of chewing and cudding were mesmerising much in the same way that you can't help but stand and watch large pieces of machinery doing their job – cement mixers and the like.

John had lived on the family farm his whole life, having one brother who moved up to Dublin quite a few years back. John's father, MJ (Michael John), and his mother, Breda, had passed away in close succession about five years previous, both elderly by that point. This left John in sole charge of the farm cottage and about fifty acres of farmland across a few neighbouring fields. The farm was set on gentle sloping hills close to Brittas Bay, just high enough above sea level to have jaw-dropping Wicklow views all around on a clear day.

I guess John's main occupation was as a farmer, but on closer inspection there wasn't so much farming occurring. It was more of a hobby, as it had been quite some time since he made much of an income from it. He was good with his hands, though, and could often be found doing odd jobs for neighbours. He was a sociable chap, and he moonlighted as a rideshare driver up in Dublin too. Many suspected that there was a bit of inheritance in the kitty from when his parents had passed and a combination of all of the above provided John with an income stream. This kept John, Mamo and Frankie the cat in food, hay and cat food, and while it wasn't an extravagant existence, they had everything they needed.

John was a familiar face in the neighbourhood. He was often found as a second pair of hands for neighbours who were doing a bit of DIY, or for older neighbours who needed a bit of work done around the house. He did a lot of gardening favours, and often thought to himself how funny it was that he didn't need to do his own garden.

Having tried his hand at keeping sheep for a few years, he had thrown in the hat, concluding that they were a lot of hard work. Despite all of his best efforts to keep them safe and healthy, they just kept inventing new ways of dying. He certainly had had a run of bad luck, all in a matter of weeks.

First, his old 'black white-head sheep' (yes, it's usually the other way round – white sheep, black head – but this is why her absence was most noticeable that day) had somehow got a bucket over her head, and in her panic had fallen into a nearby ditch and died. John wandered the fields, perplexed looking for her. Eventually his olfactory senses pinpointed her predicament a few days later. Then, close to lambing season, one of John's finest ewes, heavily pregnant, had gone for a lie-down on a gentle slope one afternoon, and had rolled onto the flat of her back. The resultant high abdominal pressure bearing down on her upside-down lungs had brought about a reasonably quick death. He found her that evening, feet in the air and stiff as a board. He was still in disbelief a few days later when I told him it wasn't that uncommon: this can happen to a ewe when she is heavily pregnant and full of food. Dear reader: if you ever see a sheep in a field with legs in the air for more than a few seconds, expect something is terribly wrong.

Then there was the day he found a ewe stuck up a tree – had he not found her for another few hours, she wouldn't have survived. A nearby straw bale was her suspected target. This isn't technical vet advice, but of all the even-toed ungulates, a sheep is the least suited to being up a tree – quite unlike its cousin the goat, who, with its agility and balance, can pull it off much better. This was the final straw for John. He concluded that sheep farming wasn't for him and sold the rest of the flock to a neighbour. His bigger paddocks were empty for now, although later in the year another neighbour was due to put in a few horses.

John, being the local 'help anyone out' sort of soul, had a lot of his goodwill reciprocated by his friends and neighbours in the form of them looking after Mamo and farm when John wanted to go travelling and exploring Ireland or Europe, and sometimes even further afield. He went off as often as he could, getting dropped off at the DART in Greystones, and would be drinking a latte in Dublin Airport awaiting a flight in no time. John's life motto was 'work hard and travel lots', and that was exactly how he lived. He would say often that he felt his life's purpose was to experience as many things as possible, and he certainly did that.

When John was getting ready to go travelling, he would drop a bag of cat food off to his old friend and nearby neighbour Mrs Murphy, Frankie's second owner. Mrs Murphy was an amiable older lady, who had a couple of cats herself (Bella and Teddy), and she was completely dedicated to them. She was delighted when Frankie would take himself over to hers for a visit. The three cats would play hide and seek around her garden all day long.

John was a well-read man; he could talk about the Qing dynasty opium wars in China, or the plight of the Aboriginals in Australia. He could talk about art and theatre well beyond what anyone would believe.

He could talk about politics from Obama's work in the States to what was going on in Russia, and although most of his facts were from reputable sources, he had travelled so much that he had a lot of first-hand knowledge too.

On John's driver runs, he loved to have a good old chat with anyone from anywhere, who was in chatting form. He especially relished the airport runs, and the range of passengers that led to. One day he collected and delivered a young American chap from the airport into Dublin city. At the pub a few days later, he told the story of how, during the forty-minute journey, the visitor mentioned that his 'job' was a cryptocurrency investor. John was interested, and initially felt this was something he could do himself, but on further investigation he was confused and sceptical.

His direct quote was, 'Only a bloody *amadán* (Irish for 'fool') would buy virtual reality currency.' John said he wasn't falling for that one and chalked it up as a scam! He would later add that the only Ripple he would be investing in would be the edible ones (the name of one cryptocurrency being shared with that of a brand of chocolate bars).

At forty-two years old, John was six foot two with a medium build and short, fair hair that tended to get a slight curl in it at times. He had a rustic look, with wind-worn skin and large, kind brown eyes. Most would say he was a handsome chap. He had big strong arms and hands like shovels. He had never fallen in love that anyone knew of, which most thought was a terrible shame, but it didn't affect John at all. He regularly said he wasn't lonely. He had great friends and family.

Mamo and Frankie were largely about as much commitment as John seemed to want. He would often joke that even buying a full bunch of bananas was a big commitment, as, 'You'd never know where you would be at the end of the week.' More than a few times there were a few spare bananas packed into luggage for trips away or were left out for his lawnmowing friend to enjoy in his absence.

John's brother Michael (Senior) his wife, Martha, and two sons lived up in Dublin. John referred to them as 'the Dubs', and they often came down to the farm for the weekend. The two nephews: Michael Junior and Patrick, often lent John a hand around the farm, and he was at times surprised at how hands-on the city kids were, from driving tractors to digging potato drills to helping with the hay harvest. He often remarked that perhaps doing a bit of farm work was in their genes.

When I first arrived into that area, John went out of his way to make me, the new vet in town back then, feel welcome. We had played a few rounds of golf, and on a few occasions enjoyed a social pint of ale at the local pub together.

It was a Saturday afternoon around 2 pm when I got the call from John to come over. Any time John rang I assumed it was a social call, but I shared his surprise when he reported that old Mamo was in labour. She was going to need a bit of help. John sounded stressed on the phone. The big concern here, was Mamo's age. She had already reached nearly triple the life expectancy of an average Irish cow. She certainly would be the oldest cow I had ever assisted with calving.

The call was brief. 'I can't believe it, Mamo's calving, can you come over? She's been trying for a few hours now and nothing is happening. It's very strange for her, as with all the calves she had years ago she never once had a problem.'

I asked John to get a few clean buckets of warm water ready and said I would be with him shortly.

I had been out to the farm to see Mamo a few times over the years to do her tuberculosis test, which is mandatory, at least once a year for cattle in Ireland. That in itself used to get John a bit twitchy with nerves, as back in the day their cattle herd had been plagued with tuberculosis (TB) and he had lost several infected cattle to mandatory slaughter. Thankfully, however, Mamo got the all-clear each time. TB testing in Ireland is carried out to identify cattle infected with the bacteria that causes tuberculosis, and in some areas, there can be wildlife infected with this bug and acting as a source of infection for cows. TB is a risk to man also, responsible for 'the consumption' back in the day.

Many countries now enjoy a TB-free status, but not Ireland or the UK. Instead, with infected wildlife acting as reservoirs perpetuating the disease, it is mandatory to test and remove infected cattle from farms, for the health of all species involved, including us. This is at times, a really tough job to do. A vet confirming a TB infection to a farmer is almost always racked with sadness and shares the farmer's disappointment and pain. It was this very experience that still lived on with John even years after he had lost most of his herd, providing a very legitimate reason for him to be anxious when it came to Mamo's annual TB test.

When I got to the farm that day John and the Dubs, who had just arrived for the weekend, were there with the buckets of water ready. Mamo was standing over by the fence, tail in the air, giving a few heaves just as I parked up. You could see she was fighting a battle between her need to push and deliver a calf versus her intense interest in what was in the buckets.

John introduced me to the Dubs; I had not met Michael Senior or his wife Martha before. The two teenage nephews, Michael Junior and Paddy, came over to say hello and offered to help with getting things ready. The Dub gang were very interested in what was going on, firstly because they loved Mamo and were concerned for her, and secondly, well, all this harsh countryside reality and goriness was such a stark contrast to their clean city lifestyles.

We knew Mamo was in her mid-thirties but knew nothing of the calf-to-be's paternity. With cattle, paternal size and breed can influence calf size quite a lot. John paced around shaking his head saying, 'That O'Halloran's bull! I'll cut his bloody balls off myself!' Yes, O'Halloran did have a bull just a few fields away, and yes, he had been known in the past to be something of an escape artist and a local bovine Lothario, and for now he was the chief father suspect.

Mamo, being a quiet old girl, didn't need much restraining. She just looked at me with a half turn of her head when I approached, almost like she expected me, or maybe again this was her hand-milking training at work. At any rate, she certainly wasn't resisting my help.

I pulled my calving gown and gloves on, applying obstetric lubricant to my hands and arms. I was calculating in the back of my mind, the degree of difficulty of this delivery. There is a whole scale of difficulty you come to learn through the years as a vet. There are large cows with small calves (easy deliveries), and small cows with big calves (hard deliveries), and then all the weird and wondrous stuff in-between, from foetal abnormalities to twins or more. With the large size of Mamo and a bit of luck, I was hopeful this would be a straightforward delivery – it wasn't as though Mamo was a maiden heifer. But I had an underlying uneasiness also, as she didn't seem to have been progressing on her own; she had been in active labour for a few hours now, but hadn't successfully advanced the calf legs or head externally yet, and at her age, calving complications could be very hard on her.

The thoughts of what could be wrong and what I could successfully do about it were bearing heavily on my mind, but I tried not to show that I was a bit worried whether everything would be OK while getting ready to do the internal exam.

I got into position and started by passing my right hand through her vaginal canal and carefully felt my way ahead towards the cervix and the uterus. It was at this junction that my progress came to an abrupt stop, having reached a tight tube of tissue that enclosed my hand and came to a narrow point through which I could only fit a finger or two. I could feel the tight bands of the uterine broad ligaments running in abnormal directions. My fingers touched the tip of a calf hoof through a tiny gap, but the space between us was almost completely sealed off. I swallowed hard.

I had encountered this problem before. It's like grasping a plastic carrier bag half full of apples – holding it at the neck in one hand and spinning it a three-quarter turn with the other, and then poking a finger through the bag's constricted neck and maybe just about getting a fingertip through the twist – you may be able to feel an apple within, but you can't easily retrieve one without untwisting the neck. I grimaced, poor old Mamo had a twisted uterus; I reckoned at least a three-quarter turn.

No doubt her older uterine ligaments and her large abdomen had a part to play in this problem, although any expectant cow could suffer this, with this bit of bad luck. The calf was there and certainly ready to come out but was going nowhere fast through that twisted-up neck of the uterus. I could feel the subtle little signs of life; my finger found the calf hoof again, which jerked away from me, at my touch. It was a good sign, I thought, but certainly too soon to declare the calf deliverable. Saving Mamo and getting a live calf delivered was going to be the challenge.

I raced through some options in my head for getting this twisted uterus unravelled. One approach I had used a few times with various degrees of success was to try to stimulate the cervix to open more, get a hand through in order to grab hold of a calf leg and use the calf to spin the uterus in the direction opposite to the twist from within. But trying to spin a forty-five-kilo calf in an enormously engorged uterus full of fluid by using one foot was not only back-breaking work, it was often just not possible.

Failing that, we would have to sedate poor old Mamo, get her down on the ground and roll her over, hoping that the uterus would do the necessary untwisting of its own accord. The third option, one that I didn't really like, was a Caesarean section – accessing the uterus from Mamo's left flank and correcting the twist from within the abdominal cavity, and then delivering the calf. A Caesarean would be hard on Mamo; for a start, how would her ancient body handle all the anaesthetic drugs? She was the oldest expectant cow I had worked with, by a good twenty years.

I was rapidly getting hot inside all the plastic protective clothing, and the adrenaline rush of the task at hand had me sweating profusely. John watched me anxiously for any updates, and the Dubs all seemed entirely baffled as to what was going on. I decided it was best to let them know.

'She's got a twisted womb, John, and we'll have to fix that first before we get the calf out,' I said. John looked at me with a very worried look; he started pacing again, hand on his forehead, saying, 'I just knew something wasn't quite right. She's been at it too long and nothing coming out.'

I agreed with him.

Martha, who had been standing beside Mamo looking anxious, came forward and said, 'Thank God you came, sure didn't I think I was going to have to do it myself.' She hastened to add that she was in fact a (human) midwife and had been nominated by the gang as chief calf deliverer, should the vet not be able to get there! Martha winced, and from behind a hand covering her mouth kept compulsively saying, 'Jeez, she's thirty-five years old.'

Now I'm a big fan of using pain relief in any way I can for my patients. I often give epidural anaesthesia for calving cows – it helps ease the pain and reduces the excessive straining, which relieves stress. And (equally important), as an old vet pointed out to me in my younger years, epidurals also help reduce the incidence rates of vets getting kicked. This last piece of information is not one you're likely to see published in a journal of bovine medicine research, but so far, within my study group of n = 1 vet (me!), my research supports this hypothesis.

Martha, extrapolating from her human patients, asked me about pethidine and gas, and I had to explain that we don't use that stuff with cattle. She watched with interest as I gave Mamo the epidural. After a few minutes, Mamo's tail had gone limp, and the straining had eased off – a sure indication that the epidural had set in – meaning that Mamo could stand relatively relaxed.

Hoping for a miraculous correction of the twist, from within the uterus, I got into position, and now that Mamo was not straining quite so much, I went back in with my right hand. In the area where I had got two fingers through earlier, I started making gentle movements against the cervix, spreading my fingers from a closed fist to an open hand. Ever so slowly, the tissue started responding by relaxing a little, and the small gap into the uterus opened just enough for me to gently fit my hand through. From there I could feel two medium-sized feet and a nose, all sitting there with the amniotic sac still intact. I gently passed my hand over the body, assessing the calf's anatomy. The calf's feet and nose tip, were still making little jerky movements – the calf was still with us.

The calf thankfully had not been waiting in that trapped position for too long, otherwise the life-giving placenta might have already detached, and the calf perishing would have been a very real risk. At last my hand was through, and it was time, hopefully, to get a hold of the calf's leg, to try and get a bit of momentum going, so as to spin the uterus and entrapped calf.

On my way in I had noted that the vaginal canal seemed to corkscrew to the left, and so a counter twist of the uterus to the right a good three-quarter turn would be needed to correct this. I felt the calf legs and head on the other side of the twist and knew there wasn't much room for the calf – that side too was twisted and narrowed. With my hand through on the calf's side of Mamo's cervix, despite the efforts to pull away from me, I managed to get a firm grasp of the calf's elbow.

In the past, on the few lucky occasions when I had managed to correct a uterine torsion from within, I had needed a good leverage point, so now, holding what I suspected to be the calf's left elbow, the job was to push hard upwards and clockwise so that the uterus spun that way too. The sweat was now pouring off me, dripping from my forehead and running down my back. I rested my head on Mamo's right hip, my left arm stretched out in the air by Mamo's side, wishing there was enough room for it to be of use in the heavy lift I was about to try with my right arm inside.

With a great big heave, I gave a push upwards on the elbow, willing it to cooperate and wishing to feel that deadly uterine noose loosening around my arm. The first attempt I got a little bit of movement, but the weight and my poor access just got the better of me, and in an instant the twist was back. It started to weigh on my mind that I could be wasting precious time; the calf could be suffocating right now, and this twist might not be corrected quick enough.

The thought of this being the only real good option for Mamo and calf, though, gave me a determination that got me through the pain of my aching muscles and tightly squeezed, numb right hand. That feeling of 'dammit this has to work' seemed to give me the strength to give it one big last lift, and as I sweated and strained, head pressed firmly once again on Mamo's hip, slowly it started – the up up up … up – and then swoooooossssshhhhh, that magical feeling of the uterus rotating and landing back in the position nature intended. The twist was gone and the pressure around my wrist was instantly relieved.

Mamo's cervix opened-up like a valley, leading to an amniotic sac, two calf legs and a head. Saving my right arm, I swapped to the left for an examination, and even in that minute or two as I changed arms, the calf was already coming into the birth canal, meaning delivery was imminent.

Mamo had carried enough calves in her past that she had sufficient room inside to fit a small elephant. This calf, which seemed to be of medium build, was now in a normal presentation. With the twist corrected she now proceeded into a normal calving, but given the delay in the labour, time was of the essence. I got John's nephews lined up with some towels and set about breaking the waters around the calf.

I had all my equipment ready, ropes, calving jack, etc., but as it would happen, none of that would be needed, for as soon as the waters were broken and I gave a gentle pull on the calf's forelegs further into the birth canal, Mamo started a few big pushes, and it couldn't have been five minutes from that point to the calf tumbling out into my arms. For one of the only times in my career, I didn't even use calving ropes on the legs.

We gave the calf a good rub-down with the towels and straight away it was coughing and spluttering the remaining amniotic fluid from the airways and taking its first nice deep breaths of air, alive and kicking. After a quick check between the back legs I declared it as a boy.

Everyone present, gave a huge sigh of relief, and John beamed with pride. In fact, John started to smile so much that he started to chuckle, all the while marvelling at the calf. He turned to Michael Senior and said, 'You know, Dad used to give me stick about giving him a grandson to pass on his name. Maybe I should call him Michael!' Michael Senior smiled at the thought.

I did another internal check of Mamo to ensure there was no surprise number two, which there wasn't, then gave Mamo a shot of anti-inflammatory pain relief; even if she wasn't in that much pain, sure it would do no harm, and in any case it would ease her arthritis for a few days.

Right around that time Michael Junior, who had been dwelling on it, piped up, saying with a cheeky grin on his face, 'Ah, Uncle John, I think with Grandad, Dad and now me, three Michaels are enough in any family!' This comment started John and Michael Senior off belly-laughing.

At that moment you could see how John and Michael Senior were brothers for sure – their similar mannerisms were uncanny. I had always admired John's hearty, jolly laugh, the kind of laugh where you couldn't help but join in. But now this was doubled with his brother, their heads tilted back, roaring with laughter to the sky. As the laughter escalated, the brothers grew louder and louder, until their combined mirth had them leaning on a nearby fence to catch their breath.

After a few minutes John finally came to and said, 'OK, OK, I accept three Michaels are plenty. Maybe we'll go with Bó? As in Irish for "cow"?'

Martha was quick to add, 'Or spell it "Beau", as in French for "beautiful"? Look at him, he's a stunner!'

To which John exclaimed, 'Right, so Beau it is.'

It was about five minutes later that John started up again with his pacing and headshaking. 'O'Halloran's bull is exonerated,' he yelled. 'He is not responsible!'

'By God you're right,' I said, the reason being fairly obvious. Before us lay a beautiful black-and-white bull calf, the kind of colouration synonymous with a dairy animal, and absolutely not the progeny of O'Halloran's red Limousin bull. Surveying the results, it was clear that some nimble-toed dairy farm suitor had negotiated the cattle grid and visited Mamo in the night! Being surrounded by dairy farms, John would never know the culprit.

Mamo went straight into her motherhood role, licking and admiring her new offspring. After years of being alone, with her only bovine contact recently being a rogue one-night stand that no one had witnessed, it was nice for her to have company again. John declared with a big grin on his face that Beau would be staying put for life, no questions about it. Already as I was leaving, Beau was up and having his first feed, Mamo standing there in pure contentment with her new arrival, her tail swinging gently in the summer breeze.

I was called to visit once again about a month later in order to castrate Beau, ensuring that his breeding career was over before it had even begun. He would go on to grow into a fine big bullock, tall and muscular; he was one of the biggest bullocks I have ever seen, a good 1.8 metres at the shoulder, though luckily, he inherited Mamo's docility and good nature – along with her lingual dexterity! With his height and sense of mischief, John had to rethink his fencing strategies, as from an open kitchen window – never mind the fruit bowl – Beau was a huge fridge-raid risk. He was great company for old Mamo. They got on so well together, they were often spotted mutual backscratching and licking each other. Mamo, in her element.

Beau's kryptonite was carrots. He would do anything for this delicious root vegetable snack. He also held hero status with young Paddy and Michael Junior ever since the day he had retrieved their orange soccer ball from being stranded on the roof of John's house; his extendible tongue, combined with his height and penchant for anything orange, had made quick work of licking the stricken ball out of the gutter along the roof.

And poor Martha was to find out the hard way, that for Beau anything orange, equals carrots. The day she wore her orange-coloured flip-flops to come and visit the farm, they were way too carroty and irresistible to Beau. Martha's lesson? Don't climb a medium-sized apple tree to escape a tall bovine that is intent on licking your footwear off, as this only increase said bovine's access to your dangling feet. And there aren't many people that have ever had a bovine lick their footwear off. It is said that Martha's screams could be heard as far as Dublin that day.

Now I have never seen an official human-age/cow-age chart like they have for dogs and cats, whereby, depending on who made the chart, a dog year is worth anything from four to seven human years, so that a ten-year-old dog, say, is considered to be aged the equivalent of seventy human years (that's breed dependent too.) But I'm going to stick my neck out regarding a human/cow chart and suggest a minimum of two human years per every cow year.

So as a cow that is at the time of writing, a good forty years old and going strong, and not looking a day over twenty, it would seem that Mamo is going to give the current longest-surviving cow ever recorded – Big Bertha (who happened also to be Irish) – a run for her money, with just another nine years to go!

After that visit I would often enquire after Mamo and Beau when I met John at the local pub. I didn't really go out his way so often on my calls, but the odd time I did drop by to deliver an apple and a scratch at the fence along the road. Last visit I had a chuckle to myself. As I approached the driveway, two shiny, brand-new stainless-steel gates adorned the entrance – no more rogue liaisons for Mamo.

CHAPTER 9

The Sow's Nest

Way back as a kid growing up in the orchard county of Armagh in Northern Ireland, our farm had a mix of cattle and horticulture. The cattle would spend the winter in the farm sheds at home, and the rest of the year out in the grazing fields away from the farm. Surrounding the farm, we had some apple orchards and, in the summer months, cultivated fields of strawberries, raspberries and blackberries. There were also crops such as potatoes, cabbage and turnips, depending on the season. With a few spare paddocks, and at times lots of leftover produce, we kids convinced my dad to get us a pet piglet. She was my tenth birthday present – I should say 'joint' birthday present (me and my twin sister). We named her Willow; the day she arrived she balanced the scales opposite a bag of spuds at ten kilos.

Willow, who was five weeks old, came from a commercial pig farm and, strictly speaking, was more of a weaner, than a piglet (a weaner pig has finished drinking their mother's milk and is ready for independent living). We fenced off one of the smaller paddocks and built her a wooden hut with a deep straw bedding. Having spent her life entirely indoors, her new enclosure was completely foreign to her. She had never seen grass or rolled in mud before; we really enjoyed watching her experience these things for the first time. In the early days she was nervous and frightened, probably wondering where all the other pigs were. She just wanted to run and hide from us, in the straw. It took a few days of food bribes and gentle encouragement before she settled in and became more friendly. Apart from one black spot on her left ear, she was pinkish-white all over. The fine white hairs covering her body soon thickened and became coarser, as she adjusted to outdoor life. As the weeks passed, she grew quickly to an impressive size, and instead of 'Willow' she became affectionately known as 'the sow'.

She was a crossbreed (Large White/Landrace), a mix mostly designed for rapid growth and meat production. We planned to have a few litters of piglets with her when she matured. Inquisitive and sociable, she communicated with a series of grunts, and we soon learned how to read her moods. She was mostly mellow and happy but could get quite cranky if expected to do something she didn't want to do. And boy, did she love her food! She had become so tame and friendly that we started to let her out of her paddock to free-range around the farm. She still went back to her hut each evening and we would lock her in her pen overnight and release her again in the mornings. With the farm being a safe distance from the main road, she could spend her days roaming the edges of the fruit fields.

We worked the free-ranging pig scenario with strategic fencing designed to keep her out of certain areas and crops, although we could also let her in certain fields to feast on the leftovers after the crops had been harvested. Soon she had fashioned a few mud wallows in the ditches around the farm. She would spend several hours each day off foraging, wallowing and exploring. We also fed her a pig cereal-mix twice a day at her trough, at her enclosure; she was always punctual for her mealtimes. Of all the horticultural leftovers on offer, her favourite snack by far was a bite-sized June drop apple (a premature apple dropped by the apple trees according to growth conditions), but she also made quick work of any stray potatoes, carrots, berries or turnips.

We kids spent many hours just hanging out with her, watching as she foraged. Coming from a musical family, some of my siblings even played their musical instruments for her. She appeared to enjoy the music, at times halting her relentless hunt for food and listening to the instruments being played. As she was out and about each day, on hearing our cheers during family football matches and games, she would come running out of nowhere doing little excited trots, sharing our excitement as though she loved her freedom and was celebrating it too. It was very entertaining for us to watch. Our Irish Water Spaniel farm dogs got on remarkably well with her too. The sow and dogs would often be found panned out sleeping in sunny spots around the farm together. She was so relaxed with us that she would wander around the farmyard at our side; it was only when visitors or customers buying produce turned up and were amazed by the pig walking around that we realised she was a pretty novel pet – well back then anyway. These days pigs are much less unusual pets, for those lucky enough to have the space for them.

When she turned one year old, we decided it was time for her to visit a boar (breeding male pig) on her next heat cycle (a hormonal state of being ready for mating) with the hope that she might have a litter of piglets. Getting her to and from that boar was a challenge.

The boar was a twenty-minute ride away, and we had purchased a trailer especially for getting her there. Later the trailer, towed by our old Massey Ferguson 35 tractor, would also be used to bring her piglets to new homes after weaning. It had a back door that came down on springs to meet the ground and served as a ramp for the sow to climb inside. With four sturdy stainless-steel sides, just high enough to be secure, the trailer top wasn't covered, and when the sow was coaxed inside the top half of her body was visible.

My dad and a neighbour were tasked with loading her up and bringing her to the boar. Now, loading a head-strong sow into a trailer can be a difficult task.

If she didn't want to do something, she could use her body weight and a loud squeal as defence mechanisms. She had never seen a trailer before and decided pretty early in the game that she was not going next to or near it, squealing and objecting if they even managed to get her close. Eventually they had to go for her Achilles heel: a handful of June drop apples from the orchard laid out in a strategic path leading up into the trailer. This worked well, as the sow followed the line of apples up the ramp door and onto the trailer – the ramp door was closed before she realised what was going on. And at the other farm, by all accounts, a mating had taken place (in pig reproduction, one mating is typically sufficient, for a pregnancy).

After the mating had occurred, the men had to do something similar with food bribes to get her back on the trailer for the trip home; luckily, they had brought a bucket of apples for this purpose.

I still remember my dad and the same neighbour howling with laughter at our farm – she gave us one of the biggest laughs of my childhood. They had gone on the boar visit trip with the sow the previous evening and this was the next morning. I had just let her out of her pen to go off exploring around the farm after breakfast. The trailer was parked in the farmyard, still attached to the tractor from the previous evening, and the spring-loaded ramp door was down, hovering just a few inches from the ground. As the three of us stood talking in the farmyard, we watched the sow come past us, grunting and snorting her way over to the trailer with obvious purpose – with love still on her mind. She looked at us, looked at the trailer, and then, pushing the ramp down to ground level with her nose, she took a step onto it. Wiggling her tail, she proceeded to walk up into the trailer and then stood looking back at us giving out a series of cheerful grunts in pig language as if to say, 'OK I'm ready, take me to my boyfriend again.'

We had to use June drop apples to get her back off the trailer that day!

The gestation of a pig is three months, three weeks, three days, a nice symmetry making it easy to remember – or you would think that, anyway. We didn't do a great job of counting her due date or keeping any records. In a very short time, we certainly knew she was pregnant, as her tummy swelled and her mammaries enlarged. Also, the fact that she didn't come into heat again three weeks later was a good sign she was pregnant (when in heat, pigs will go off their food and tend to stand still for long periods; the heat can last two to three days). She went about her daily routine of eating two meals a day and we let her go on roaming the farm fields and orchards as before.

Then one autumn evening, heavily pregnant, she didn't turn up for her evening food. I recruited some of the siblings and we searched high and low, sending the twin sister off towards the orchards and the brother to the hay barn, but we couldn't find her. With bucket in hand and a couple of little apples inside, I gave it a good shake and shouted her name. By now she would normally have knocked me down in a drooling frenzy, but this time there was not even a grunt.

Where had she gone? We were sure she had a few days still to go, but the anxiety started to rise that there had been a miscalculation and she was farrowing (giving birth) somewhere. We regrouped at the main farmyard; it turned out no one had seen her all that day, since her morning feed. We hoped maybe she would still turn up that evening like she always did but was just running late.

We continued to keep a watchful eye out for the sow, but we also had to finish some work in the raspberry fields. Autumn was a time for pruning the raspberry and blackberry bushes ahead of winter. Over the previous days we had been busy in the fields, pruning and gathering huge piles of old raspberry canes to be collected by tractor later; the big masses of cuttings would make an impressive Halloween bonfire after a few months of drying: a bit of a tradition for us.

The raspberry field was only a few minutes from the farmyard, past the Bramley apple orchards (commercial type of apple for baking/cider.) In any case, getting a bit of work done down that way would help distract me from the excitement of the imminent sow farrowing. Not fully realising the raspberry field gate had been left slightly open the previous day, I returned to the raspberry field and got back to work pruning the raspberry canes. I slowly made my way through the rows of plants towards the middle of the field, and that was when I discovered where the sow had got to.

As I approached the clearing in the middle where all the discarded bush clippings were being collected, I noticed that the previous days' collection of pruned branches and canes had all been moved and reorganised in a completely different way from how we had left them – the sow had made an enormous nest out of them. She must have been at it all day, as she had nearly cleared half an acre of cuttings. Gathered in the most elaborate nest around her, she lay in it with her back to me. The nest was piled high a couple of metres off the ground – it truly was a sight to behold. I stood, marvelling at her creation, impressed with her handiwork. As I got closer, gazing in amazement, I could see she had got into the middle and chewed the bushes – thorns and all – into a fine wood-shaving consistency. She lay in the middle of this enormous nest mound, and there, suckling on her teats, were three tiny little pink piglets.

She was just delivering a fourth piglet onto the nest behind her as I arrived. I stood at the side of her nest, adrenalin pumping with the shock and wonder of it all. I had never laid eyes on a newborn piglet before.

The sow was on her side, but she briefly turned and acknowledged me, and because we were good friends, I could tell that she was at ease with my presence, as she kept focused on her labour and didn't stir. With a couple of grunts, she went back into a trance of rhythmic breathing; she was pushing and straining, getting ready for the next delivery.

I watched the little piglet that had just been delivered. Breaking free from the placental sac, the umbilical cord was naturally getting stretched and disconnected as he made his way along the sow's back leg, clambering towards her tummy. The piglets had the finest covering of white hair, their little twitching noses instinctively searching out a teat to suckle.

The sow didn't move, just stayed lying there, her labour coming in waves. The piglets, on making their way in search of milk, visited her head and were greeted with a few gentle nudges with her nose, her grunts becoming more of a chattering. The babies responded too; it was their porcine way of greeting each other for the first time. Her big nose and powerful jowls that could demolish a whole turnip in two crunches, now tenderly comforted and guided the little piglets back to the sow's warm underbelly milk bar. It was truly heart-warming to watch. Because she was largely a free-ranging pig on our farm, it just seemed so lovely that she was able to show natural nesting behaviour. That certainly would not be seen in a more commercial pig enclosure with limited nesting materials.

The newly arrived piglet instinctively knew to go looking for a teat and at not even ten minutes old he was already latched on. One little piglet who must have been born a while, had already had his fill and was asleep on the nest, lined up beside two of the others who were happily suckling. I couldn't resist – I had to pick him up and have a closer look.

Although perfectly formed, he was so small he fitted in my cupped hands. His skin was so soft, almost like a baby human. Holding him in front of my face I looked on in amazement as he stared back at me, wriggling his little nose back and forth, taking in the smell of me. His little sleepy eyes looked at me. I imagined he was thinking, *who was I? and why was he in my hands?* Taking a few moments to pet him and look at him up close, I played with his little feet and his long curly tail, his ears being perfect little triangles no bigger than tea bags. Holding him in my hand with the sow in the nest just a couple feet away, I couldn't help but compare and take in the wonder of how his little trotters, and all his little body parts for that matter, were one day going to be as big – if not bigger – than hers. I just had to go and find the rest of my family to come and see this spectacle.

Leaving the raspberry field and running up to the farmhouse door, I breathlessly announced that I had found her, and that she was pigging! Everyone was so excited by the news that we all ran back to her. In the time it took for me to go and fetch my family, there were three new arrivals at the nest. The sow now had seven piglets. We gathered around in open-mouthed amazement at the sow and babies and the huge nest she had made, standing in stunned silence. My dad now joined us and, being a practical thinker, suggested we bring the sow's food trough and drinker down and make a temporary cover for her nest. She wouldn't want to leave that for a few days at least, and although the high sides were good at wind breaking, the top was open to the never distant Irish rain. We went off to the farm sheds and got wooden fencing posts and stretched some tarpaulin between them to cover the nest a few feet above the occupants and hammered it all in place. It seemed completely snug and safe under there now, in that wonderful nest.

The next piglet head count was eight. My dad had been around pigs quite a lot in his childhood, and asked expectantly, 'Where is the runt?' As we had been distracted by getting the cover in place, no one had noticed there had actually been a ninth arrival (a farrowing sow will usually have anywhere from six to fourteen piglets). If we thought the others were small, this little runt was only half their size. She may have been small, but she was up and determined for some milk pretty quickly (the space in a sow's uterus and therefore the nourishment of the developing piglets is not always even, therefore one or two smaller runts are not uncommon in a litter). My sisters couldn't resist picking the little runt up and giving her a cuddle. My dad let us know that the sow only had eight teats (some have more) and the runt may not be able to fight her way in to get milk, meaning she may not make it. We did a bit of the leg work for her and put her onto a good full teat so that she got a feed.

I kept a vigil that evening by the sow and piglets, sitting with them under the canopy until dark. There were no more piglets; she had finished her labour, and nine was her lot. I sat on the side of the nest just watching the sow and her family. At one stage, when the piglets had had their fill and were mostly asleep in a neat little mound, with the runt at the top (I put her there especially), the sow gave a few grunts, and with a few heaves, she sat up. I took that as a cue that she might be ready for some food. I got a bucket of food in her trough and she pulled herself up onto her feet and came over and had a few big drinks of water and ate her food – she looked so thin now.

In the coming days, the sow would alternate between feeding at her trough, nosing through the nearby undergrowth for tasty roots, and nesting with her piglets. Within a matter of days, the piglets were following her on her forays through the fruit fields, staying close to her underbelly as she nosed along. Later, the piglets became braver, and would venture away from her too, in search of roots and the odd piece of fruit on the ground, left behind from the harvest a few weeks previous. The sow was regularly seen stacking up and building more to her nest. The piglets, although generally friendly and playful, if startled in any way would all go running from wherever they were in the field and dive head-first into the safety of the nest. Only when they deemed it safe, the first few would pop their heads out and grunt their approval for the rest to follow back out, danger gone. This nest was right in the middle of the fruit fields and, realistically, not a great place for a gang of pigs to be long term. At about two weeks old, with offerings from buckets, we managed to entice the whole family up into their own paddock back at the farmyard. There the sow's hut

– complete with heat lamp – would be a much more suitable option, as they were growing rapidly.

The piglets were good fun for us kids. We spent hours watching them wallow in the mud and playing pig tag with each other. Incredibly, all nine of them survived, the runt mostly catching up in growth. From about six weeks old we started to find them new homes at other farms. In a matter of weeks, all the piglets had been sold and the sow was back to having her food trough and our farm all to herself again. She wasn't fazed by the piglets going away. She was still her happy-go-lucky self, getting back to free ranging our farm and hanging out with us kids.

She came into heat soon again, but we decided to give her a few months of recuperation before having more piglets. Her cycles came and went every three weeks. About six months later, with her reproductive hormones surging, we loaded her up on the trailer once again with relative ease, and she had another visit to the boar. This time we kept a better record of her due date and fixed up a farrowing area in a vacant cowshed next to her paddock. Excitedly, we anticipated our next set of piglets. On her due day, and with a more moderate straw nest, right on cue, she went into labour and started delivering piglets. After the fourth piglet arrived things started to go wrong – her delivery stopped. It became apparent we needed to call a vet to come and give her a hand.

It was a late spring Saturday evening and, as we were in the Irish countryside, it could be a difficult time getting hold of a vet. Many of the hard-working vets who had been busy all week would be trying to have a night off, and some of them would be with other calls. My dad called a few of the local practices, but they were busy. He knew of an old retired vet, about a thirty-minute drive away in the neighbouring county, who you could sometimes call upon if you were stuck. I didn't know much about this vet, but my dad knew of him through his farming circles. We would get his number and try to find him. The vet's nickname preceded him in the local area – Cranky Davey. Davey was actually his surname, and his first name was Alister, but everyone referred to him as Cranky Davey – though definitely not to his face! Back then it wasn't that unusual to refer to vets by their surname. The Cranky bit was more of a character reference. I didn't realise at the time how unusual the interaction with Cranky Davey would be that evening, but I still smile looking back, thinking just how cranky and old-school he turned out to be. This was almost thirty years ago now.

My father got the phone number of Davey's old practice, and it turned out that this was also where he lived. The practice had been closed for a few years, but Davey did his best to participate in an on-call roster, letting the other local vets have a night off, and at nearly eighty years old, that indeed was very noble of him. His wife answered the call and gave my dad another number to call, telling him he would need to do the driving as Davey was beyond it. My dad called and made arrangements to go and get Davey, and off he went. I stayed at the sow's side. About an hour later my dad reappeared with a red-faced Davey walking beside him. Dad and Davey had stopped by Davey's premises, and when they got back to our farm, he was carrying a leather bag of veterinary implements and bottles of potions.

Cranky Davey was a medium-sized man, with bushy eyebrows and a long grey moustache. The open neck of his navy overalls revealed a checked shirt underneath. This was the first time I had ever met him. Having such a high opinion of vets and harbouring a secret ambition of one day being one, I was very impressionable. I greeted Davey with a hearty 'Good evening,' but he mostly ignored me. I knew of his reputation for being cranky, but I didn't really know just what to expect, so I favoured keeping quiet and out of his way and just observed him with intrigue. I was twelve years old then, perhaps in Davey's eyes still being in the 'seen and not heard' child category. I couldn't help it, as my eyes searched his face for a sign of anything other than grumpiness, but he just got to work and addressed my dad only.

You couldn't say he was mean-spirited; he just wasn't for saying hello or smiling. He walked with a constant head nod, and as he went, he emitted a low-grade mumble in conversation with himself, an ongoing speech that seemed to come out in loud, abrupt outbursts of the odd word. Arriving at the sow, he looked at me and then turned to look at my dad with a stare and silence that felt like, 'What to hell are you people doing pig farming?'

Then he placed his bag down and took his jacket off. I was well used to the cattle vets needing buckets of fresh water, so I gingerly asked if he wanted some. He barked, 'No, I'm planning on digging a small well here, of course I do, boy!'

I was a bit shocked at just how cranky he was – he had already surpassed my expectations. The four piglets that had been born earlier were now mostly asleep under the heat lamp, and the sow was doing some strong grunting in the throes of a now unproductive labour. I had a bad feeling that something was wrong; she did not look happy at all.

The shed lighting wasn't great, so we used torchlight to help illuminate the rear end of the sow for Davey. He let out a steady series of loud grumps as he put on his gloves. Being old school, he pulled back his overalls and applied soap from a wet bar, to his arms (most of us use lubricant these days) then got on his knees behind the sow. Quickly he was reaching far enough into the sow's birth canal that he needed to lie on the straw on one side next to her. The sow grunted as Davey continued his exam of her birth canal. I squeezed my eyes shut tight, hoping there would be a simple explanation for why the labour had stopped. Perhaps two piglets were coming at once, or one big one was coming sideways. I was using cow-calving scenarios I had seen other vets successfully manage on our farm in the past as a reference for what was happening here. Davey started extracting something, and I didn't dare ask what it was. I stared at his arm emerging from the sow: even in the poor lighting, what he took out from the sow didn't look anything like a piglet. Davey turned to my dad and said, 'Some of them have gone bad in there, that one was,' he loudly exclaimed, 'A mummified foetus, and there will probably be more. I'll give her a shot of oxytocin (a drug used to stimulate uterine contractions) and we'll give her a break, and then I'll try again.'

Davey gave the sow an injection in her hip muscle and he and my dad headed off towards our house with talk of tea. I stayed with the sow. She didn't look happy and wasn't showing the same attention to the piglets as she had before. Her large mammaries looked a bit empty, like she had stopped producing milk. I was starting to get worried – if the last one was stillborn, had any more survived inside?

After about fifteen minutes Davey and my dad came back and Davey got into position once more. With the oxytocin, the sow was now giving some big heaves. I had my fingers crossed, hoping more live piglets were on the way. I didn't realise at that point that soon I would be praying for the sow's life.

Davey was lying on the straw with his hand in the sow's birth canal once again, sweating and grunting. I nervously watched his facial expression for updates, but he didn't give much away. With a bit of head shaking, he started delivering the next arrival. Dad and I got closer with the torches, awaiting eagerly. I had a towel ready to deliver some rubs, knowing the coming piglets would need all the help we could give. This time Davey pulled something small out and put it on the ground before I could see it, then immediately went back in with his hand, shaking his head as he delivered the silent but firmly negative message – no, no this wasn't good. Standing back up and now holding another shrivelled foetus, he just said to my dad, 'She's in a bit of trouble here. The rest of her piglets are coming stillborn and underdeveloped.' He bent down and picked up the first thing that he had put on the ground – I now know it was a fleshless piglet's jawbone. I couldn't believe my eyes.

My heart sank – this was all becoming a nightmare.

Davey said, 'Something has gone wrong with the pregnancy and it would seem the remaining piglets inside have perished and are coming out in bits.' He gave the sow some antibiotics and then gave us more to give her over the course of the next few days. He suggested we would have to let nature take its course and let the stillborn babies pass when ready. He added there was nothing more he could do.

I was very worried now for the sow, as this all looked like it was very hard on her. My dad said, 'OK, let's all go and drop Davey back and give the sow some space.' The three of us got in the car and headed off through the dark of the night. After getting into the car, in a closed airspace with Davey, I realised there was quite a strong smell of booze off him. I didn't know then, but in my mind's nose now, it was a strong whisky smell.

On the journey the three of us were relatively silent, my dad and Davey in the front seats, and me sitting in the back. I couldn't stop thinking about the sow. At least the time I was away from her allowed space for some glimmer of hope to creep in, that something good might have happened by the time we got back to her. My dad, trying to lighten the mood in the car, said to Davey, 'The boy here wants to be a vit too, you know.' Davey just grumbled and turned from his seat in the front and looked me over and then turned back again. I decided then, of all the inspiring vets I had met, he was probably not going to be one of them, for me. I got a very cold feeling from him, almost as though he was thinking, 'What a ridiculous ambition to have.'

I wasn't familiar with the area where Davey lived, so I was even more surprised when we arrived at what I thought was his house, only to find it was actually a country pub, pretty much in the middle of nowhere. My dad parked in the car park and told me to wait a couple of minutes and he would be right back. We all got out of the car and I went to move up to the front seat. Davey came past me to get his bag from the car boot. As he walked by, he stopped once more and looked at me and said, 'You want to be a vet do you, boy?' and he beckoned me over. Leaning over and covering the gap between my ear and his mouth with his hand, and in a miasma of distillery grade alcohol breath, he whispered, 'Don't do it, go and be a feckin dentist.'

He said this with such conviction that my eyes involuntarily widened.

My dad didn't hear the comment.

Dad and Davey headed off towards the pub and opened the door, releasing a few blasts of laughter and music from the patrons within, then went inside. I lowered myself into the car seat, still processing the sow's predicament and now Davey's sentiments, taking a bit of wind from my sail. I felt especially lonely in those moments, waiting on my dad to come back. Closing my eyes and leaning back into the chair, I turned up the car radio a notch or two to try to blank it all out. A couple of minutes later my dad came back and got into the driver's seat. He turned the music down and off we went for home.

Dad filled me in more about Cranky Davey on the way home.

Turns out it was customary for farmers who called upon Davey to both collect and deliver him back to his local pub – his actual house was just a few doors down. Upon returning Davey, it was also customary to buy him a couple of drinks. My dad was very matter-of-fact, about it all.

I was still in a bit of a spin from the encounter with Cranky Davey, but still thankful that he had tried his best at helping the sow. Driving along, my dad said, 'When it comes to Davey there is a very sad story …'

He continued, 'Davey had one son, Christopher Davey, trained as a vet in Scotland, and came back to his father's practice to take over some years back, well before you were born. Unfortunately, there was a tragedy. Christopher died in his early thirties, and his father has never been quite the same since. He was always a bit of a grump beforehand, he didn't cope with the loss very well, with years of alcoholism ever since.'

Dad pulled up at a junction and paused for a moment or two longer than he needed to. 'Austin,' he said, 'the young vet, Christopher, died at his own hands. It was suicide. People say the pressure of all the long hours, the isolation of the countryside and the task of filling his father's shoes was all too much for him.'

In my relatively young years, I had heard the word 'suicide' only once before. The previous year Kurt Cobain (the rock star) had died by suicide, and there had been lots of media coverage. This news about Christopher hit me hard. I was so saddened to hear that this happened to everyday people much closer to home too.

I don't know what my dad was thinking then, but his recalling of a story where a father loses his son in such a way had made him go very quiet, no doubt bringing up difficult thoughts and feelings. My heart was wrenching for poor old Davey now. I didn't know what I could have said or done differently, had I known that earlier, but I sure did feel sorry for him.

I was also troubled by the thought that a vet could be so unhappy with the job that this could happen. My images of working with puppies and kittens and having endless successes, curing sick animals and having great job satisfaction with hordes of happy customers – was this not the reality? The shows on television suggested otherwise. When did it all get so sad? More about that another time, but right there, that weekend, the sow was about to show us that sometimes, veterinary endeavours, and wishful owners, do not always win.

Arriving home, we parked at the farmyard and made our way back to the sow. She had passed more foetal material and looked like she had been up for a drink and was now in a different position on her side. She was unusually quiet, still having signs of active labour, but despite her straining, there wasn't much coming out. It was getting late at night, so we got her piglets onto her for some milk and left her for the night. I hoped that whatever needed to come out would pass overnight.

Next day, Sunday morning, I was up first thing to go and see her. The sow was not looking good at all. There were purple blotches on her skin and her milk was drying up. The piglets looked hungry, moving between her teats frequently. We gave her the morning antibiotic injection. With this dreadful skin colour and her depressed demeanour, I was now very worried. She had stopped straining. I think the remaining foetal materials had passed, but she looked very sick. Now she wouldn't eat, and despite lots of encouragement, she wasn't willing to stand. We brought blankets and moved the heat lamp closer, and I stayed with her.

Once the afternoon arrived, I reluctantly left her for forty minutes to have my lunch. Afterwards, when

I came back and opened the barn door, I noticed that the piglets were back, lined up against her belly going from teat to teat now frantic in search of milk.

I looked at the sow, her body now completely covered in purple and red blotches. She looked dreadful. It was unusually quiet in there, and it took me a moment or two to fully realise: that damn trick your eyes play on you when you see a deceased remains and you are sure you can see breathing. It hit me like a hammer in the guts – the sow had passed away.

I threw myself along her back and wailed. I just couldn't believe that this could happen. She was still warm and must have gone only minutes earlier. With tears streaming from my eyes, I looked over her belly at the four little piglets still trying to suckle – they had no idea what had happened. I just couldn't stop staring at her, wishing this wasn't the case, willing her to take a breath and come back. I cried so hard I thought I might never be able to take a full breath again myself, holding my stomach against the waves of paralysing emotional pains. I couldn't stop the tears. It all seemed so unjust, those little orphan piglets trying to suckle their deceased mother, they looked so helpless and vulnerable. I just couldn't accept that she wasn't coming back. After some time, I went to break the news to my family.

Reeling in a state of shock, my whole family were gripped with the grief of Willow passing away. No one knew what to say or do. Willow's absence around the farmyard was undeniable, like a repeated punch in the guts every time we went through the farmyard.

Determined that this was some sort of nightmare that I was going to wake from any moment, a few times my eyes were still keen on playing tricks, imagining her in the form of shadows moving around the yard. It was weird and eerie, but I wasn't scared. Like chasing the end of a rainbow, whenever I let myself go to follow these, they were gone. The menacing wind even recreated some of her noises, rustling in the bushes and tossing empty buckets. But the only trace we now had of Willow, was her four little piglets.

Looking back, getting thrown head-first into hand raising the piglets was a necessary distraction. Willow's loss would take years, to fully accept.

I started to try and find some positives in this horror, thinking that at least the little orphan piglets had got some of her colostrum (first milk, rich in antibodies), which would give them a good start. We got them on regular feeds of powdered formula milk with a bottle, by hand, and in no time, they got the hang of it. After a few days they had learned how to drink the milk straight out of a bucket on their own. My dad showed me how to teach them that trick, getting them to suck a finger and then slowly lower their mouths into the milk; soon they would be sucking up the milk. As they grew, they would spend periods of time off exploring around the farmyard, often running back into the comforts of their straw-lined shed. Being hand-raised, they were much more friendly and sociable than the other piglets before them, and they spent quite a bit of their day following us around the farm, perhaps thinking of us as their parents. They often could be found having a snooze in warm spots around the farm, the glass houses, or on the hay bales in the midday sun, just like their mother.

I still remember the look of outrage on our broody bronze turkey's face. Every day she gathered up whatever eggs she could find on the hen house floor, which may only have been one or two, with her mind set on brooding them. Cue some small, rambunctious piglets, loving a bit of heat. They must have gotten into her nest and fallen straight asleep while she was out eating her grain. On her return, the turkey didn't know what to make of it all, getting up and sitting back down, puffing her feathers out repeatedly, each time appearing to check if the long pink eggs that were snoring under her, in her nest, were still there!

After many funny encounters like this, eventually, at six weeks old, the four piglets went on to new homes. After that we gave up on pig farming.

It would be some years later before I really understood what had happened to the sow. In vet school in Dublin and learning about pig health, I found there was a whole range of diseases that could have caused this. There are several viruses, one being a relative of the deadly canine parvovirus that causes severe disease in unvaccinated dogs. There is an equivalent in pigs, also called parvovirus, only in this instance it causes developing piglets to pass away in the womb. There is also a porcine enterovirus that can cause this too. Then a range of bacterial infections is also on the list of possibilities. Looking back, it was pretty incredible that any of that litter survived, but I would find an explanation for that later too. A sow's uterus is divided into two horns – each side capable of holding developing piglets. If an infection occurs close to farrowing, it is feasible that it can be contained to one side of the uterus only, so that one uterine horn is able to deliver live piglets while the other side has only undeveloped foetal material.

Cranky Davey had done his best to get the material out of the affected side. Even now with my long arms, I'm not sure I could have done any different to what he managed. My vet brain then also reasons that what happened with the sow, is that she then developed septicaemia, and that's what caused her death. Those images of purple and red blotches all over her body stayed with me for a long time. I would later learn that they were signs that nasty toxins had been produced inside her by bacteria and were coursing through her bloodstream.

One final vet thought also. Given that we were having a go at pig farming and blissfully ignorant to these diseases, we were inadvertently remiss with getting her vaccinations against these pathogens, and some of these diseases are entirely preventable. It is possible that, had we been better informed, we might have been able to protect her from this. Given that the sow lived on her own on our farm, she was not going to get many opportunities to build natural immunity until something as catastrophic as this happened, and unfortunately overwhelmed her system. A harsh lesson learned in hindsight.

Back at the very start of my stories I told you that I studied dentistry for a year, and here I am telling you that an old vet advised me to do just that. I know it looks suspect, but as it happens, Davey's advice was never part of my thinking or rationale for my choice of career. I studied dentistry by default as it was just so difficult to get a place in vet school, although my luck later changed.

However, something else equally poignant happened in my transition from dentistry to veterinary medicine, and in both cases this story, and the circumstances of Christopher Davey's death, again weighed heavily on my mind.

On day one of dental school, my entire year group were asked to attend a lecture by the Dean of Dentistry. One of the important topics discussed was our mental health as future dentists, and the fact that back then the dentistry profession had the highest rate of suicide of all the medical professions, that year in the United Kingdom. There was discussion of how we could look out for ourselves and each other better. There were some very scary statistics also involving rates of mental distress and unhealthy coping mechanisms, such as drug abuse and alcoholism. An uncomfortable topic, so sad and difficult to talk about for us all.

One year later I changed to vet school, and during my first week, as it would happen, I attended an uncannily similar lecture. This time, vets had overtaken all the other professions as having the highest rate of suicide (using UK statistics). I began to feel like somehow someone was playing a cruel joke on me, about my life choices. As it happens, vets have maintained the highest suicide rate of all the medical professions ever since (worldwide) – a devastating reality for many veterinary families around the world. Cranky Davey has long since passed, but this was my first encounter of a veterinary family devastated by this reality, and it breaks my heart to say it certainly wasn't the last.

I look back on my encounter that night with Cranky Davey with perhaps now more reasoned insight. He had every right to be cranky, I guess if similar circumstances had arisen in my life, I can't promise I would be any different. But what strikes me, every time my thoughts drift that way, was his reaction to my father saying that his son was hoping to become a vet.

It makes me a little sad thinking that on some level this must have been very difficult for Davey to hear, having lost his son who also chose that path. Hence his reaction.

Mental health and the grief from such a loss in life are not always things we handle very well. I know that for many, using alcohol to numb the pain or to sidestep these difficult conversations is a coping mechanism. Perhaps some could judge Davey for not coping too

WHISKERS FEATHERS AND FUR

well with what he was dealt, with his grumpiness and likely alcoholism, but I also cannot deny, coming from a position of more mature understanding, the difficulty of his situation, and I respect him much more now than I did back then.

It is well known that men (and some women too) are reluctant to speak about their feelings. I also think that this custom of local farmers picking Davey up and dropping him back at his local pub when he was needed after hours, and buying him a couple of drinks, was for many of them an unspoken way of sympathising with him. The words in these circumstances are always hard to find.

In fact, even now, the adult me sometimes thinks I would have bought him a few drinks myself.

CHAPTER 10

The Hairy Fairy Goat Dairy

During my time in the Southern Hemisphere, I had always felt drawn to go see New Zealand, having heard great things about it on my travels from so many Kiwis – the moniker 'Kiwi' being mostly a term of endearment for the people of New Zealand arising from their national symbol, the nocturnal, flightless and hairily feathered bird, the kiwi. For some time, I had wondered, could the term also have something to do with the hairy- kiwi fruit? But I soon learned that the naming of the fruit plants, having been imported and grown in New Zealand since the early 1900s, was more of a marketing campaign for the fruit (which is actually a kind of gooseberry), as it turned out it grew really well there.

Some compared New Zealand to Ireland, both being green and rugged, and I was excited to see it for myself. Up to that point, the Kiwi people I had met on my travels mostly had a good sense of humour, and were easy-going, likeable sorts, so I had a feeling I would get along just fine in their motherland. I was getting towards the later part of my stay in Australia working as a vet locum, and from there it was just a three-hour flight across the Tasman Sea.

New Zealand is two large islands set close together – the North and South Island. I wanted to see each island individually, so I decided to head to the North Island first, where I found a one-person rural vet clinic run by a heavily pregnant vet who was in need of a maternity cover locum. I signed up for six months and excitedly headed off.

My plan was to land at Wellington in the southern end of the North Island a few weeks before I was needed, then travel northwards by road, taking in the incredible sights along the way. The fun and camaraderie began with the Kiwis onboard the plane from Melbourne. This was the start of the *kia ora*, the traditional Maori greeting. Arriving in New Zealand, there was a warm welcome all around, from the airport staff to the taxi driver to the hotel staff – and the local people I met just seemed so very friendly and helpful. This theme would continue throughout my entire stay in New Zealand – a feeling about as close as it gets to being at home and in good company, even though I was travelling alone and on the other side of the world.

I explored the famously windy Wellington for a few days, then headed north. I spent a few days at Lake Taupo, kayaking and swimming in the crystal clear, naturally tepid geothermal streams, in some places as warm as you would want a bath, but just a few breast strokes away from cooler currents. I stopped in at the volcanic geysers and mud pools of Rotorua, where I also went to a kiwi-breeding facility to see the birds for myself. It was incredible to see them out at night snorting and sniffing around, using their long beaks and sense of smell on the hunt for tasty morsels in the leaf litter. I spent days hiking into the forests and mountains, cooling off in some of the most stunning waterfalls along the way. I called by Hobbiton and observed its magic, taking the mandatory hobbit-house selfie of course. Then I headed on to Auckland for a few nights, and eventually arrived a few hours north to begin work, coinciding with the start of spring that year.

The practice was in the heart of the countryside. We saw a good mix of farm clients and held regular small animal clinics. After a few days the boss handed over the reins and went off to get ready for her other new arrival. I quickly got into the swing of things, working with a nice team of people at the practice – country Kiwi types that included a receptionist (Megs) and two vet nurses (Kate and Shell) – and I soon felt very much part of the team. The practice was reasonably small and therefore offered a very personal service, and, as I would discover, it had lovely clientele too. Clients dropped in to say hello and welcome me to their town. It turned out that a shortage of vets in the area had made everyone a little anxious that the head vet was going to have to close her practice for a few months in order to have time with her newborn baby; they were visibly relieved that I was there to cover, and keen to make me feel welcome. Some even brought me gifts of fresh produce – eggs, potatoes, tomatoes and preserves. My New Zealand experience had started to feel like I was in an advert for Tourism New Zealand; the friendly welcome just seemed to keep on coming.

Being in a new country where many things differed to Ireland or Australia, I had lots of interesting things to see on my rounds, from enormous rotating dairy cattle milking parlours, to deer farms, harvesting antler velvet for the Chinese medicine market. Agriculture was a busy part of the practice workload, and each day I had a list of farm visits, satnav at the ready – a big change from finding my way on the signless roads of the Wicklow mountains! The clinic staff knew the clients really well and would be able to tell me in good detail about who I was going to see and what each call-out entailed, from castrating piglets to doing dental work on horses to treating lame dairy cows. I really enjoyed getting out on the road and meeting the animals and clients.

I had been working there for a couple of months when a call came in for me to visit Ian and Dave's farm – the practice's only goat dairy. On my rounds I had heard a lot about Ian and Dave from the locals, as they were at the heart of the community. From charity work to participation in the theatrical society group, they had earned a reputation as being both local comedy kings and treasured citizens. Ian was also known for running a stall on the weekends at the town farmers' market, where he would sell his goats cheese. I had heard so many great things about the couple, I felt like I already knew them before I ever met them.

On this first visit they were doing an exchange of some high-genetic-merit dairy goats with another New Zealand goat dairy to help improve each other's breeding lines. The exchange goats would need blood tests before travelling to ensure they were free of certain diseases (this is a regular practice with goat farming). The receptionist, Megs, smiled as I headed off out the clinic door and said, 'You are going to love these guys. Secretly, they are some of our favourite clients; you'll see why for yourself.' As I was leaving, Megs added, 'When you're out there, will you tell Ian and Dave I said hello, and I am looking forward to seeing them at drama class on Thursday night.'

The notes gave me satellite coordinates, with a brief mention of a hillside and a phone number. I arrived about fifteen minutes later to the mentioned hillside location and turned onto the driveway up to the farm. The one thing the notes failed to mention was an enormous wooden cut-out on the hillside near the start of the driveway, of a man fairy and a large prominent sign that read, 'Welcome to the Hairy Fairy Goat Dairy'.

Now, when I say it was a 'man fairy,' I am talking a ten-foot smiling caricature cut-out of a burly man with impressive large, white fairy wings at the back – big enough to carry a man with such a stature, and holding a happy-looking goatling under one arm. The fairy, who wore a toga, had bulging muscles, grizzlyesque body hair, a spiky beard and a good crop of long hair projecting out from under a shiny crown.

I didn't know what to expect ahead! But the intrigue made me smile as I drove up the laneway. *Hairy birds, hairy fruit and now … why not a hairy fairy too?* I thought to myself.

Arriving at the main courtyard, in the centre of the farm buildings, I parked up and was getting my kit organised when I heard an exuberant, 'Hellllloooooo! Welcome to Kiwi land! You must be the new vet! You are most welcome!'

Ian appeared from one of the nearby doorways and introduced himself with a firm handshake. He was tall and slim, with a shaved head, and I quickly picked up on a northern English (Geordie) accent; he appeared to be in his early forties. It was a nice sunny morning and he was making the most of it, wearing dungarees with sawn-off arms and legs and a pair of hobnail boots. I remember thinking that it was quite a fashionable look, for a goat farmer.

Enthusiastically, he asked, 'So, do you like it? My new sign! It's just been installed yesterday.'

I said, 'You know what Ian, I think it's great,' adding, 'Coming all the way from Ireland, I feel privileged to visit a hairy fairy goat dairy.'

To which Ian replied, 'Oh my God, you're Irish?' he then said, 'I bet you're wondering where the fairy is,' and he stood back and did a little dance, somewhat like the floss dance tossed up with a bit of ballet, performed with a beaming smile and hands cupped occasionally about his face, much like petals on a flower. He then loudly exclaimed, 'It's me!' And with a quick spin and a curtsey, he added, 'I'm the hairy fairy!'

I smiled and said, 'I am most humbled to meet you, Mr Ian the hairy fairy.' And we both had a giggle.

'Wait to you meet my husband Dave and he finds out you are Irish,' Ian said. 'He's going to die! He loves Irish people – what with his ancestors being Irish convicts back in the day.' He made these comments with a cheeky grin and it all sounded funnier in Ian's Geordie accent than it should have. Again, we both laughed.

He then said, 'This can only mean one thing – cocktails! Do you have time for a mimosa now?'

It's not like me to say no to a cocktail, but it was 11 am on a Tuesday, and I had a day's work ahead. We agreed we would all definitely catch up for a cocktail after work soon thereafter. Ian was so friendly, spirited and flamboyant, I couldn't help but instantly warm to him. I could see what all the neighbours meant; he truly was both fun and entertaining to be around.

Ian then invited me to have a look around his farm, and as we walked, we had a chat. He explained that he was a chef by trade, trained in England, and that he had travelled and worked in a few different countries before meeting Dave and settling in New Zealand a few years back. Growing up on an English dairy cattle farm, he had always had ambitions to run a small farm of his own and produce high-quality food, and this was his dream in progress. He then said, 'Come meet some of my goats – the girls! They're a friendly bunch.' Excited at the prospect, he exclaimed, 'The girls are going to love you!'

The farm overlooked a spectacular hillside, part of a valley with green rolling hills on either side with a deep blue river in the centre. The height gave a great vantage point over the local town on one side and looked onto miles of hills and forests on the other. The farm itself consisted of a series of rectangular buildings forming a courtyard in the middle. Some of the buildings were older with modern improvements, while others were brand-new builds, mostly wooden and goat-sized with lowered roofs and smaller doors than you would get away with for larger farm animals. Ian and Dave's house sat only a short distance from the farm courtyard, through a flower-lined garden path. I could see the house was a nice old Victorian-style farmhouse, featuring modern extensions and a sunny veranda. There was cast steel garden furniture and a giant chess game set on the lawn.

All the farm buildings and the courtyard were well kept, spotlessly clean and freshly painted, with lots of hanging baskets of beautiful, colourful flowers – just out of goat reach, of course.

Dotted around in the nearby wooden-fenced paddocks were many small buildings, almost like little log cabins. Some had stores of square hay bales and others were goat shelters accessible from the paddocks, which all connected to a central lane, the main walkway for the goats to get to the milking parlour. In the distant fields were lots of goats, grazing contentedly.

There were about a dozen chickens in one of the nearby paddocks, a mix of breeds, mostly ISA browns, a few black Leghorns and a couple of light Sussex. Some pecked busily amongst the grass while others enjoyed a dust bath in the shade near the buildings. As we crossed the courtyard, a ginger-and-white cat appeared from one of the buildings, walked along behind my car and disappeared over a yellow half door into a building that looked like an old horse stable.

In another shed I could hear the playful bleats of goat kids – this was the nursery for the youngsters, Ian pointed out. The kids, about fifteen of them in total and all of them white, ranged from a few weeks old, to six months old. They had a straw-bedded shed attached to a small paddock, with lots of little mounds and logs for them to climb and jump on; it looked like they were enjoying a game of tag, frolicking and running around at high speed as we looked on. Some were still having milk, and it was feeding time. Ian set up their milk train drinker (a long plastic tank with a series of teats), fetched a bucket of milk and poured it in. In no time, every one of the teats had a kid enthusiastically suckling, their row of tails cheerfully wagging as the milk bubbled through. They were quick drinkers; in just a couple of minutes they had nearly finished the whole thing. Already some had got their fill and were making their way back to their comrades outside. We continued our tour.

As we walked through the courtyard, we looked down over the grazing paddocks; the field closest to us had about forty grazing nanny goats, all busy munching on the beautiful green grass. We went for a stroll through the field with the grazing goats – all the same breed. They were Saanen dairy goats, white and mostly hornless apart from the occasional stub. Ian pointed out one goat in particular, with one singular large horn, and said it was his pet unicorn! The goats were busily grazing and as we approached individuals they would come and briefly said hello, for a chin scratch. Ian pointed out his first-ever goat – one of the matriarchs of the flock. He introduced me to several different goats by name (an impressive skill, given they all looked identical to me) and pointed out daughters and granddaughters. I smiled as I noticed a lot of music culture names coming up: Shakira, Beyoncé, Nicki and so on. I don't think it was just because they were pleased to meet me, but these were some happy-looking goats.

As we walked, I asked Ian whether, given his dairy farm background did he ever consider keeping cattle? He said maybe one day, but for now he was concentrating on goats and expanding his poultry. 'Come, let me show you,' he said, and we went off towards the courtyard again to have a look. Ian had taken delivery of a baker's dozen (thirteen) day-old goslings just four days before my visit. He explained they were all the same breed – Emden geese – a common farmyard breed. He added that although they were all yellow and fluffy now, they would eventually turn snow white as they grew into adults. This was a new venture for Ian, having geese grazing the paddocks in rotation with his goats.

Walking back through the courtyard, Ian said, 'Hopefully, you get to meet Stella too. She's our recently adopted cat. She's an interesting cat for sure. We only got her six weeks ago from our neighbour, who had a few too many cats.' No one knew for sure, but they guessed she was around two years old. Ian said that just as they were getting her organised to go to the vets for neutering, they noticed her tummy getting bigger, and they realised she was in fact pregnant. Just a few days before my visit she had produced one little kitten. Ian led me over and opened the farm office door (complete with a shiny new cat flap) to show me a little ginger-and-white kitten fast asleep on a snug cat bed, beside a radiator. As the kitten was getting all the milk for himself, he was already pudgy and just looked so cosy and peaceful, perhaps just after a large feed. Ian whispered behind his hand, so as not to wake the kitten, 'We shall call him Prince,'(after the pop idol.)

Stella herself was nowhere to be seen. As I had noticed her earlier in the courtyard, I asked whether she might have been going off to have some food too.

'Well, here's the thing,' Ian said, pausing. 'Come and see for yourself. I bet you she's in with the goslings.' We gently closed the office door and left the kitten in his dreamy slumber and went off across the courtyard towards the horse stable. Ian explained that this stable used to be for a pony many years previously, but now it was going to be the goose shed. Conveniently, it opened at the back also, onto a paddock for when the geese were much more grown.

As we approached the yellow half door of the goose shed with the top door latched open, Ian told me of a very peculiar thing that was going on within: as well as mothering the kitten, they were starting to think Stella had also adopted the goslings! Ever since the goslings had arrived, she was spending hours with them snuggled on the hay; she had even made a nest for them. I was slightly sceptical about all of this and was keen to see it for myself. Thinking back to my childhood poultry farming enterprises, the farm cats had liked my hatchlings a little too much, but in a totally different way. We had to build Fort Knox to stop the cats from eating them. This suggestion that Stella was mothering goslings, was pretty incredible.

Peering over the half door, I saw that one end of the shed was shadowy and dim while the other end, having a large, bright brooder lamp overhanging to provide heat, was well-lit. Some of the goslings were up and about, adorable little fluff balls acknowledging us with a series of cheeps and whistles, all while chatting with each other. There was the occasional splashing noise as some of them played around with their water and food bowls. Ian said Stella split her time between the kitten and the goslings, doing a good job of mothering both.

A gang of about six goslings were in one corner all nestled together, asleep on the bedding of straw and wood chip, but nowhere near their heat lamp. As my eyes adjusted to the dim lighting at that end of the shed, I could just make out a cat tail and some paws projecting from within – it was Stella, buried in a blanket of baby goslings. They were sleeping on top of her in what appeared to be a circular cat nest made in the straw!

Ian turned on the main shed light for us to get a better look, and there Stella was, fast asleep in the exquisitely fluffy and furry ball. Even the startled swallows making a quick, screechy exit as the lights went on didn't wake them. We stared on in amazement for a few minutes before turning off the light and quietly retreating. I was completely speechless; it certainly was the first time I had ever witnessed such a spectacle.

The only explanation I could come up with was that, as she had had a kitten at the same time that the fluffy little goslings arrived, perhaps Stella, overcome with maternal instinct and perhaps a little confused, had decided to spread the motherly love a little – although a lot more than is traditional in the feline world.

We then made our way over to take the samples from the three goats. I was amused to find that they had music-world names as well, with Whitney, Aretha and (in a surprise Irish touch) Enya. As I tried to concentrate on taking the jugular blood samples, I was replaying all the marvellous things that had happened in the previous fifteen minutes, primarily the hairy fairy and Stella the cat. I had one thing I really wanted to ask

Ian, and was a bit apprehensive, but I decided to fire ahead and asked him anyway: in the goat dairy name – why was there the 'fairy' bit? Surely this could be considered offensive, or even derogatory, to members of the LGBTQIA (Lesbian, Gay, Bisexual, Transgender, Queer/Questioning, Intersex, Asexual) community?

When I asked Ian, he smiled and gave me an answer I certainly didn't anticipate. He said, 'Yes, of course it is a risqué name!' He went on to explain that back when it was decided to put the Q in LGBTQIA, amongst the motivations, one was to help detoxify a previously hurtful word. 'It doesn't hurt anywhere as much if we use it ourselves,' Ian explained.

He exclaimed, 'And I've decided I'm claiming the term "fairy" – I'm the fairy on the hill! By the time I'm done, "fairy" will be a term of endearment, and my LGBTQIA brothers and sisters will smile if they hear it!' Then he added with a grin, 'But I won't be pushing for LGBTQIAF – it's too much of a mouthful. I'll just spread my message from my little Kiwi hillside goat farm.'

And I found myself smiling in admiration for the third time that visit.

After I finished collecting the goat samples, I bid Ian farewell and drove off down the lane, back past the sign. I was awestruck at the fantastic character I had just met, along with his astonishing animals. It truly was a marvellous experience to have visited that farm, I thought to myself, I could see why the neighbours were keen for me to see it for myself.

I did have one last thought burning in the back of my mind, though – as the hairy fairy, he wasn't that hairy, was he? Ian was beardless and had a closely shorn head. The only evidence of hairiness I witnessed was when he held the goats as I collected the blood samples, and I saw the dark hair of his upper arms peeping out from under his high-riding dungaree sleeves.

I thought to myself, maybe he had plans on holding off shaving for a while, or something in else in store – or maybe the caricature was more fitting for Dave, whom I had not yet met?

Going back to the vet clinic later, I told the ladies about Ian's new sign, and they all seemed eager to keep an eye out for it while driving home that evening. Megs came to me and asked, smiling in anticipation, 'I don't suppose you got invited for cocktails, did you?' The way she said it, I quickly gathered this must have been a regular occurrence, so I just winked at her and said, 'Of course I did. I'm going tomorrow night.' As we closed-up the practice that evening, the ladies recalled many a cocktail party they had attended over the years up at the goat dairy.

The next evening Megs gave me a lift over to the goat dairy for that cocktail, and when I arrived Ian and Dave were in their garden with a third person, a teenage girl, playing a game of garden chess. Megs dropped me in the farm courtyard right at the garden gate and shouted Hello! to Ian and Dave, blowing a few kisses before driving off. Dave came to greet me with a good strong handshake and a firm pat on the shoulder, issuing another hearty, 'Welcome to New Zealand'. It was a balmy evening, with a clear sky overhead and a pleasant breeze rustling through the paddocks and hedges. As we walked along the garden path, I heard some nice chill-out music playing through speakers at the veranda nearby, giving a very peaceful vibe. The only other sound for miles was the occasional bark from a dog playing fetch with its owner down in the river valley.

Dave was a similar age to Ian, with a larger build, big strong arms, a bit of stubble and short black hair. You wouldn't call him hairy either, I thought to myself, slightly disappointed, and weighing up the reality that I was probably the hairiest man present. Dave, who was the strong, gentle sort, had us laughing as he issued a few witty quips about his Irish convict heritage. It was quickly apparent that he and Ian shared the same sharp sense of humour. We walked along the path and arrived at a garden table setting, where they introduced me to the girl: Emma.

Although at first appearing quite shy, Emma came over and shook my hand too with a smile and a, 'Pleased to meet ya.' She was tall, thin and pale, with long black hair and patches of teenage acne on her cheeks and wore baggy blue jeans and a red T-shirt that was too big for her frame. Ian put a hand on Emma's shoulder in a proud, fatherly way and said with a smile, 'Emma is here to stay with us for a while. She is fantastic helping me out with the animals and you want to see what she can do in the kitchen. I think we might have another chef in our midst! In fact, we can't keep her out of the kitchen. We have been busy getting some snacks ready for your arrival,' Ian said with a wink to Emma, who blushed a little from all the praise.

Ian and Emma returned to playing chess – I seem to have arrived at a crucial moment in their game – and a short time later Emma was declared the winner. She celebrated with loud cheering and a bit of fist pumping. None too crestfallen, Ian declared it time for dribbles and nibbles, beckoning Emma to help him in the kitchen, and off they went.

In no time Ian and Emma reappeared with a gin and tonic for everyone, served in enormous wide-bellied gin glasses with lots of ice and decorative adornments. Emma had a booze-free mocktail and went off to find a comfortable spot to enjoy it. Dave must have been thirsty, as he drank his in a couple of gulps, and was soon picking a rose petal from between his teeth. He looked at me with a smirk, rolling his eyes, then laughed and looked at Ian and said, 'That's what happens when the chefs make the drinks! You get a load of trumpery floating around in them.' He plucked a rosemary-speared olive from the bottom of his glass, and as if to prove his point, he quickly de-herbed and gobbled it in such a theatrical way that we all had a giggle.

Shortly afterwards, Emma confessed, from her prone position on a nearby garden hammock, that the dried rose petals were her idea, and wanted to know didn't we think they were pretty?

Every one of us smiled.

Next up was a mimosa – definitely one of the tastiest I have ever had – ice cold with crisp, tangy-yet-sweet citrus flavours from freshly squeezed orange juice and made with the most effervescent smooth champagne. It was delicious.

Ian took his mimosa with him and once again called upon his apprentice, and off he and Emma went to the kitchen. Shortly afterwards the surround-sound music changed to pop, and their kitchen-curtain silhouettes made the occasional dance move as they laughed and joked while organising the food. In the meantime, Dave and I enjoyed our drinks and chatted.

He told me he was a surgical nurse working in a large hospital in the city about thirty minutes away. One of a family of three, both of his parents being deceased, the goat dairy site was his original family home. It was previously a cattle dairy but had not been for many years. Dave said that nowadays, Ian was definitely the resident farmer. Although, Dave added, he certainly was not afraid to get his hands dirty when he was off duty, in order to help Ian out, around the place. Having done some travelling together, he and Ian had moved back to New Zealand and established the goat dairy eight years previously and had slowly been building it up ever since.

Since their return they had refurbished the house and some of the farm buildings, as well as building a few new ones, including a cheese shed for onsite production, and a spanking-new upgraded milking parlour. Ian had started out supplying goat milk to the local dairy and now, in addition, he was also making his own cheese. He had taken a big leap of faith and jumped into it and given it all of his effort. Even in only a couple of years, Ian's goat cheese range was proving very popular at the local markets, and he was now supplying delicatessens as far as the city with a nice mix of cheeses, including feta, halloumi, cheddar, a triple-cream brie and soft fresh goat cheese, alongside his newest addition to the range – an ash rind. Dave said he was really proud of what Ian had achieved, given that a few years previously Ian had battled with depression and had really struggled to overcome it. Now, with his feet firmly on the ground and his dairy up and running, Ian was like a changed man and full of the joys of life once again.

Dave went on to explain that with Ian working from home mostly and him working alternative weeks at the hospital, this meant they had time to look after and provide a home for foster kids, Emma being their most recent arrival. In recent years, they had opened their door and provided transitional foster care for teenagers in need, with some staying with them for up to six months, and also on occasion offering respite foster care for children in crisis. Dave had a pensive smile as he reflected on the others that had already shared their home. He recalled some of Emma's predecessors – mostly disadvantaged kids from the city – on their time at the farm, and how he and Ian had tried their best to show them a bit of the countryside, good food and a loving home. Dave added, 'Ian sees having the goat dairy as another way to help kids, and I guess some adults too. Some people can't have cow's milk, but they can have goat's milk, and you know also, there's the well-known benefits of goat's milk for certain allergies and skin conditions.'

I smiled and said, 'That's such a nice way of looking at it.'

Dave teared up a little and beamed. 'Emma's only been here three weeks and it truly is humbling to watch her grow even in that time. She's cooking with Ian daily, she's so gentle and caring, helping to look after the animals. She's coming out of her shell and she's such a lovely kid.' A few tears rolled down Dave's cheeks as he said, 'It's just not fair the crappy hand she was dealt, her family being pulled apart by drug addiction.'

Thinking about the magnitude of what Dave said, I was feeling emotional too, as we sat in a brief silence with Emma and Ian's laughter in the background, right then, it was such a contrast to the picture Dave painted of her previous years. Drying his eyes with a napkin, Dave said with a shaky voice, 'This is what makes it all so worthwhile – giving something back.'

My heart just swelled with that sentiment; this couple were so exemplary and commendable. The thought of their inspirational, selfless endeavours gave me goose bumps. In that moment, it was crystal clear to me why everyone in the community had nothing but great things to say about this wonderful couple.

Shortly afterwards the kitchen doors opened, and beautiful cooking aromas drifted across the veranda into the garden. The tantalising smells quickly made me realise that, unusually for me, in my hurry to get out after work, I had overlooked dinner that day. The scent of baked goods and exotic spices suggested that great things lay ahead.

I have always visualised my appetite like a chubby little inner Buddha; he gets happy or sad depending on the different dining experiences I encounter. Delicious experiences make him smile and even laugh, but hunger makes him very sad. Especially with the fresh hit of booze, my stomach was now rumbling – my poor little Buddha was famished! In my mind's eye, I pictured him with his napkin on, sitting at a dining table, knife and fork in hand, tapping on the table expectedly. In fact, with these aromas, Buddha was now salivating in anticipation. I tried to contain my excitement for whatever food was coming, as it sure smelled great.

Moments later, the chefs appeared, Ian carrying a large, varnished, carved-out pine chopping board with an eye-catching spread. On a plate in the centre of the board was homemade feta, baby asparagus and shortcrust mini tartlets. Arranged around these were bite-sized quail Scotch eggs, a mix of juicy olives and a variety of home-grown cherry tomatoes in a lovely blend of vibrant reds and deep yellows and even a few tigerellas, with a decorative splash of balsamic glaze and a handful of big basil leaves. The chefs joined us, and we made a start. The tartlets were melt-in-the-mouth, the cubes of feta were crisp on the outside but creamy in the middle, with the perfect amount of saltiness, and the asparagus spears still had a crunch in them, and being home-grown, they were juicy sweet with freshness. I hadn't had Scotch eggs since I was a kid, and though I had always enjoyed them, Ian's offering – the gourmet version – were sensational, with a crunchy outer layer of herbed breadcrumbs, a delicious, moist sausage meat layer, and a core of egg whose yolk was still a little runny – just the way I like them.

Ian popped back into the kitchen and returned this time a chunky mahogany board with a freshly baked sourdough loaf on it, with one end already arranged in slices, still hot. This was accompanied by a range of freshly prepared dips, including a black olive tapenade and a thick, creamy hummus topped with caramelised red onions. This was complemented with a dipping bowl of extra virgin olive oil, which was a lovely, buttery yellow with a wonderful floral fragrance, and a scoop of cracked sea salt in a small bowl on the side. There was a still smaller, covered bowl, which Ian opened to reveal a dukkah (a dry dip of seeds and spices) that he had tossed in a hot pan before serving. The aroma of cumin, coriander seed and toasted cashew nuts was incredible, and everything was delicious.

After we devoured the first two trays Emma went off to the kitchen to get the dessert course. Arriving at the table, it truly was a magnificent sight to behold: a tray bearing miniature white chocolate and raspberry crèmes brûlées and a stacked mound of freshly baked bite-sized chocolate brownie squares, festooned with sprigs of mint and with a small saucepan on the side. After placing the tray on the table Emma poured the contents of the pan – warm, luxurious chocolate sauce – all over the brownies. Lining the tray's outer edges were a colourful assortment of flowers from the garden, purple and white borage and vibrant yellow Indian cress blossoms. 'Such a pretty touch,' I said to Emma, who shyly accepted my compliment.

It was fare one would have expected from a fine dining restaurant and was certainly more than what I would have considered to be nibbles! The brownies were warm and moist, and the sauce silky smooth. The crèmes brûlées were light and fluffy, with little hits of sweetness from the squares of white chocolate and raspberry within, an inspired combination of sweet and tart flavours. Just when I thought we were done, Ian appeared with a plate full of walnut-sized buttermilk scones, sliced and topped with generous dollops of home-made clotted cream and raspberry jam. He said he had been waiting for an occasion to make something from back home in England. The whole thing was fantastic – the setting, the drinks, the food – such deliciosity that my inner Buddha was now in a merry coma. They say the ambiance is a big part of a memorable dining experience, and in this case, everything was superb – a feast up there on my list of those I will never forget.

After the food and another couple of drinks we were all getting a bit giddy, and with some Dutch courage I decided to broach the subject of the lack of fairy hairiness at the Hairy Fairy Goat Dairy. I asked Ian straight up – Why, as the hairy fairy, was he not really that hairy?

Ian and Dave responded by laughing so much that they each had to hold their noses to try and stop. In the moments of laughter that ensued, they successfully skirted the issue completely, but added, 'You're here for another few months – maybe you'll get to find out!' At that, I left off any further questioning.

While the sun set, I admired the scenery, the fading light highlighting various aspects as it dropped, including the peaceful grazing goats in the distant fields and this lovely couple, and Emma; it had been such a nice evening, spent with good company.

That night, Ian and Dave told me of their love story. They had been together fifteen years and, having dreamed of getting married for a long time, were one of the first gay couples to marry in 2013, when same-sex marriage was written into law in New Zealand. Anyone could see that the men were still madly in love with one another: finishing each other's stories, a bit of flirting, recalling tales of time well spent together, and knowing the backstory showed their wonderful teamwork, with the farm and with foster care. Even though this was only my second visit to their place, I could see what fantastic role models they were for their foster kids. Some people just warm your heart. They showed what generosity, charity and humanity can look like. Dave and Ian reminded me, and many others no doubt, of the ways in which we can make a difference in the world, even from a little hillside Kiwi farm.

A short time later my taxi arrived, and as I bid them farewell, I thanked them for the most fabulous evening. As I had only been on a working goat dairy a handful of times before, I asked if I could come and help out one morning with a milking to see the whole thing in action, and we agreed to do that one weekend, a few weeks later.

During the following week back at the clinic, Megs, who saw the guys regularly, let me know that, as it happened, Emma had just learned that a more permanent home had been found for her, with a family about three hours' drive away. Emma had spent some time with this family previously, and now the formalities were underway. She was excited by this news, although the move was still a few months away. This meant that Ian and Dave really wanted to make the most of her remaining stay and spend some extra-special quality time with her. They got a neighbour in who provided relief milking on a few occasions, and the three of them took trips to some of Emma's wish-list destinations, including going up the Auckland Sky Tower and spending a day at Auckland Zoo. There were other things Emma wished for of the remaining time she had with Ian and Dave, and I would find those out in due course.

As the trio had spent a few weekends away it was about six weeks later, before I got a chance to visit the Hairy Fairy Goat Dairy, to see a milking in action. This meant an early start on a Saturday, with me arriving at the dairy at 6.30 am. It was a nice bright sunny morning, with mist rising off the nearby hills when I arrived at the courtyard and parked up. As I made my way over to the parlour, the first thing I could hear in the distance was music – Britney Spears, 'Baby One More Time'. It was pretty loud, too. As I opened the milking parlour doors and went through, I felt like I was going into a disco! A queue of goats standing at the large gates above the paddocks on the far end of the milking parlour awaited their turn for milking as their freshly milked comrades made their way back down to the paddocks in the other lane.

Ian and Emma were busy applying milking clusters and organising buckets of dairy nuts for the goats to eat, while being milked by the machine. Dave must have been on a weekend off from the hospital, as he was there helping too.

I shouted hello, through the music and goat noise. They beckoned me over to their area in the parlour pit behind a row of milking goats. The guys had to wait on that wave of milkers to finish, so Dave and Emma were being entertained at Ian's efforts at miming to the music, using the handle of a large sweeping brush as his microphone and doing a pretty good Britney impersonation, with the pit as his dance floor.

I greeted the gang and got ready to try and make myself useful, and then it was time to let that run of milkers off and fetch in the next batch. Ian shouted out goat names and everyone seemed to know who, was who. It was like a comedy sketch hearing him shout, 'No no, Mariah, you go in this stall today! Hey, call it off Katy! Look Emma, Katy and Taylor are butting heads again! Just like in real life!'

In no time, the next gang were all hooked up to the milking machine and eating their breakfast.

The music played on, and halfway through Nicki Minaj's, 'Pound the Alarm', Dave took over the dance floor and brush, throwing shapes, and everyone, some of the goats included, had a laugh. He had some moves.

Ian and I talked as we worked, and he explained he had started with five goats, all milked by hand in the early days, but now that he had his milking parlour up and running, he was up to forty-five milkers, and was planning on increasing in the future. The flock looked healthy, and the good grazing pastures were an important factor in this. Hearing about the success of Ian's goat cheese I was curious to ask him what his secret to success was. He said that good genetics were important and good food was essential, as was a bit of luck, but his secret ingredient......... Pop music!

On hearing that, Dave, who was standing nearby, rolled his eyes and had a bit of a chuckle.

Ian piped up, 'You better believe it, hun. It's the secret ingredient! You won't be saying that when I get speakers installed in the pastures for the girls to enjoy music all day long, and not just at milking time.'

Dave had a good hearty laugh and then said, 'Yes dear, let's do that sometime' – perhaps in jest, but I couldn't be certain.

Looking on, I was fascinated at how it all worked. The goats, keen to get into the stalls, battled to be at the front of the queue and be next in to have their meal. Their engorged udders delivered pipes full of creamy white milk, which whizzed in multiple directions through transparent tubes overhead. It was all very smooth and efficient, and when they were done, the girls just trotted off down to their fresh grazing paddock looking reinvigorated. Watching the system in action – maybe it was my imagination, but I would say – the goats really did seem to enjoy the music, there was such a jovial atmosphere. It wouldn't have been quite the same without the music.

An hour or so later the morning's milking was over, and we scrubbed the parlour clean from top to bottom. Afterwards they asked if I would like to have a walk over to feed the male (billy) goats, and we headed off to one of the upper fields. I was aware that you can often smell entire (uncastrated) billy goats well before you see them, especially around breeding season, and these guys met this expectation – a very pungent lot, we could smell them downwind on approach.

Ian introduced the billy goats – there was three of them – on the far side of the hill, each in a fenced paddock with their own individual sleeping quarters. Ian explained that, apart from breeding season, they needed to be isolated from the milking females, as their stench can rub off on the females and make its way into the milk.

They were three fine-looking billies, well-built and strong, with intelligent eyes and good deep chests and back confirmation. All handsome chaps, they looked well equipped for the job, with their enormous, dangling scrotums. It's a funny thing, that billy goat musk. Being not unlike rotting onions mixed with ammonia, it can make your eyes weep at close proximity, and gets into your pores, where it lingers for a day or two. Part of me suspected that the girls were happy with this living arrangement too. After we fed the boys, we went back to the farmhouse for a quick cup of tea as Emma went to feed the goat kids.

Ian and Dave filled me in on Emma's new plans, her wish list, and their trips to the city since my previous visit. Ian said that Emma, in her previous life, had spent nights on the streets, homeless. Because of this she wanted to help other people down on their luck, and so Ian and Emma had gone on a few trips to the city and spent time preparing meals for the homeless in charity kitchens. While there, Emma let Ian in on one of her secrets – how she used to get food while living rough: dumpster diving. She brought him to some of her past haunts to see all the good-quality discarded supermarket food, and he said it was hard to see all that food going to waste when it could have been put to good use, at the shelter. After a few weekends of volunteering, Ian and Emma were inspired to start a charity of their own closer to home.

Being a producer of delicious goat cheese products, and having a few other friends in the food industry, Ian, Dave and Emma wanted to make use of food surplus, so they started a Friday night food drop to their elderly neighbours – six of them, mostly living alone. In just a few weeks, this became a more regular routine for the trio, with many of those elderly people already looking forward to their Friday night visit.

'It only takes a couple of hours out of my day, and you want to see the joy it brings,' Ian said. Even in just a few short weeks, they had started to think of ways to enhance the food drop experience. Being very comical, fun people, and having a house full of party costumes, it was a natural progression to doing the food drops in fancy dress. The old folk loved it. The previous Friday night, they had taken it a step further, with Ian doing the food drop in drag – dress, make-up, shoes, the whole lot. He declared, 'And so, Meals on Heels, has been born.'

Members of the local community were offering help and support too. It wasn't an official charity, just a community looking out for its elderly members, and it was proving to be both rewarding and fun – they planned for it to be a long-term venture.

After the cup of tea, it was time to head home. I left once again, blown away by just how special these people were.

Back at the office the next week, a shiny envelope arrived. Megs opened it and happily announced to the practice staff that we had been cordially invited to a mid-summer party at the goat dairy. There was a theme, too – Wacky Charity Shop Disco. The party was only a few weeks away, and as I was nearing the end of my time at that clinic, I was delighted that I would still be around for the party before heading back to Australia.

It came to the night of the party. I had searched far and wide through the local charity shops and had come up with a patriotic number – a leprechaun outfit. As a six-foot-five leprechaun I had a good old laugh at myself. It was a good choice, I felt, as I was going to a party hosted by a fairy, after all. It ended up being a huge novelty for all the Kiwis in attendance, and I had to feign granting a lot of wishes that night – I didn't have the heart to tell them that leprechauns aren't known for granting wishes, and are probably frustrated that everyone seems to confuse them with genies. In any case, it was easier just to comply.

I was joined in the taxi by the ladies in the office, which meant I was accompanied by a glamorous trio: Madonna, Marilyn Monroe and Tina Turner. We arrived at the house, and in the garden was a delicious spread of goat dairy-themed canapés and a glass of bubbles for everyone. There were plenty of locals in attendance, many of whom I recognised from being out and around the neighbourhood farms, as well as a few lovely eccentric people I hadn't met yet, presumably from the ever-popular local theatre troupe. There was a hilarious mix of costumes and I was impressed by the creativity – the fancy-dress challenge certainly was a hit, and of course another great way to support charity. At the start of the evening a crowd of us gathered indoors, enjoying the music in the living room, with more people spilling out onto the adjoining veranda.

To our surprise, we were treated to an impromptu theatrical performance by Ian and Dave. It started with Ian shouting loudly, from out of sight at the top of the stairs, 'I'm not ready, I'm not ready!'

We were all slightly concerned that he wasn't fully clothed! Having grabbed everyone's attention, Ian appeared at the top of the stairs, then ran down them dressed in a fluorescent-yellow mankini – a sight to behold! Famed for being a revealing garment, it certainly didn't leave much to the imagination, and by that, I mean my search for the hairy fairy's hairiness was well and truly over. That mankini revealed abundant areas of voluminous dark body hair all along Ian's back and shoulders.

Ian ran around the room posturing and posing and putting up dance moves to the music, all while occasionally stroking his hairy shoulders and upper back, showing off his self-confessed man cape while the crowd shrieked with laughter.

Dave appeared moments later, coming down the stairs and chasing after Ian with an imaginary butterfly net, shouting, 'I am in hair-suit pursuit. Hair-suit pursuit!' in a hysterical comedy duo act. And just like that, they ran back up the stairs, leaving the guests applauding and cheering. We all laughed for quite some time. It just seemed to click in for everyone at the same time – after all that, the hairy fairy *was* hairy!

I'm sure the hairy back cover could have all been sorted with a quick shave, but I admired the way the two men instead turned it into a comedy sketch to celebrate its presence. About ten minutes later, Ian reappeared dressed in drag as a fairy, complete with wings, although this time his man cape was well concealed. Dave was dressed as Freddie Mercury (his idol).

There was a lovely fire lit in the garden firepit, and the party moved outdoors to make the most of the summer evening. Emma stepped up as DJ and played a fantastically cheesy disco playlist. Everyone was up dancing from early evening; there were many cocktails and much laughter.

At around 9 pm I took a few minutes on the veranda to catch some air and watch the sun set over the hills. As I looked on at the goats grazing in the distant paddocks and listened to the birds in the garden chattering with each other as they settled in for a night's roost, my attention was drawn to the paddock immediately beside the garden fence, where the thirteen geese came marching in procession until they were almost level with me, and then spread out through the field, busily grazing. They were halfway grown at least, having replaced most of their fluffy down with feathers, and had achieved much of their adult height. They were constantly talking to each other, in a mix of adult goose and the odd gosling noise. From where I stood, I could see their sleeping quarters, recognising the half-hatch stable door at the far end of the paddock a few hundred metres away.

As the geese made their way through the field back towards the shed, Stella appeared from within and walked up to meet them, followed closely by Prince the kitten, already nearly half grown. While Prince stopped to play with a leaf, the goslings formed a circle around Stella, necks outstretched, whistling and chattering to her, much in the way that young geese greet their parents. Stella lifted her tail in the air and wove her way through the goslings, who were already tall enough to tower over her, and as she walked, she rubbed against them, much as she might have greeted her owner's legs. It was a remarkable thing to see. Just as it got dark the goslings headed towards their sleeping quarters, and in they went. In a matter of minutes, they were all quietly preening and getting ready for sleep, Stella watching from her position on a nearby tree branch – like a proud mother, and with Prince by her side playfully tapping at her with his paw.

I couldn't help but think of the parallels: the two men and their history of opening their home to foster kids, and how they had adopted Stella the cat – who had in turn adopted the geese.

A few weeks later my time at the practice was up, and it was time to head back to Australia. The Hairy Fairy Goat Dairy will always hold a special place in my memories of North Island New Zealand.

CHAPTER 11

Nancy Reilly and the Fine Pair of Wellingtons

I had a stroll down to Molloy's shop to get a sandwich for lunch and a carton of milk for Lindy back at the office. This was day three of my new job in a town on the west coast of Ireland. Walking down the main street, I admired the natural beauty of the surrounding countryside, with jagged limestone mountain peaks ahead of me and stunning views of the Atlantic Ocean on the other side. I arrived at the shop at the same time as Pascal Molloy, the owner. He had just pulled up with a delivery and had some boxes in his hands, so I held the door for him.

As we walked into the shop Pascal shouted towards the storeroom at the back, 'There's coleslaw spilled all over the front counter, Margaret!' (Mrs Molloy). Then, putting down his boxes, 'What to hell is after happening here at all? Where is Vanka?'

'She's out the back having a moment,' Margaret shouted.

Margaret then appeared from the storeroom towing a mop bucket behind her, as she too came to survey the damage. I was the only customer in the store.

At that point Vanka appeared from a walk-in fridge at the rear, nervously sobbing. She rushed towards Pascal saying in broken English, with a Polish accent, 'The lady, the last customer, she, she went craaaazzzzzy. The lady, she slammed her basket of groceries on the counter and hurled a tub of coleslaw at the wall because I told her it was not at special price anymore. Then she said she hated me because I'm stupid foreigner and she say I stole her jobs and the government moneys too and then she stormed out.'

Feeling as though I was a part of the discussion, I couldn't help but stand there in front of the deli counter beside the Molloys and look on at the mess, listening to poor Vanka's account of what had happened.

Just then a big dollop of coleslaw fell from an overhead fan behind the counter, as if to prove the point: whoever threw it, really meant it.

Pascal, who had been silently shaking his head, hastily asked, 'What lady? Who to hell did this?'

Vanka limped her way through the mess on the floor to the nearby window overlooking the town and pointed with a shaky finger to the hill in the distance at the far end of town. With a wail she cried, 'It waaaassss her, the lady on the hill!'

We all gathered a bit closer to the window, looking at the far end of the high street. I squinted without my glasses and could just make out the outline of a little old lady scurrying off in that direction.

Pascal thumped his fist on the wooden window frame and shouted, 'Right, that's enough outta her, Nancy Reilly is not welcome here anymore. She can go and shop at Gleeson's [the other grocery shop in town] from now on, and good enough for them too!'

A couple of minutes passed before Margaret Molloy pushed a freshly made wrapped sandwich into my hand. 'Made exactly the same as the previous two days,' she said with a brief smile. In my three days in town, she had already learned what I was after for lunch. I didn't have the heart to tell her I was going for something different that day; I just complied. Margaret was a talker, but she was quiet that day. I guess she had been silenced by the incident. So far, all the people I had met around town seemed to be lovely, but I would quickly find there was at least one who wasn't, and that was Nancy Reilly.

At this vet clinic I was working with two senior male vets. Their younger female vet, Nora, was drawn to do a bit of travelling and had set off bound for the southern hemisphere, and I was her enthusiastic replacement. I didn't know it then, but I was only a year or two from heading to the southern hemisphere myself.

The vet clinic was along the main street. The town was about a kilometre long, starting at a bridge over a river (close to our clinic) and ending at the far side with a large stone church and graveyard. Beyond the church the landscape changed abruptly, to large rocks and jagged hills, with a couple of houses nestled in-between. The high ground was not very fertile, with large exposed areas of shale and scrub. The one cattle farm over that way, belonged to Nancy.

The vet clinic had a laneway along the side that led to a rear car park. This car park was shared with one other business: the local mechanic, Terry Logan, who had his workshop there. Beyond the buildings, the car park backed onto some paddocks. As I parked there daily, I soon got to know Terry well. Now in his sixties, he had been in the army in his younger years, before becoming a mechanic. Around Terry's end of the car park there was always a collection of cars at various stages of repair. He was a fan of vintage cars, and spent hours fixing them up, wheeling and dealing antique cars and bikes.

Terry, who was separated from his wife and had adult children in the area, lived in a flat just above his workshop, and he shared the flat with his beautiful tricolour Bernese Mountain Dog named Shamrock. Terry was also the proud owner of five-year-old Bertie and twenty-five-year-old Charlie, the two donkeys who lived in the paddocks adjacent to his workshop. He was the only mechanic for quite some distance, and as a result, he knew many of the locals from working on their cars. Many clients parking at our rear car park would bring Terry's donkeys treats and stop to give them a pat on their way. Some people came by, just to visit the donkeys.

One evening, on my second week in town, I stopped over to Terry's for a chat. We leaned on the fence along the paddocks and the donkeys came over for a rub. As we talked, we were interrupted by a few loud gunshots in the distance, after which a group of jackdaws made a hasty exit from the oak trees at the far end of town and flew in to shelter in the trees overhead where we stood. Just as they got settled, they were startled into flight once again with another series of shots, and this time Bertie started freaking out, spooked by the noise. He ran back and across the far end of the paddock while Terry, Charlie and I looked on.

Terry said, 'Whatever it is about Bertie, he is a flighty one alright. Donkeys are supposed to freeze when scared.' He rubbed the back of his head in frustration and added, 'No, not my Bertie. No, he is a runner.' I asked who was shooting what, up on the hill, and Terry came over a bit funny, saying, 'Ah, it will be Nancy Reilly at it again, I suppose. She's handy with that gun alright.' Terry then went a bit quiet in thought, and after a few moments abruptly threw his hands in the air and said, 'She's too handy with that gun, in fact.'

I was surprised at his reaction. Nancy Reilly's shooting seemed to have really triggered Terry (so to speak), although I did wonder whether perhaps it was his army days that caused his discomfort. I left as Terry went off to get a few carrots in an attempt to comfort and distract poor Bertie.

As the weeks passed, it became clear that Terry was a very community-spirited man. He was often doing extra jobs around town, like picking up litter on the days the council wasn't around and trimming the odd hedge. He also did a job that not many would envy: he was the local gravedigger. When they needed a grave dug, bereaved family members would come to see Terry – bottle of whiskey in hand. Terry would then organise a few other local men and they would gather at the cemetery to dig the grave, drinking the whiskey as they worked. It was an old graveyard, and with space at a premium, the men would need a few stiff drinks, especially for when they got down to the bottom of the grave, where there could be bones. Not a job for the faint of heart.

Getting settled into work at the vet clinic one day, about a month into the job, I answered the phone as Lindy was busy on another call.

The female caller shouted angrily, 'Who to hell is that? … What? Anyway, I don't care. You are needed out here and I'm expecting you next Tuesday at 9 am. I have got a few helpers lined up. The cattle are up for testing again – and don't dare send a female vet or any foreigners up here or I will run them with my pitchfork…'

'Now I have a few questions,' I interjected. 'First of all, who is speaking?'

'It's Nancy Reilly here.'

'OK, and I believe you need to book a TB test for your herd?'

'Yes, next Tuesday morning, and tell himself he can get the pay after it's done.' Himself was what some people called one of the bosses at the clinic, in this case, Henry. 'There will be at least 200 head of cattle here too,' she added. 'If you're a new vet, you better be up to it. My cattle don't like people.'

Slam! The phone went dead.

I turned to Lindy, who had finished her call a few minutes earlier and so had heard most of mine. She looked at me and said, 'Ah, you've encountered Nancy. So, go on, tell me, what horrible things did she say?'

'Jeez she sure is angry, racist and sexist all in one hit,' I said. 'What a bundle of joy.'

After that phone call, my heart was low in my chest. Nancy's noxious words resounded in my ears and I was a bit shaken. The racism was distasteful, but what she had said about not sending a female vet cut me more. I had heard it before, and I hated it. Nancy would be one of a number of sexist vet clients I would encounter who had a problem with female vets. The rage flowed through me with no obvious outlet, and I was beginning to tremble. Nancy had effortlessly reached right inside my head and pushed one of my big red buttons, and I was fuming. In the years since I had qualified, I could never comprehend why the worst cases of sexism against female vets, seemed to come from female clients. From day one of vet school, I had learned that a vet's genitalia are completely inconsequential to our work. It was very unfair. With the bosses on holidays, that work at Nancy's the next week would be for me.

Lindy got up and put on the kettle. 'Himself won't be best pleased either,' she said. 'He has endured years of Nancy's raging demands. Nancy Reilly owes half the county money, never paying her fair dues anywhere really. Henry has done hours of back-breaking vet work for Nancy and her large herd over the years, and she hasn't come close to paying even fifty per cent of her bills. There's always a broken promise when it comes to Nancy.' Then, pouring hot water into the tea pot, she added, 'Nancy isn't stuck for money either, mind you.'

Lindy gathered the biscuit tin and two cups and sat down beside me. 'Nancy is by far our worst client. She's a widow and lives in a cottage up on that hill by herself. The fields surrounding her house are filled with scrap and her cattle live wild, roaming the hills and mountains behind. Poor grazing land, they are half starved for most of the year. She's no good at farming. She won't make enough fodder to get the cattle through the winter and certainly wouldn't be buying any. More than a few winters now Nancy has put out calls for donations of silage, expecting others to bail her out instead. The last time she did that the department threatened to seize her cattle, but she just managed to do the bare minimum to get by them. It's always bordering on cruel up there. She would be much better to sell all and put her feet up. No one knows why she persists.' Tossing her eyes upwards Lindy added, 'Let's call it cattle hoarding, rather than farming.'

Lindy opened a file from the bookshelf and retrieved an old black-and-white photo of a group of young men and women. Quick to point out herself, all of nineteen years old, she now clasped her hands and smiled at the happy memories. Lindy pointed out a stunning young lady at the edge of the photo wearing an elegant hat and holding a cigarette in a holder, not unlike a glamorous model of old. Lindy held her finger on that part of the photo and, gazing at me, said, 'That was Nancy Reilly back in the day.' Nancy was ten years older than Lindy, but they had briefly been buddies back then. This photo was them and their gang of friends at a local disco. 'Nancy, an only child of a well-to-do family, had all the nicest clothes and make-up. Many said her parents were too good to her, Nancy growing up very spoiled,' Lindy adding with a sigh, 'But it never brought her any happiness. Many a man's heart Nancy broke over the years. Men swarmed around her. Nancy had quite a few tumultuous romantic relationships over the years. There were even a few broken engagements, with the men later claiming she was unbearable. Nancy eventually settled down and got married later in life to an older eligible bachelor, Tommy Reilly. A very nice man he was too. I never understood what he saw in Nancy – she wasn't known to be good to him.'

After a brief pause Lindy added, 'God rest his soul.' Deep in thought, she looked at her teacup and said, 'Me and Nancy lost touch years ago. She barely speaks to me now, only when she has to, here at the vets. Nancy just became so mean over the years. It's as if, as age caught up on Nancy and as her looks faded, her inner demons came to the surface. She got crazier and angrier as she got older, and she took it out on everyone she came across, around these parts.' Lindy gently shook her head, saying, 'No, Nancy didn't love anyone or anything. I just don't understand it. She inherited a fortune from her parents when they passed, and she could have had anything she wanted. But she chose to live a very reclusive life, up on that hill.'

Lindy continued, 'Nancy insisted on growing their herd far beyond what their land could manage, with Tommy doing all of the back-breaking work on his own. Nancy wasn't keen on the actual farm work herself.' Lindy looked off into the distance with a sigh, swirled the tea in her cup and said, 'Oh, and the awful circumstances of Tommy's death...'

She paused in thought once more and I had to interrupt her trance, asking, 'What happened to Tommy?'

Lindy's mind returned to the room and she said, 'Tommy died in one of the fields on the hill behind the house. They say he was dead before he hit the ground, a big heart attack from all the years of working too hard.'

She added in a pensive tone, 'The ambulance that came to get him had to park at the farmyard and take a stretcher to him. As he got wheeled back to the ambulance, a gang of the neighbours gathered in time to pay their respects. Nancy came from the house yelling at the paramedics to stop because she needed to see Tommy one last time before they put him in the ambulance. Everyone thought the grief-stricken widow wanted to say goodbye to her beloved, but no. No, she didn't do that. Instead, in front of everyone, Nancy went about pulling the welly boots (wellingtons / gumboots) off Tommy's feet, muttering to herself about how they were a fine pair of wellingtons and she could now make good use of them, not one bit ashamed to tell the gathered crowd she was afraid the boots would get lost at the morgue! Many people lost respect for Nancy after that stunt. Many couldn't stand to see such disrespect for a dead man.'

Lindy's eyes widened. 'But that's not the worst of it. What Nancy did next was even worse.'

I continued swallowing gulps of tea in anticipation.

'Shortly after Tommy passed, an advert appeared in the death notices section of the local newspaper.' (Lindy made sure I understood this was where local bereaved families gave notice of funeral arrangements and mentioned flowers or donations to charity.) 'Now Nancy did the unthinkable. With her sitting up on the hill with plenty of money. In the death notice, she put a request for cash donations to be sent direct to her. Sounding like she had fallen on hard times, there was many a local person felt obliged to donate. There were a few who sent an empty sympathy card, some in defiance and others not realising the strange request.' Lindy then said, 'You will never believe what Nancy did next – all of the empty cards Nancy received were returned to sender with a note asking about the missing donation!'

Lindy packed away the sugar bowl and biscuit tin. 'There is a sombre cloud that hangs over the Reilly farm place now. Local people will only go up there if it's really necessary. Some say with Nancy's advancing madness, there's even been some sorcery going on. She's always been known for hunting and shooting in the hills around her farm. She regards most wild animal as vermin.' Lindy added, 'Nancy took to stringing up some of the animals she had shot – foxes, crows, magpies – and hanging them from trees and fences along her laneway, like some kind of dark warning to other animals, and, I suppose, to keep humans away. Nancy sure has a troubled soul.'

Lindy walked back to her desk and sat at her computer. Then, slightly distracted by her efforts at getting back to work, she said one last thing on the matter that has given me years of thought ever since: 'They say people like Nancy who are cruel to animals, and other people for that matter, are either......... mad, bad or sad.'

At that, the phone rang, and the conversation finished.

In the days that followed I was feeling apprehensive about going up to Nancy Reilly's. I mentioned to Terry, chatting outside his workshop, that I was due there the following week. He looked at me with an uneasiness and said, 'Be careful up there. There is only one word for Nancy.' He paused, then, shaking his head, said, 'Everyone in this town has at some stage or other been burned by Nancy Reilly. No one can stand by and watch an old lady struggle, but she's just so difficult. 'How's your Irish?' he asked. I admitted it wasn't great, and he said, 'Well, Nancy is an easóg' (pronounced 'yass-og').

Noticing my raised eyebrow, he said, 'Nancy is just as cranky and quarrelsome as an easóg in a bad mood.' Terry then explained that this was Irish for 'stoat' (sometimes called a weasel in Ireland). I let out an involuntary laugh.

'Follow me,' Terry said, then beckoned me out onto the main street. With both of us looking up towards the church, he pointed to a laneway that passed by the graveyard and led to a house partly hidden amongst trees at the bottom of the mountain. 'That is where you will find Nancy Reilly,' he said.

He then added, 'Now as it happens, when it comes to talk of an easóg, their much scarcer cousin, the pine marten, has been spotted visiting the stone walls of the graveyard right beside that laneway up to Nancy's place.' (Pine martens are members of the mustelid family, endangered relatives of the stoat and the weasel. Very nimble climbers, they hunt birds and small mammals and are notoriously difficult to spot. They're mostly active at dusk but rarely can be seen during daylight too). Terry suggested that if I visit just after sundown, I might be lucky enough to see one. And at that he was off back to his workshop.

That night I had a walk up to the graveyard. The sun was just starting to set. Behind the cemetery's eye-level stone walls there was only a gentle breeze. The tall conifer trees overhead told a different story as they swayed widely from side to side, taking the brunt of the coastal Atlantic winds. From within the graveyard, standing on my tiptoes, looking over the stone wall through the trees, I could see some of Nancy's cattle in the fields leading up to her farmyard. Lindy was right: the cattle were thin and puny, looking like they needed a good dose of deworming too. Noticing me, the cattle grew wary, foot stomping and calling to each other. I sure was dreading my visit up there the following week.

I moved further along the wall, trying my best not to appear as creepy as a lone guy hanging out around a graveyard at dusk usually would be. My only company turned out to be a family of barn owls, though, screeching from an opening high up on the old church wall and flying off into the twilight. Exploring along the wall of the graveyard, I found a narrow gap in the trees leading to a path. I decided to squeeze through and have a closer look. It was surrounded by tall fir trees, and there wasn't a whole lot to see apart from tracks through the undergrowth that were probably used by wildlife. In the last of the falling light I saw a few empty galvanised dog food bowls strewn around. Assuming someone must have been feeding the wildlife at some point, I didn't think too much more about it. Time spent in nature is never wasted in my book, but with no pine marten in sight, I headed off; in any case the barn owls were worth the trip.

I went back to work the next day, as usual. All along I had been getting accustomed to Lindy's motherly ways. She was prim and proper, and I had grown to admire that about her. This day was a bit different, however. For a start, Lindy had got me to man the phones while she went off for a few minutes and reappeared with a couple of pieces of carrot cake from Molloy's deli. Unusually, there was no sign of them being shared with me. By twelve o'clock Lindy was wearing red lipstick, also not a regular occurrence. It was about one o'clock,

I was pottering around the storeroom when the high-pitched laughter started – that my Spidey sense was triggered; Lindy was putting on a bit of a show for someone.

As I got myself organised to go and see a few sick farm animals. I stopped by the reception desk just as a middle-aged man in a suit was heading out the front door and Lindy was cleaning up the plates of cake crumbs. She shouted after him, 'I'll be right out there with you!' Perhaps feeling a bit put out, I decided to ask Lindy who this guy was. To which Lindy said, with what appeared to be a smitten smile, 'Oh, that's Brian, the sales rep from the pet and farm supplies company.' She then applied more lipstick and pouted into a small mirror. It was all so strange, like watching your happily married mother flirting; What was she doing? It was too much – I had to ask her what was going on.

Lindy just smiled and said, 'Ah, never mind me, I'm just buttering him up. Brian gives me cheap food for my dogs, especially the damaged bags back at the depot, still perfectly good stuff. Today I've managed to swindle a few dog de-wormers out of him too.' Going out the door, she pressed her lips together to even out the lipstick, then said, 'Watch and learn, son, watch and learn.'

I left the two of them in the car park, organising his van and her car, in an atmosphere of high-pitched laughter. I didn't think much more about Lindy and her friend Brian that day, as I headed off and got busy with work.

It came to me like a strange dream that night. I had awoken at about midnight and was just nodding off again when it hit me. Hang on a minute – Lindy didn't have any dogs! What was really going on? I wasn't so sure anymore.

The day of the TB test at Nancy's farm arrived. As I drove into the farmyard, I was pleasantly surprised to find three local lads there waiting to help. It was a wet, miserable, overcast February morning. An ankle-deep layer of sloppy mud had already formed underfoot by the cattle milling around. The yard looked like it hadn't been cleaned, ever. There must have been several years' worth of foetid mud, now freshly churned up again, all over the yard. The broken, rusted gates and fences were just about fit to hold the cattle in. The cattle were mostly rounded up into holding pens and waiting in the long race was the first batch for us to attend to. The lads didn't seem to be particularly happy to be there, with lots of head shaking and disbelieving looks around at the mess of the place, not their doing at all. I guess they knew that their time would be mostly unpaid, but they were likely there also through a feeling of obligation, to help an old lady in need. In any case, back in the recession with not much local work available for them, the prospect of getting some pay was better than nothing.

As I got my equipment ready at the back of the car, I could hear a lot of dogs barking from a nearby hay barn. A few holes had been gnawed in different parts of the doors, and some very angry border collies were taking turns sticking their heads through to bark at us. One of the helpers shouted over to me, 'Ah, they'll settle in a minute. They usually roam free around this place, but Nancy has just locked them in this morning to keep them out of our way.' He then added, 'God help us if they ever got out though – they would definitely bite. They're ferocious.'

The dogs blasted us with a mix of baying, growls and yelps. The sounds they produced had notes of anxiety and despair, as though they were angry about their circumstances and were shouting about it. They seemed especially annoyed by us being there. I took a moment to consider that they probably hadn't had the best life with Nancy, and that they must have thought we were just as mean-spirited as her. The uneasiness of the dogs made me nervous, giving way to a feeling of sadness. I couldn't help but think about how unpleasant their existence must have been. The dogs did eventually settle, though they still took turns popping heads through the holes. Going by the various popped-through heads, I counted five adult border collies inside: four black-and-white and one brown-and-white.

Testing cattle for TB takes place over two visits. On day one, we measure the thickness of the skin on the side of the animals' necks, then inject an extract of bovine TB (tuberculin) and avian tuberculin in two different sites near each other. At a revisit three days later, the difference in size between the two injection reactions is measured. Animals infected with bovine TB will have a larger reaction at the bovine tuberculin injection site. Carrying out this test at Nancy's was a difficult task, as her Limousin cattle were as wild as they come. These cattle really were not used to human contact, and we had to go slow and steady getting them through the race so they wouldn't panic and injure themselves. As the morning rain gave way to afternoon sleet and hail, we had endured several hours of hard work and were now up to our knees in mud. With such a big day of work, many a farmer would throw on a bit of a spread – sandwiches or even a mug of tea for the workers – but there was no sign of any such thing coming from Nancy. Just as the last cattle were coming through that afternoon Nancy turned up. This was the first time I had ever laid eyes on her up close.

Nancy, I guessed, was elderly. She was small and thin with sparse fair hair coiled in a loose bun. Despite the weather she wore a pair of sunglasses. Although the sunglasses had a large frame, they didn't hide Nancy's persistent frown. She had on a long, black waterproof coat that went as far as her knees, and her narrow legs were tucked into Tommy's old wellington boots, which looked far too big for her. The squelch emanating from within the boots as she walked, confirmed this. Knowing the backstory of her taking them off Tommy's corpse spooked me a little. For some reason I had thought Nancy would be frail, but she had much more of a step about her than I expected. I was nervous as she approached, thinking of all her antics and trying to second guess what she would be up to next; I hadn't gotten over the unpleasant phone conversation with her either.

Silently, Nancy looked over my equipment and my handheld computer. Casting her eyes over me and the helpers, all of us standing in the filth of her farmyard, she had an unexpected air of snootiness about her. There was no talk, as the cattle were already stressed, and we were suitably distracted trying to keep them moving. Nancy hung around for a bit and soon we had finished that batch and the helpers went to get the last few cattle in.

In the few minutes of downtime, I didn't really know what to say to Nancy, so I decided to ask her whether she had seen the pine marten down at the graveyard wall. After some consideration pacing back and forwards, she came up to me with a look of outrage on her face and said, 'You know what I call them yokes? (things) Target practice! For my rifle!' Turning to pace another few steps away from me, she then added, 'Mind you, years ago I got one in the hay barn with my pitchfork.'

Nancy then set about recreating the scene, in which she had killed the pine marten. I couldn't bear to hear it, but the fact that she was now acting out how she did it overcame my disbelief and I couldn't help but watch. Holding an imaginary pitchfork, she charged at an imaginary pine marten in the yard before me. Her animated steps splattered mud everywhere, perhaps even metaphorically speaking too. Lindy's words, 'mad, bad and sad', began to whir in my mind, and as I tried to decide which one it was, the act continued.

Nancy's face scrunched up, and with her couple of remaining blackened front teeth on show, she really looked the picture of a provoked easóg. As Nancy charged the imaginary animal, she momentarily stopped to face me, and using her hands she gestured how the pine marten had looked up and opened its mouth at the wrong time. She then demonstrated how one prong of the fork had impaled the pine marten through its open mouth and, cackling with glee, she pretended to brandish her pitchfork with the stricken pine marten in the air before her. Then she turned and walked off. A few minutes later I saw her go into her cottage, and we didn't see her again that day. I can't say for sure, but I think she was all three of Lindy's words.

That evening after work I decided to have another go at spotting the pine marten, so I headed back to the graveyard. I was sitting at the far end of the yard on some rocks, trying to be discreet, when a car pulled up and parked on the other side of the wall a few hundred meters away. Through the low sunlight shining in my eyes I saw a lady organising something at the car boot and then make her way through the small side gate entrance into the graveyard. I couldn't make out much more than an outline, but the shape appeared edgy and nervous, engaging in lots of furtive gestures and glances all round. I didn't think too much more about it at the time. Once again there was no sign of a marten, so I decided it was time to head off. As I passed by the parked car, I realised it was Lindy's.

Assuming Lindy must be in visiting her family grave, I thought I would pop down and say 'hello' before I left. As I walked back into the graveyard, she went down one of the paths into the bushes along the back wall, and I was halfway towards her before I had fully thought it through. Once I was closer to the bushy path where she had just disappeared, I heard lots of lip smacking and heavy breathing. I lost my nerve as I neared the bushes – what to hell was she up to in there? Did she have company?

I decided I no longer needed to say hello, so turned to leave.

As I started back up the path, two black-and-white border collies came from across the road, walked right past me, and went into the bushes where Lindy was. I thought back to the dog bowls I had found in that area a few weeks before and what Lindy had said about feeding dogs and I talked myself back into having another look.

Peeking through the bushes I saw Lindy organising bowls of food and recognised all five of Nancy Reilly's dogs (the four black-and-whites and the one brown-and-white). Given the proximity to Nancy's farmyard there could be no doubt who they belonged to. They ate greedily, stopping only to rub against Lindy's legs, showing their great affection for her. Lindy went around each of the dogs as they ate and gave them a few pats, talking to them. She then unravelled a bag from her pocket and presented each dog with a cooked sausage, explaining to each of them that they needed to have their sausages as they had worming tablets in them to help keep them healthy. The dogs didn't display a hint of the aggression I had seen up at the farm. I smiled to myself, thinking, God bless Lindy, what a lovely thing to do. Not letting Lindy see me, I headed off; I would let her keep this secret.

It got to day three of the TB test up at Nancy's – time to check the cattle for any TB reactions. It was much like the first day, with the dogs locked up and barking and the same group of helpers, and we worked our way through the herd. After about three hours, as we got close to finishing the last race of cattle (they all had been clear, with no sign of TB reactions), Nancy came down the path from her house and walked up beside me.

Looking me up and down and walking back and forth with her hands behind her back, avoiding eye contact, she said, 'I expect you have carried out this test in a professional and correct way? I expect your observations and assertions regarding the tuberculosis status of my herd are in line with the department of agriculture guidelines and European regulation number blah blah blah?' She had entered into legalese, perhaps getting ready to challenge my conclusions and mount a fight. As I completed the last few cattle checks, again with no TB reactions, I decided to stop Nancy's legal spiel. I let her know that the test had been carried out to the letter of the law, and that her cattle were free of TB. The words registered in slow motion across her face, and she almost smiled. Almost.

Nancy pointed to a nearby gate and said to one of the lads, 'Close that up there and we'll send these last five straight to the market. I have a few bills to settle.' Then, as she made her way past me, she paused and turned to look at me. Wearing a smile that didn't suit her, she said, 'The vits will have to be paid too I suppose.' And then she walked off briskly.

As I packed up to leave, I glanced at the group of cattle in the pen and thought to myself, lucky them, getting to escape this sorry place. Another part of me considered that this was perhaps just an act too, and that Nancy would not be selling them at all. It would be easy for her to open the gate once we left and keep her hoard, the talk of selling them like dangling a big carrot for all the people present who wouldn't mind getting paid.

Lindy told me a couple of days later that Nancy had done her usual, drop into the office and pay a few coins off her bill before leaving again, saying she would need to sell cattle to pay any more, and as usual the rest of the bill went unpaid. She wasn't known for selling cattle until things got very desperate.

A few evenings later I was chatting with Terry out at the car park. He was asking how things had gone up at Nancy's. I mentioned Nancy's pine marten target practice comment, to which Terry screwed his face up and said, 'That woman has no shame. Someone needs to take the bloody guns off her!' He then said, 'I spent years in the army and never had a gun pointed at me once, not until I left and was back in my own hometown, did that happen. By Nancy Reilly of course.' I couldn't believe my ears.

Terry went on to explain. A few months previous he had been up in the graveyard with a newly bereaved widow. Himself and the widow had been marking out with tape where Terry and the men were to dig a grave that evening for her deceased husband. When Terry arrived to get started later that evening, Nancy Reilly was sitting on a nearby gravestone, waiting for him. As Terry got closer, she pulled a gun on him and threatened to shoot him if he was to dig that grave. Terry said that Nancy had jumped up and down in a such a temper, as that was the spot, she wanted for herself. She yelled that she was an only child, and that she deserved her *own* grave no matter what the widow thought. She was so angry and threatening that Terry had no choice but to call the cops.

'By the time the local sergeant arrived,' Terry said, 'Nancy had got rid of the gun and put on an Oscar-worthy performance of poor her.' His eyes got wide and disturbed as he recalled how Nancy wailed and was so convincing – he had even started to believe her himself, saying it was making him forget that moments earlier she had been pointing a gun at his face. 'For all the eye rubbing and tissues she used during her performance, there wasn't a single tear shed. It was all an act. Crocodile tears, they call them, I believe. The priest then turned up too, and Nancy's wails escalated so much that another site was found for the deceased man pretty quickly.'

As it would happen, later that year, as autumn turned to winter, Nancy went on to make use of that purloined plot, perhaps a bit sooner than people in the area might have predicted. Her dreadful end came with the onset of a particularly chilly blast of winter weather. I was away on a winter sun holiday for two weeks at the time, and it was all over and done by the time I got back.

Lindy filled me in on what had happened.

Nancy had been found dead in her living room by a couple of neighbours who had checked to see if she needed anything with the bad weather. The cause of death was inconclusive and the subject of some local speculation. Many said she had frozen to death. She was found sitting in her armchair at the hearth beside the ashes of a few turf briquettes. On a night as bad as the one in question, most people would burn a few bales of briquettes, but not Nancy. Although she had three bales at the ready, she had taken to burning them one piece at a time. That was never going to be enough to warm that room on that night.

At this point in Lindy's description of the events Terry arrived at the vet clinic reception room and joined the conversation. On hearing the subject was Nancy, he took off his hat and held it at waist level as a mark of respect. 'Some say her heart gave out in the end,' he said, 'So filled with hatred and gall. It just stopped.'

Terry and Lindy agreed that it could certainly have been both a troubled heart and the chill. Terry said, 'The neighbours rallied around after to try and give her a decent wake and there was a big enough turnout of locals for the burial too. Of course, she got her own -brand-new grave in the end.' He then added with a cheeky grin, 'Sure, didn't I dig it. Funny though, we didn't need the whiskey for that one.'

'You'll never believe it,' Lindy said. 'Nancy wasn't cold in the ground till a nephew on the Reilly side turned up from England, the sole benefactor of her will. Of course, Nancy overlooked a handful of local nieces, to leave her will to the only male, even though she had never met him, they say. The priest and a few of the locals took the nephew up to the house. Straight away the nephew said, "There will be no more farming up on that barren hill." Just this week the whole herd was sent to the market.' Lindy punched her clasped fists into the air in celebration, adding, 'The cattle will be much better looked after by real farmers now.'

Terry gazed off through the side window of the reception room and said, 'Fine young chap the nephew turned out to be too. He took the money from the sale of the cattle and visited every creditor that Nancy owed money to and paid them all in full.'

Lindy smiled and said she would see to it that the dogs up there were looked after.

Terry said, 'And they say when it's all settled, the nephew is going to be splitting it fairly and writing a few cheques to the nieces. He's keen on rewriting a bit of history from beyond the grave for Nancy too.'

On hearing this news, I don't know what came over me, but I took a notion to drop by and visit Nancy's grave in the coming days. Maybe I was still in shock.

That weekend, I went to the cemetery. It was noon on a nice sunny Saturday (by Irish winter standards). Nancy's grave had been freshly decorated by parishioners with bunches of mixed-colour carnations. I was alone in the graveyard this time, just me and some chirping birds. As I looked at the flowers on her grave, I felt sad for Nancy. After a few moments of reflection, I was distracted by the low-level 'chip chip chip' alarm call of a pair of blackbirds over by the wall. It's a very distinctive call that ever since childhood has inspired me to immediately look around for a nearby bird of prey or, failing that, a cat in the vicinity. But in this instance, there was nothing but an aeroplane high above hurtling towards America, leaving a vapour trail in its wake. It wasn't obvious what had frightened the birds; perhaps whatever it was had passed by, as the birds settled again.

I spent a couple more minutes at Nancy's graveside, thinking about her sad ending.

As I got ready to leave, the birds once again began a frenzied alarm – all of them this time: the robins, thrushes and blackbirds went straight into their agitated 'chip chip chip' sounds; even a solitary wren got involved in the chorus of outrage. I scanned the area again. There's a predator here, I thought, but where? Then I spotted it, curled up in a cosy-looking nest of moss between some rocks. Awakening from a nap, it rubbed its eyes with both of its front paws at the same time, before taking a really good look at me. Then it stood and gave a bit of a shake and – in typical pine marten fashion – in a heartbeat it disappeared up over the wall with a flash of its bushy tail. I ran to the wall to watch for it on the other side, but it was gone.

I smiled, thinking about those evenings I had spent up there. Our local pine marten turned out to be a daytime creature! It sure was great it had managed to avoid Nancy too! As luck would have it for the pine marten, Nancy's farm (which was undoubtedly his patch) was later sold to a wealthy retired couple who were mad about nature. Not only was there no more farming on those hills, they spent a fortune planting native trees and plants and re-wilding the parched, bare hillsides. In the months and years that followed, this pine marten would find itself living in a sanctuary for nature, once again rewriting some of Nancy's legacy.

CHAPTER 12

The Tassie Twins and the Orgling Debacle

'You're not serious? Surely, you're having me on, Rose? I just can't quite believe it,' I said.

We were standing on the patio at the front of Rose Harte's cottage. Rose was stroking Butters, her podgy Russian blue cat. He was freshly brushed and mostly asleep on the garden bench but enjoying the attention.

'That's some kind of perverse cycle of life stuff right here,' I said, still trying to get my head around it. 'Butters hunts the wild birds (I presume). You brush Butters and peg the little tufts of his excess fur onto your clothesline for the birds. The birds pick it up for their nests, and then the cycle perpetuates...... Butters eats the birds ... The premise of some sort of horror film perhaps?'

I had a chuckle, but Rose just looked at me kind of funny.

As we spoke the birds were in a frenzy to get the fur no more than a couple of metres away from us. Looking on at Butters and his close proximity to the birds, my laugher slowly changed to alarm as I started to fear that there could to be a showdown right there and then. An avian massacre in the making ...

Discreetly I started tapping my foot to try to shoo the birds away from Butters, an attempt to avert the impending bloodbath. My theory was quickly dismantled, alas, when, in the rush of birds grabbing beaks full of fur off the clothes line, one of them, a yellow-throated honeyeater, landed right beside Butters and helped herself to a few tufts of fur directly from Butters' rump, perhaps not fully realising this fur was still attached to the cat! But Butters just sat there in sleepy indifference, looking at the bird. I don't think Butters was into bird-hunting after all.

Tasmania (Tassie), Australia's island state, is a land of manic weather and stunning natural beauty, and is teaming with native animals, some being unique to that part of Australia. I was there working at a clinic in the middle north, often travelling large distances to deliver vet services to remote towns. I was never far from the Bass Strait, though, the body of water between Tassie and mainland Australia. As Tassie is closer to Antarctica than the rest of Australia, it often has a mix of high and low temperatures, and on occasions, able to deliver all four seasons in one day. The weather was often quite manic, I remember witnessing a raging mountain bush fire one morning that threatened to burn up a huge amount of forest, only for it to be completely quenched by a blanket of snow that same afternoon.

During my time there I got to meet some Tassie local wildlife, including Tasmanian devils, quolls and a few platypus. Tassie is a really nice place to spend some time, and can look very different depending on the season; it can get quite green in the winter months, and tends to revert to a dry rusty brown in the summer, as the heat and sometimes lacklustre rain can leave it all a bit dry, which is not helped any, by a huge gap in the ozone layer above.

I had been asked to stop in with the Harte sisters on my way past while doing the outreach run. They were very good clients of the vet practice, with a menagerie of animals, and if we were over that way there was almost always a new instalment of medicine for one of their animals to be dropped off, or an animal to be looked at. Over the years the sisters had so many animals under our care that if we were doing one of our trips over to eastern Tasmania, we gave them a courtesy call just to make sure they were all good. This time I was to help Rose trim the hooves of her pet sheep Sally, as they were getting a bit long. Rose knew well how to do the trimming, but was nervous she would cut them too short, and in any case she needed a hand to hold Sally too.

We made our way over to the paddocks, and it was a fairly routine hoof trim. When we finished with Sally, we put her back into her paddock where she lived with two of Rose's elderly rescued alpacas. There was a wether (a castrated male alpaca) called Dalai (his first owner's kids having made the common mistake of thinking he was a llama, and thus having named him after His Holiness) and a female called Alice, both of whom were snowy white. As we stood at the gate the alpacas came over for a chin scratch and to say hello. Being gentle, inquisitive creatures, they made constant reassuring humming noises to each other. Rose said she was just about to receive two more alpacas, a mother and son, rescued from an abandoned property a few miles away. They were arriving that afternoon. 'That will be it,' Rose added, 'No more after that – four alpacas are enough.'

Rose had a tendency to take in rescue animals, and each came with its own story. There was a Muscovy duck that had come from the local vicar, the vicar's flock having aged and dwindled down to one, which he then sent over to live with Rose, saying it was only right, because she had access to a pond. As it happened, Rose had a fine big pond, a rainwater reservoir with an adjoining stream that helped fill it in the winter months. She also had a rescue Shetland pony called Toby, who had turned up some years previous, left behind by a travelling circus, and had been at the Harte's ever since. Toby could still do nimble-toed circus tricks when he needed to, making it a nightmare to get deworming paste into his mouth. You would want to see his ability to rear up and dance around, making for quite some job for me and Rose a few times each year.

The Harte sisters, Rose and Daisy, were twins, young-looking for their early fifties and although not identical they were damned close. They lived a couple hours' drive away from our clinic, well and truly out on the sticks. When it came to their animals, the Harte cottage's interior was reserved for Butters the cat and Eric, their rescue greyhound only. The rules proved to be loose, however, as over my time there I witnessed many critters that had made it inside, from orphan lambs in heat boxes to local wildlife rescues. The Harte's hobby farm was a collection of veggie patches and small, neatly fenced paddocks. Bordering their property stood a forest of large karri and eucalyptus trees. These enormous trees gave off a wondrous psithurism (the sound of wind moving through trees) all around. Although always sounding windy high up in the tree canopies, at ground level there was only ever a gentle breeze as the trees provided a nice shelter from the coast, the forest being all that stood between the Harte's place and the sea. With all this natural habitat, their gardens were alive with local bird life and the odd native animal.

The sisters, both unmarried, were tall and thin and shared a penchant for wearing bright, colourful garments. The exterior walls of their cottage and their roadside garden fencing were painted in an equally bright mix of colours, a melange of sea blue, lime green, mustard yellow and cherry red reminiscent of the psychedelic era. The cottage easily could have been mistaken for an artists' retreat. The sisters had brown eyes and long, fair hair, usually tucked up under a hat or a scarf. Rose was fresh faced, with sparkly eyes and a peachy complexion, while Daisy was paler, with dark circles around her eyes that augmented a naturally meek disposition. You might say both sisters were easy on the eye, and would have been many a Tasmanian bachelor's dream, not that either of the sisters seemed to be on the lookout for one.

Rose was a well-known local herbalist and reflexologist and did massages at a studio at one end of her cottage. She had a reputation for treating many afflictions with her concoctions of herbs, essences and massage. When it came to the Harte's animals and their ailments the veterinary medications and treatments that I prescribed were regularly complemented with lotions and potions from Rose's garden too. Rose also made a range of Harte family recipe preserves, from fruit jams to chutneys and relishes. Having green fingers, Rose made a small living off her veggie patch and herb gardens as well, selling these from a small wooden cabinet with an honesty box at the edge of her garden fence. Depending on the season, there could be anything in that cabinet – apples, cherries, garlic bulbs, bags of herbs and even the odd beanie hat whenever she found time to knit. People would drop by and help themselves to the home-grown produce. Many came for a massage and left with some spuds, a dozen eggs, a new hat and a couple of bags of herbs. It was like life before supermarkets.

After Sally's pedicure was done and she was back with the alpacas, Rose brought me on a walk to show me around her vegetable gardens, which were a series of raised beds and two large polytunnels, nice and close to the pond for irrigation. The pond and stream provided a nice backdrop to the vegetable beds and also served as a natural barrier to wallabies and wombats coming from the forest for a snack. As we walked around, I noticed Rose had lots of mixed plant types growing together and she explained that this practice was part of her permaculture methods. She knew exactly which plants benefitted from growing alongside others. To the untrained eye, it was all a bit haphazard, but what she had was really clever. Coming from a horticultural background myself, and at times having green fingers, I was naturally curious as to what she had going. I noted the marigolds and nasturtiums plants placed in-between cabbage, and Rose explained that it was sacrificial pest control in order to keep the bugs off the cabbage. As we walked, I saw an abundance of herbs I had heard of but never got to see before, and we spent some time picking, sniffing and rubbing different leaves. Rose was excited to show me some of her plant varieties for cooking. There must have been ten different kinds of mint, and Rose had a different use for each. There was sage and rosemary, a plethora of thymes and basils to beat the band.

In the medicinal herb areas, Rose pointed out St John's wort, arnica flowers with their soft, lamb-tongue-like leaves, and some big potted aloe veras. She had so many plant varieties I couldn't keep up: there was borage in flower and milk thistle ('Great for a hangover,' Rose quipped), lemon balm and tea tree, saffron flowers, and many varieties of eucalyptus.

As we approached the polytunnels, I noticed several wooden shelves inside the first one, with lots of jars and bottles of different-sized plants. It turned out Rose was a dab hand at making terrariums, and even on occasion held terrarium workshops throughout Tassie, showing others how to make their own. She pointed out some newly potted ones and some more established ones. After completing a terrarium, Rose would sell it through one of the local garden centres and planned to do a few mornings at the big Tassie farmers' markets when she found time.

We peeked from the half-open door into the other polytunnel, which was for food; on one side she had rows of tomato plants and on the other were some baby salad leaves. Through the back door I could see the alpaca paddocks. The polytunnel was just a few metres at the other side of their fence, almost close enough for them to swipe the occasional tomato, with a reach of their long necks.

Passing from the vegetable gardens, we walked along the stream to have a look at Rose's fruit trees. These were arranged in rows, with some of the trees slightly overhanging the reservoir banks. As is standard practice in Tassie, the trees were enclosed in netting to keep the fruit-eating birds out. One such culprit is the European blackbird, which some bright spark introduced to Tasmania in the early 1900s to eat horticultural parasites, only to discover that they like to gobble up the fruit too! At the Harte's, the nets also helped to keep most of the fruit out of the stream.

Of the twins, Rose was the talker. Daisy was more the shy, quiet type, with a tendency to pull at her jacket sleeves nervously during reluctant conversations. In her younger years Daisy had been a ballet dancer, gaining some fame around Australia back then, but had given it up to live the quiet Tassie life with her sister. I think the dance never left her, however, as she regularly could be seen gently swaying to an inner rhythm while Rose and I chatted. In any case, Daisy smiled a lot through her shyness, and she certainly shared her sister's love for animals. Any time you saw the Harte's old yellow panel van roll into town, Daisy, never having learned to drive, would always be in the front passenger seat, keeping Rose company.

I found out pretty early on that Daisy had been through a battle with cancer. Rose was afraid she might get sick again, so she fussed after her and forbade her from exerting herself in any way. It was clear the sisters cared for each other dearly. Daisy tended to hide one side of her face in her scarf, or her hair or hand. Initially, I thought this was purely due to her shy disposition, but I later found out that that was where her cancer had been, in her left cheekbone, and although the surgical scars were minimal, Daisy was clearly self-conscious about them. Thankfully, surgery, chemotherapy and radiotherapy had been successful in treating the tumour – along with, of course, Rose's remedies from the garden.

A lovely smell of essential oils permeated the air around the sisters: an intriguing aura of evening primrose, mint, lavender and sandalwood, amongst others. Rose always had a healthy glow, like she had just had a wonderful massage, even though she was the masseuse. A shed in their garden that backed onto a little horse stable had an adjoining canopy at the front, and under the canopy Rose hung masses of herbs to dry in the open air. The shed also provided storage for pots and jars of herbs and seed; the whole thing gave off a fantastic smell, should you happen to be downwind. Whenever I visited the Harte's they invariably were holding cups of home-made herbal tea. They seemed to have an endless pot brewing on a wood-fired stove on their patio, just beside the front door. The tea, their garden, the herb store, the ladies – the entire combination gave the area around their house the most beautiful fragrance, which reached as far as the garden gate a few hundred metres away. When I visited, I would always have a cup of herbal tea too, and I rarely left without gratefully receiving a few dabs of essential oils on my temples and wrists 'to fend off stress.'

Many of the trees that lined the paths around the Harte's garden had been given little colourful knitted makeovers, with many wearing handmade tree jackets. An array of various styles of wooden wind chimes hung around the garden, gently plunking in the wind, giving the easy sea breeze a lovely, earthy rhythm. The whole place was an oasis of tranquillity, vivid colours and happy animals.

Rose and Daisy's cottage was actually the Harte family ancestral home. The ladies were the only daughters of two English botanists who had moved to Tasmania back in the 1950s. Their parents became well-known in the area for their work with native flora. Their father was a political activist and had even spent a spell or two in jail for impeding logging companies back in the day. I am told that some of the native Australian plants Rose and Daisy's parents discovered were named after them, a nod to their life's work. It was only natural then that their parents dished out flowery names to their twin girls too. The Harte's cottage was 270 Broccoli Street – they had named the street too. You knew green-fingered people lived here, as the house number digits, instead of being on a conventional sign, were sculpted in the hedging along the garden fence. There were no other houses for miles, which contributed to my early confusion at Tassie house numbers. I soon learnt that 270 was the distance in metres from the junction off the main highway; this was a way of helping attentive odometer-reading travellers find Tassie addresses. The Harte's parents had carefully chosen a site by the forest edge on which to build their cottage, mindful of the local flora and fauna and – my gosh – what a stunning location it was.

Over the years I came to think of Rose and Daisy as local animal guardians. To be fair, they did their share of helping their human neighbours too, but what really captivated me from my first encounter with the Hartes, was their voluntary work with animals. Every day the sisters travelled great distances, visiting often remote neighbours whose animals needed daily medications, to help administer them. They even brought their neighbours' pets all the way to our vet clinic, should they need attention before we got up that way. There were many examples of people the Hartes helped out, such as old Mrs Watts on the hill, who, crippled with arthritis in her hands, was unable to give her cat Jarvis his medication. Rose and Daisy dropped by every day and did this for her. Then there was Mr Murphy, elderly and afflicted by cataracts, who needed help for his dog Boris, who had required ear ointment twice a day, every day for two weeks. The Hartes saw to that too. The sisters certainly were a godsend for both the animals and their neighbours.

A few weeks after my visit to help with Sally the sheep, I received a phone call from Rose.

'Austin, that young male alpaca – I've named him Pablo – he turned out to be eighteen months old and fully grown. I had to separate him immediately from the others; he is behaving like a brute. For a start, he was harassing poor old Dalai, chasing after him and trying to wrestle him to the ground! Then he was trying out his luck with Alice! At her age! He just goes around all day long pacing his fences trying to get out, making the most hideous noises. It's like he's possessed!'

Rose went silent for a moment, then said with a serious tone, 'Anyway, I've been gurgling, and I think he's oogling ... *ahum, ahum* ... let me try that again, Austin. I have been googling – and I think he's orgling, making those alpaca mating calls all day long. We can't get him to stop! I've been feeding him peppermint leaves and my tranquil essences, but it's not working, so I gave him cumin seeds. Dammit I even gave him some of my good turmeric root, but it's actually worse he's getting! He's orgling at the other animals too: Sally, Toby, and that's not all, even poor Daisy. He's driving us crazy! Will this debacle ever end? Help!'

I said I would drop by later that week when I was back over her way and we would have a look at what could be done to help.

Later that week I went to see the Hartes and meet Pablo, and I needed to drop some medication off also. I parked at the edge of the roadway and made my way through the garden gate. The well-kept hedges that bordered the garden path were taller than me, and I noticed as I walked that there were a few side paths coming off the main path and leading into smaller gardens. One was filled with beautiful red and yellow roses, and on the other side was an area with an old stone fountain over some rocks and a few cast-iron sculptures. It looked like the perfect relaxation spot. I walked along the path towards the cottage, still a few hundred meters ahead; the morning sun shone through the hedge, causing spiderwebs to sparkle with dewdrops as they danced in the gentle heat. I became aware of music playing near the front patio, which was still out of my view, and as I come into earshot, I stopped. Could it be? Really?

Yes, it was – Pavarotti's 'Nel Blu Dipinto di Blu'! (I'm a bit of a Pav fan.)

Right there in the music and sun I was overcome with a feeling of tranquillity, looking around at the vibrant flowers, the hedgerow's wall of leaves swaying in the breeze, and a chorus of friendly little birds chit-chatting and darting around, excited by my arrival.

Making my way towards the house and getting ever more lost in the beautiful tune, I turned the last hedge corner, and there, about fifteen metres in front of me, was Daisy, with her back to me and Butters cradled in her arms. There were clippers and a comb on a table, beside a little pile of Butters' blue fur. I momentarily thought to myself, jeez, grooming time again – that's one well-groomed cat!

The music being quite loud, Daisy hadn't heard me arrive. I thought about how best to announce my presence without causing a heart attack. I stood for just a moment before realising that, not only was Daisy holding Butters, she was dancing with him – swaying with him cradled in her arms, weaving from side to side, doing little circles on the patio. As Pavarotti let out a few high rolls while the song played, Daisy lifted Butters, one hand under each of his armpits, held him out in the air in front of her and began to make bigger circles, smiling and singing to his face, lifting him high into the air and burying her face into his portly belly. They were having too much fun – I couldn't disturb them! I noticed Daisy was repeatedly saying something to Butters that I couldn't quite hear. Each time she said it, she would snuggle him close and stroke one side of his face.

Conveniently realising that I had left the medication I was to deliver in the car, I popped back to get it. On the way I caught a strong scent coming from the kitchen door. Something was cooking, but I couldn't quite put my finger on what. It smelled almost like jam, but there was a strong smell of onions too; my nose couldn't quite make sense of it. By the time I returned to the house, the music had finished, and Butters was now on the table as Daisy swept up the patio. The garden gate hinge let out a screech as I opened it, and Daisy gave a wave and invited me over.

I said hello and Daisy said, 'Oh I was just giving Butters his weekend makeover.'

Butters looked at me, his head playfully tilting from side to side, with an inquisitive look on his face. He looked a bit different, I thought, thinking he'd had a bit of a trim. I said to Daisy, 'Ah, he looks well!'

To which she cast her eyes up to the clouds and, covering her mouth with one hand, said, 'Oh Austin, it's a dreadful thing I've done, isn't it?'

I looked at her in slight surprise. 'Sorry, come again?'

She said, 'It's so obvious isn't it? Look at his poor little face – a whole side of whiskers gone! My hand slipped with the clippers!'

Keen to comfort Daisy, I said, 'They'll grow back, sure. Accidents happen.'

She set her brush down and embraced Butters, stroking his good, whiskery side, saying, 'Oh I'm sorry, sorry, sorry!' I realised that that's what she had been saying to him earlier – apologising for the whisker mishap.

As Daisy begged for forgiveness Butters just looked at me as if to ask what all the fuss was about. And before

Daisy could get the patio swept up, an army of little birds had begun fighting over Butters' fur. It was quite a sight – blue fairywrens carrying tufts of Butters' fur almost as big as the birds themselves! Those birds truly are stunning to see in breeding season, their iridescent electric blue in the morning sun is both mystical and magical.

Rose appeared at the half-hitch kitchen door, wiping her hands with a tea towel, shouting Hello, apologising for the cloud of what turned out to be onion jam fumes, saying she would just turn her stove down and be right over. She popped back inside, and in a few moments returned with a small plate of cheese, crackers and the aforementioned onion jam. She called me and Daisy over and invited us to try her latest batch of jam. Daisy got a cracker with a nice big chunk of cheddar and a generous dollop of cooled onion jam on it and put the whole thing in her mouth at once, then stood back to enjoy. Rose set down the plate and I made a similar one for myself.

The combination was revelatory – not too sweet, still a little crunchy, with a sharp cheddar tang. 'Delicious,' I declared. Daisy nodded in agreement and said quietly, 'Go on Rose, try some for Austin.' Rose, blushing a little, glanced at me, looked at the plate and then back at me and said, 'Ah, don't mind me, sure I'm a funny old thing. I love making onion jam but by God you'll never find me eating it.' She screwed her face up and stuck her tongue out, saying, 'Onions! Yuck!' We all had a laugh. Then she added, 'OK, let's go see my naughty alpaca!'

I followed Rose along the garden path to the back of the cottage, looking onto the neat little paddocks. One paddock held Dalai and Alice, who had been joined by Cinnamon, Pablo's mother. Cinnamon was a fawn colour and was a very woolly specimen. Pablo was separated in the adjacent paddock all on his own, just beside the polytunnels. He was bigger than I had expected, his coat much neater than his mother's, and was dark brown all over.

Rose mentioned again that he was now coming of age and said, 'You want to hear the racket he makes when he starts. I'm afraid he'll get out one day and injure someone.' Pablo, happily grazing, occasionally lifted his head to masticate and watch us watch him. Just then I noticed Rose's pet Muscovy duck waddle towards us. She was very purposefully avoiding Pablo's field, taking the long way around the fence to get over to the pond. Rose pointed out that even the poor old Muscovy was living in fear, having had a few orgling chases around the field earlier that week. 'When the urge is upon him, he makes a deep, throaty noise, somewhere between a dying goat and a dinosaur.'

At that, Pablo went running to the fence nearest the Muscovy and let out a territorial bawl, throwing himself at the fence and scaring the wits out of the duck. Rose started shaking her fist in the air and shouted, 'Off ya! Off ya, you brute!', turning to me to reinforce her message.

Rose said there was a problem with Cinnamon too. A few times Rose had found her in the paddock lying on her side, unable to stand up. We entered the paddock with the three alpacas. The gang were friendly and inquisitive, and made their way over to us. As I stood there, pondering Cinnamon's predicament I got to running my hands along her back and down her sides, and found masses of knotted wool all over. She hadn't been shorn for a long time. The wool on her underbelly and legs was wet and heavy from the long, dewy grass.

I stood for a minute racking my brain as to why Cinnamon was fine on some mornings and unable to rise on others. An ear infection causing vertigo? A brain tumour? A bad back? Dodgy feet? None of these seemed likely, mostly because they wouldn't just cause sporadic immobility. I noticed Alice had less wool and was much more mobile on her feet, and something dawned on me. I said to Rose, 'I don't suppose she's only stuck down to the ground and unable to rise after it rains?'

Rose thought back and said, 'You could be right. Last wet day was on Friday, and she didn't get up until the afternoon that day.' We both twigged at the same time – The poor thing had been sponging up rain and had been unable to stand with all the weight of soaked wool! The visit from a shearer to clip three years of wool off her, was already imminent. Rose seemed relieved, saying she would make some beanies from all the wool when it came off.

Then as we headed back past Pablo's paddock Rose asked me, 'What are we going to do with this character?'

The most immediate answer I could come up with was that perhaps castrating him would help settle him down a bit and take away his testosterone-fuelled urges. I let Rose know that I would make some enquiries and get back to her.

Back in the office at the vet clinic, I decided to enquire about what the other vets thought about my idea of desexing Pablo to stop all this orgling. Alpacas were still a bit new to me, and apart from doing a few pet alpaca castrations and clipping a few overgrown hooves along the way, I was still gaining experience with their vet needs. In that practice I worked with two senior female vets (Liz and Bree), both of whom had years of experience with a range of species, on several continents. It would be fair to say they both had a great sense of humour too, and the three of us would often get lost in regaling stories from our work as vets. Liz, the most senior vet, had an infectious laugh and a wealth of stories from nearly thirty years working as a vet. I was also still getting used to the ladies' numerous attempts at taking the piss out of me, their more junior and perhaps more gullible Irish counterpart. Even though I had been in Australia for years by that point, they seemed to think I had just arrived fresh off the plane and was a sitting duck for their jokes.

I told Liz about Pablo. 'I think he has loving on his mind, and he has the Hartes on edge, making sexual noises at them and all their other animals.'

Bree overheard us and came to the office door already starting to laugh at the parts of our conversation she had picked up. The thought of Pablo orgling at pretty much everything had us all in stitches. Following Rose's lead Googling 'orgling', I decided it was time I educated myself on this matter too. I found a fact page about alpacas and quickly learned that this was a noise male alpaca make throughout the mating process; these calls stimulate the female to be more receptive. Poor Pablo's lilting was wasted on his confusion with other species. The same fact sheet also informed me of a brand-new gem that was so outrageous I couldn't help but laugh. As all the other vet staff now gathered around us, we erupted in laughter as I told them, 'A female alpaca giving birth was termed alpaca unpacking.' Some of them already knew that, but we all laughed anyway. Just as we were getting a grip on our mirth, Liz piped up and said she once had to treat a bovine patient that had got orgled. Well this only added to our laughter. Surely not! Was she taking the piss? Was this even a thing? There was no other option but to turn to the Internet to see if this was even possible. And still to this day, it's one of the most random five minutes of my life I have ever spent on YouTube, watching male alpacas cross the species love barrier. Liz wasn't taking the piss out of me after all!

Well, not that time, anyway.

We decided there and then – castration it shall be. That and a few months of Pablo being kept separate from the other animals while his testosterone levels dropped. But as it happened, I didn't need to make that phone call to Rose and Daisy at all. I bumped into them the next day at their book club get-together at the local café, where I had popped in to get some lunch. Their group was sitting to one side of the room and they called me over to say hello to their fellow book readers, about a dozen of them in total, a mix of men and women mostly of retirement age. I love a bit of a read myself, so I asked them what that month's book was. That month it was local Tassie history. Francis (well-known locally as the friendly waving lollipop man), who was seated at the top of the table, opened a large Tupperware box of brownies and beckoned me over, saying, 'Here, have that with your lunch', and handed me one wrapped in a napkin. Rose smiled at me saying she had baked them freshly that morning and, unlike other brownies, 'These ones are good for you.' As I approached to collect the brownie, I noticed a handbag on the floor rammed full of children's fairy tale books. Francis noticed me spot them, then just winked and said, 'Ah, those are for next month's reading.' I smiled in acknowledgment. I didn't want to interrupt, so I asked Rose for a quick word. She followed me out and I let her know that Pablo would probably be best off castrated to stop all this orgling.

We planned to do the surgery on the next outreach visit ten days later.

The following week, while I was at the clinic one afternoon, the secretary came to ask me if I could take a call from Rose. It seemed she needed some advice on a sensitive matter. I took the call and Rose, sounding quite distressed, said, 'Austin, could cannabis butter be harmful for a dog if eaten?' She then was quick to add, 'I'm asking for a friend who lives remotely and can't get to a vet clinic.'

I said, 'Well, Rose, cannabis can cause a dog to be very dull and sleepy, and it can give it dilated pupils and urinary incontinence that can last for several days. What size of dog and how much would he have had? In any case, a large amount of butter is not good for them either.'

Rose said as far as she knew he was a greyhound and he had eaten a couple of pieces of toast slathered with cannabis butter. It had happened the previous night, about twelve hours ago, and so far, he seemed OK.

I had seen a few dogs intoxicated with cannabis over the years. My advice was to keep him indoors and well hydrated, and no more cannabis butter.

I did have a question though. 'What the hell is cannabis butter?' I asked.

Rose just laughed and said she believed some people infused butter with cannabis and then used it for everyday purposes, baking and the like. We finished the call laughing, wondering how those people ever got any work done, if every time they had butter, they were high!

I didn't hear anything back about the dog in the days that followed. Being an eternal optimist, I took that to mean he never had any ill effects.

Then came the day of Pablo's castration. I arrived and parked on the roadway at the front and made my way through to the back of the cottage. I could see Rose sitting on a stool at the edge of the pond on the far side of the vegetable beds with a washing basin at her feet. She had in her hand, a tree branch with a cotton string attached to one end. It wasn't unlike something a child would construct to try to catch a fish. As I approached, she let out a little cheer and lifted her fishing stick. Out of the pond at the end of her string emerged a half-eaten red cherry with two yabbies (crayfish) dangling in tow. Interested in the cherry, they had latched on, and were now making their way to Rose's bucket.

I enquired whether Rose was fishing for her dinner, but she just laughed and said it was more of a pest control mission: they were an introduced species and were doing damage to her dam walls. In an attempt to keep her mind preoccupied before Pablo's castration she thought she would fish some out for Butters' dinner. She asked if I wanted to have a go at catching a yabby, so I took up the stick and, leaning over the bank, dangled in a juicy cherry. Through the silty water I could just make out the cherry touching the bottom, and in a minute a few dark little shapes made their way over to it. Rose looked over my shoulder and, pointing to some reeds to our left, whispered, 'There's George coming! You're in luck.'

I leaned in to get a closer look at who or what George was, but all I could see was a few ripples in the water, which was otherwise calm as a bowl of milk. The ripples started moving our way, and shortly after the most comical little long face popped up about a metre away and looked straight at me. I turned to Rose, who looked back at me with a huge smile. 'Austin meet George, our resident platypus! He's no doubt chancing his luck for a yabby. Here, let's give him one of these ones.' She popped her hand in her basin and grabbed me a yabby, saying, 'Kneel down there and hold it in the water for a while and he'll come get it.' I did just that, and George came right into the shallows immediately beneath me, stood on his back paws for a second and shook himself free of a bit of excess water. Then he nuzzled side to side with his beak, gently nibbling the yabby, before popping it out of my fingers with a yank and swimming off with it, his chubby little arse wiggling with glee.

From behind me Rose laughed and said, 'Isn't he just the most delightful little creature? Georgy Porgy is his full name because – well he's as fat as mud with all them yabbies to eat. George has been living in my dam for a couple years now. He turned up one night during a bad flood, washed in from the river nearby.'

This was the closest I have ever got to a platypus – I was blown away!

We turned our attention back to the pressing matter at hand – Pablo – and headed off towards his paddock.

Pablo's castration would involve giving him a sedative injection in the muscle, followed by an intravenous anaesthetic twenty minutes later. Once we got the first sedation on board it would hopefully be plain sailing from there. As we arrived at his paddock the dreaded yodelling and pacing began. Trying to catch an orgling Alpaca that has other notions on his mind, takes a bit of logistical planning. I decided to get Rose to stand at the far side of the gate to act as bait while I entered the field from the fence at the far side. Once Rose was in position Pablo lay on the ground with his neck outstretched, wailing like he was possessed and entirely focused on her, I seized my moment, running over and jabbing the dose of sedative into his right hip muscle. Pablo was not too happy about this. He hopped back up onto his feet to give me an angry stare and some deep growls as I made a quick exit.

I had given him a fairly strong dose (I wasn't taking any chances), and thankfully after about twenty minutes he went completely silent and wobbly on his feet like a drunken sailor. This time Rose came with me into his paddock and we got his head collar on. Then we laid some towels down on a dry, flat area of the paddock and I gave him some intravenous ketamine (used to induce anaesthesia). Pablo slowly went down, making little orgling groans as he went, almost out of defeat. In no time he was fast asleep. Rose moved in, placing a towel to support his neck and another to cover his eyes. Taking a small bottle of oil from her pocket, Rose proceeded to massage Pablo's head and neck while talking to him soothingly. I moved to his hindquarters and quickly got the area around his testicles clipped and surgically scrubbed up, then applied local anaesthetic to the area to help keep Pablo comfortable. A few minutes later I cut into Pablo's scrotum and removed his testicles. The surgery having gone down without a hitch, I stitched the skin up and gave Pablo a tetanus shot and pain relief. Soon enough he started to stir. We retreated to safety and watched as he stood up, shook himself off and immediately started into orgling at us again! Yes, it was going to be weeks before that stopped.

Rose, who had been at his head throughout the surgery, shouted 'Thank you' to me over Pablo's roars as I held the surgical kit in an empty bucket against the base of my chest. When I bent over to pick up the towels from the pathway Rose caught sight of Pablo's testicles in my bucket and looked at me in disbelief. 'You've got to be kidding,' she said, pointing. 'Is that all the size of his testicles?' She dipped her hand in and scooped them up in one hand.

'They're like cherries,' she exclaimed. 'Butters the cat had bigger balls when he got done!'

We both laughed and I decided to release another of my alpaca learnings.

'They must have the smallest balls-to-beast ratio of all the species, Rose,' I said. 'A billy goat or maybe a boar is probably the winner when it comes to animals with big balls!'

Rose's incredulity now spilled over into laughter. I left her still standing there laughing, repeating to herself, 'All that racket over two little cherries. I've seen it all now!' She may never get over the size of Pablo's nuts.

A couple of weeks later I heard from Rose. All was going well, and Pablo was starting to lose his reproductive notions. Rose had even been brave enough to go into his paddock and give him a few clips with the shears to try to get him used to it. Over their way, the old vicar's cat Lucy, had been diagnosed with hyperthyroidism and was hugely averse to taking any tablet medication. We had got the medication made into a special cream that could be applied to Lucy's ear. Rose, who was going to be coming on the trip over our way, had telephoned us to say that she would collect the medication after her monthly book club meeting and help show the vicar how to use it. Rose was well versed in feline hyperthyroidism management, having helped out with a few cats with this condition over the years. She said she loved to see how the cats responded to treatment, as their bony little frames grew back a bit of flesh, and she enjoyed watching them become nice and relaxed and calm, free from their high blood pressure and erratic heart rates. Then a very strange thing happened: Rose never arrived to make that collection; it was very unlike her.

The next day came and went and again, no sign of Rose. It got to the third morning and I still hadn't heard what had happened. Rita from the book group dropped in to buy some cat food and as she stood at the front counter, she put both hands on it and visibly steadied herself. Taking a deep breath, she audibly said to herself, 'This too will pass – this too will pass.'

I asked Rita if she was OK and she looked at me square in the eye and said, 'Dearest Austin, I am high as a kite and have been for two days now! I've been seeing butterflies and it's unseasonal, and also my cat was talking to me last night. He wants more food.' She then had to steady herself on the rail again, as she took a fit of giggles punctuated with snorts and then she turned and off she went! As I was getting used to the local comical characters I worked with on a daily basis, I didn't think too much more about it.

It wasn't until Regina Hayes, a distant neighbour of the Harte sisters, came in later that day and said, 'I believe you have something for the vicar's, Lucy. I shall take it to him.' Now I was suspicious where Rose was and what had happened, so I asked Regina where she had got to. Regina said with a little catty sneer, 'Well, I trust she is in bloody jail!'

And without a care in the world she made her way out the door. I followed her out to the car park and asked, 'Why would Rose Harte be in jail?' Regina said, 'Well she got the whole book group high on Wednesday afternoon with her bloody space cakes, didn't she?'

I couldn't believe my ears!

Regina went on to say that Rose had turned up to the book club with a big box of homemade brownies, and they had all been getting into their chats about fairy tales and storybooks when they decided to stop for a coffee and a brownie. Well shortly after that the whole gang of them had lost their minds! Mr Reynolds was going around the café flapping his arms like a seagull in *James and the Giant Peach*! Old Maggie got into a fit of laughing that couldn't be stopped, something to do with getting her Rapunzels and her Cinderellas mixed up. They usually finish up at 2 pm, but come 4.30, Mary behind the counter was having to send out for extra staff to be brought in after they got a fit of the munchies and ate ten pizzas. It all came to a close at 6, when the local sergeant came looking for his wife and found the delirious gang. He confiscated some of the hash cakes and sent a few of his cronies over to do a bloody drug bust at the Harte's – and no one had seen Rose since!

Deep in my inner mind some little flashbulbs started to light up. It was all starting to make sense … The friend's greyhound with the cannabis butter problem, even 'Butters' the cat's name. The herb growing and all those psychedelic colours. It all fell into place. How had I never made the connection myself? I was slightly impressed to be honest; I had definitely thought that when it came to Rose Harte, butter wouldn't melt.

It got to Friday evening and it was time to finish up at the clinic for the evening when the phone went. It was Rose on the line. I didn't want to say anything about the information I had just heard, and in any case, I was more concerned that Rose wasn't in jail and that her animals were being looked after OK. Rose said, 'Austin you know the question I had before about the cannabis butter? Can I ask another?'

I swallowed hard, starting to feel a bit like I was culpable in a crime, associate to a criminal. But the rebellious part of me was also slightly excited by the imminent risk and danger of it all.

'How can I help you, Rose?'

'Well Austin, what would happen if an alpaca ate a few cannabis plants?'

Thinking for a moment, all I could say was, 'It's a new one on me, Rose!' For sure, it was.

Her voice went a bit shaky on the phone as she said, 'Dammit I don't care if they have me bugged. Austin, Pablo's got out and into the tomato tunnel and eaten my hash plants. He's dancing around here the last three days in slow motion and his orgling has gone up three octaves. He's singing like an opera singer now. You wouldn't believe the noise he's making – Pavarotti would be proud,' she laughed.

Rose then asked if I could keep a secret, and I assured her I could. She said, 'You know I will be forever grateful to that alpaca. He's only gone and saved me from a term in jail. My supplier mixed up medicinal and recreational cannabis seeds and didn't I get the whole book group high, with my medicinal brownies. Well, they were supposed to be medicinal, but instead they were bloody space cakes. We've been self-medicating for years on medicinal cannabis here:

Mr Reynolds with his early Alzheimer's, Maggie Mortlock has sworn by it ever since her breast cancer surgery, and not to mention poor Daisy and her cancer too. But no, this time I had a mishap and we ended up with a batch full of the psychedelic cannabinoids instead of the medicinal ones! The sergeant caught me red-handed and came looking for my stash, and by the time they got to my place our bloody wonderful alpaca, Pablo boy, had got out of his paddock and eaten the lot – destroyed the evidence, and I'm a free woman. Marvellous Pablo,' Rose said, before shouting 'You are marvellous!' to Pablo in the background.

'Well Rose, can you tell me what symptoms you are seeing with Pablo?'

'He's just spaced out. His bottom lip is extra dangly. I see him licking at thin air occasionally. His big black eyes are mellow, and he looks kind of … happy. Sometimes he does a bit of dancing, his back feet not keeping up with his front feet so well. He sways around a bit.'

'Perhaps it's best for him to be indoors in the stable for a few days,' I advised. 'Keep the sun out of his eyes, and make sure he has plenty of water and hay. The effects will hopefully wear off in a day or two.'

I was going to be over that way again the following week. I arranged to drop by and make sure all was going well with Pablo. I met Rose at her garden path, and we made our way over to Pablo, who was in his paddock eating hay. Rose smiled as she opened the gate to his paddock and demonstrated how she could now walk right up and pet him. I joined her beside Pablo. His surgical wound had healed nicely, and the effects of the cannabis had worn off completely. He didn't even attempt to mutter an orgle. Rose, putting her arm around Pablo's neck, beamed and said that he was already becoming a very well-behaved alpaca. She was fully convinced that Pablo had saved her from a trip to jail, and he was a fan of her head and back massages now too. I smiled, thinking what a lucky alpaca Pablo was! Rose planned to introduce him back with the other gang in the coming weeks. We left him munching his hay and headed off towards the cottage.

As we headed up to the garden a clutch of little blue wrens appeared on the path before us – three males and two females. The males darted around, continually chit chatting and gesturing after the females, trying to impress them. We were close to the side of the cottage where I had been just a couple of weeks before, with Daisy singing to Butters after the whisker mishap. I said to Rose, 'It's lovely how friendly the local creatures are here in your garden – it's like a haven.'

She smiled at me and pointed to a clearance under the wooden decking adjoining the foundations of the cottage, then said, 'Well, if you came here a couple of years back, we had even more wildlife. There was a couple of Tasmanian devils living right there in that hole. They are from a long generation of devils that have lived here over the years, right here in our garden.

Sometimes they head off for a year or two back into the forest but like in the past I hope they will be back sometime.'

I imagined the devils wandering around, the Harte sisters leaving them out tasty treats, and how magical that must be. I wouldn't get to meet those ones in my time there but seeing their vacant hole under the cottage was special enough.

Rose, also noticing how captivated I was with the blue wrens, then said, 'I may not have a Tassie devil to show you today Austin, but I do have something else you might like. Come, follow me.' Growing along the gable wall of her cottage was a climbing clematis plant, abound with beautiful pink flowers. The plant was well established, with quite a thick base and bushy areas towards the bottom, getting thinner as it stretched towards the roof. Rose said, 'I was out here doing some pruning yesterday and I discovered one of the blue wren's nests. It's very visible when you know where it is – let me show you. Don't worry, we won't be disturbing them – yesterday I nearly accidentally pruned it off!'

With Rose pointing out the general whereabouts we carefully approached, looking into a fork in the branches in a bushy part of the plant. 'There it is,' she said excitedly. 'Mum must be off for a snack. Look at the little eggs.' There, amongst the leaves about a metre from the ground, was the nest. It was no bigger than a lime – a perfect little cup shape, carefully woven between the clematis sprigs. In it were five little eggs, pale blue with brown speckles, no bigger than garden peas. I popped on my glasses to get a better look. The exterior of the nest consisted mostly of a mix of leaves, spider webs and dried grass. Around the top edge of the nest, and projecting from within the nest, were dark-grey strands of a material that I couldn't immediately identify. Some feathers were tucked in under the eggs inside the nest, along with a snug-looking blue woven material. 'What could those other longer grey strands be?' I asked Rose. 'They almost look like fishing line or the likes.'

Rose, being a bit unsure now, donned her glasses too, then said, 'Well, the feathers are from the garden. The blue strands are Butter's fur, and wait … no … it couldn't be …'

She looked at me and laughed. 'Those grey strands are Butters' whiskers!'

I looked at her in disbelief and said, 'So, it's a nest made with whiskers, feathers and fur.'

Rose laughed and said, 'It sure is!'

Acknowledgements

I have a whole lot of people to thank, for helping me write this collection.

I offer, in no particular order, my sincere gratitude as follows:

To my sisters Annette Donnelly and Maire Donnelly, and my mother Kathleen Donnelly, thank you so much for being my long-suffering early readers, advice-givers, and rememberers of some of the goings-on from our childhood on the family farm.

To my good friend and fellow veterinary colleague, Dr Jimmy Wiseman, you were another early reader of the text, and a provider of honest opinions and advice. This collection would not be half of what it is today without your erudite and insightful input. Thank you.

To Ms Terri Mertz, over in Austin, Texas, you came to me as a beta reader and stayed on as an early editor. Your warm and caring approach to my text, and as a reader new to the Irish vernacular, helped me make this text accessible to many readers. Thank you.

To Mr Neil Burkey, you carried out a professional copy-edit of the text, in a very timely manner. You really helped walk this debut author through the editing process. Thank you.

To Ms Ruth Cadden, artist and illustrator of the text, your wonderful art, and enthusiasm for the stories and the animals, has brought me so much joy. I smile thinking also that if someone were to check your Internet history, they would find you've been searching for bull penis hair images (apparently – don't Google that!) and sheep's Mary. You're welcome! And thanks for everything.

To Ms Sue Hedley OAM, Founder and President of the Australian animal charity SAFE (Saving Animals From Euthanasia – Western Australia). During the writing process, over many cups of coffee and the occasional glass of wine, you always managed to say the right things to help me keep at it, and, just as importantly, remind me of the amazing universe out there.

Psychologist to the veterinary profession and instigator of positive change, Dr Nadine Hamilton, of (Love Your Pet, Love Your Vet.) Thank you for reading and giving me your thoughts on some of the more hard-hitting material.

To the multitude of beta readers who read my stories and offered me their thoughts and opinions, I will be forever grateful.

Finally, to the many, many veterinary professionals I have worked with over the years (nurses, receptionists, vets and anyone else), I wholeheartedly thank you for all the fun and laughter. For some of you, a few of your anecdotes have appeared in this text, outlining the fun we have had working together: You know who you are.

I wish to acknowledge in the story of the Craic'd sheep farmers, that although I may have told the story in a way that brings into question Irish folklore, I do so to remind us all that our ancestors had beliefs we may not hold in the same regard today, but they still very much have their place.

Since writing the Marmalade Karma story I have been told a few more stories about deceased animals going missing en route to vet clinics, in stolen handbags, boxes or even cars. Indeed, it seems to be almost something of an urban legend. All I can say is, if you set out on such a trip and someone offers to assist you, make sure you trust the help !

Thank you for reading.

Austin Donnelly
March 2020

Index of Images

Zone
of
Repugnance

Red Kite

Mackeral
Fish

Red
Limousin
Heifer

Honey
Bee

Cheviot
Sheep

Suffolk
Sheep

Old English
Sheep Dog

Lambs

Pheasant

Hare

Fox

Robin

Pine
Marten

Blackbird

Kangaroo

Wombat

Duck-Billed
Platypus

Phascogale

Antechinus

Quokka

Drop
Bear!!!

Kangaroo Joey

Koala

Sow

Piglet

Bronze Turkey

Irish Water Spaniel

Gosling

Black Leghorn Chicken

Isa Brown Chicken

Light Sussex Chicken

Saanen Goat

Charolais Cow

Dairy Bullock

Barn Owl

Wren (Irish)

Border Collie

Bernese Mountain Dog

Jackdaw

Stoat

Blue Wren

Tasmanian Devil

Alpaca

Author Biography

A uthor, Austin Donnelly is an Irish veterinarian and more recently an Australian citizen.

He enjoys writing stories from his work and international travels. Having spent 7 years travelling and working all over Australia, these days Austin has now returned to work in rural Ireland. Austin is passionate about working with animals and animal people.

Whiskers, Feathers & Fur Veterinary Tales is Austin's debut veterinary story collection. Austin now writes towards the next veterinary story collection.

With plans for much more writing in the coming years, look out for Austin's children's books and adult fiction / comedy also.

If you have enjoyed reading this story collection please consider leaving a review on Goodreads or Amazon. It would be greatly appreciated.

Keep up to date with future publication from Austin.

Instagram and Facebook @austindonnellywrites. And also check out Austin's blog for a few short animal stories and articles.

https://austindonnellywrites.blog/

Twitter @Austin_writes

Disclaimer

This book reflects the author's present recollections of experiences over time. The names and characteristics have been changed, some events have been compressed, and some dialogue has been recreated. In some instances all of the events detailed may not have happened simultaneously but at different points in time. Also the expressions and actions of some of the characters may be a collage of more than one personality.